BRAZILIAN AUTHORITARIANISM

Brazilian Authoritarianism

PAST AND PRESENT

LILIA MORITZ SCHWARCZ

TRANSLATED BY
ERIC M. B. BECKER

PRINCETON UNIVERSITY PRESS
PRINCETON & OXFORD

Published by Princeton University Press
41 William Street, Princeton, New Jersey 08540
99 Banbury Road, Oxford OX2 6JX

press.princeton.edu

All Rights Reserved

Library of Congress Cataloging-in-Publication Data

Names: Schwarcz, Lilia Moritz, author.
Title: Brazilian authoritarianism : past and present / Lilia Moritz Schwarcz;
    translated by Eric M. B. Becker.
Other titles: Sobre o autoritarismo brasileiro. English
Description: Princeton : Princeton University Press, 2022. |
    Includes bibliographical references and index.
Identifiers: LCCN 2021051259 (print) | LCCN 2021051260 (ebook) |
    ISBN 9780691210919 (Hardback) | ISBN 9780691238760 (eBook)
Subjects: LCSH: Authoritarianism—Brazil. | Authoritarianism—Brazil—
    History. | Brazil—Politics and government. | Brazil—Social conditions. |
    BISAC: POLITICAL SCIENCE / Political Ideologies / Fascism &
    Totalitarianism | HISTORY / Latin America / South America
Classification: LCC JC481 .S44 2022 (print) | LCC JC481 (ebook) |
    DDC 320.530981—dc23/eng/20220112
LC record available at https://lccn.loc.gov/2021051259
LC ebook record available at https://lccn.loc.gov/2021051260

British Library Cataloging-in-Publication Data is available

Editorial: Fred Appel and James Collier
Production Editorial: Natalie Baan
Jacket Design: Lauren Smith
Production: Erin Suydam
Publicity: Kate Hensley, Kathryn Stevens, and Maria Whelan

This book has been composed in Arno

Printed on acid-free paper. ∞

Printed in the United States of America

10 9 8 7 6 5 4 3 2 1

We Brazilians are like Robinson Crusoe: forever awaiting
the ship which will rescue us from the island where we
have been shipwrecked.

—LIMA BARRETO, "TRANSATLANTICISM," CARETA

Those who cannot remember the past are condemned to repeat it.

—GEORGE SANTAYANA, THE LIFE OF REASON

CONTENTS

When Fears Become Reality

BRAZILIAN AUTHORITARIANISM was first published, in Portuguese, in May 2019. It was written "in the heat of the moment," soon after the November 2018 presidential poll that resulted in the election of the far-right candidate Jair Bolsonaro in the second round. At the time of publication, the book was one of the first to reflect on Brazil's hard swing to the right: after thirty years of progressive governments that defended the resumption and reconstruction of democracy, the country was to have a retired military captain in the presidency, a man who had served in the Congress for twenty-eight years and had achieved little beyond sowing political division and hate. During this time, he managed to pass only two bills. It was this same man who, in 2016, on the occasion of the vote to impeach President Dilma Rousseff, then serving her second term, had hailed the actions of General Brilhante Ustra (1932–2015), an individual who had been revealed as a torturer, thanks to the work of the Truth Commission,[1] but who had never faced any consequences, despite being known to have tortured Rousseff herself when she was a political prisoner of the military dictatorship that ruled the country from 1964 to 1985.

In the original version of the book that readers of English now have before them, the name Bolsonaro appeared only infrequently—cited more commonly as a "symptom" of the transformation of Brazil into an authoritarian country than as a "cause." The intention (then and now) was to avoid dating the work, instead demonstrating how Bolsonaro's rise was the result of historical circumstances, echoes of the past in the present: a past stretching back to the time when Brazil was still a Portuguese colony, and when hierarchies of command and subordination became ingrained. In the first place, slavery, widespread throughout this country of continental proportions, took for granted the influence of the few and the subjugation of the many. The plantation model meant that the absolute power of landowners—social, cultural, political, and religious—resulted in a profoundly unjust and hierarchical society. These models created enduring structures that resonate to this day in contemporary forms of bossism, clientelism, racism, misogyny, and sexism, very much routine elements of national life.

Since the book's publication in Portuguese, Jair Bolsonaro has been president of Brazil for more than three years, and what was once conjecture is today reality. In the first place, the current government has promoted a veritable dismantling, and the simultaneous bureaucratic and ideological takeover, of Brazilian cultural and educational institutions. Since the new president entered office on January 1, 2019, Brazilians have witnessed a growing authoritarianism and systematic control of various cultural, scientific, and educational institutions, involving the appointment of ministers and secretaries lacking the requisite technical and professional expertise, who are there for no other reason than their commitment to the government's moral and ideological agenda. These actions amount to a power grab, a sort of culture war, which has no intention of mirroring the plurality of the Brazilian people and which works through intimidation.

There are many examples. Soon after the government took power, a federal deputy from the president's former party, the far-right Social Liberal Party—it is important to note that since November 12, 2019, Jair Bolsonaro himself has had no party affiliation—made a public appeal to students to film their professors and denounce them for ideological indoctrination, incentivizing attacks on and the discrediting of educators, the consequences of which continue to this day. In another declaration, the president asserted that Brazil's school textbooks "say many things" and that everything would change "once we finish ours," making clear his intent to directly interfere in public school materials, and in a most sectarian way. The Brazilian government even removed more than 130 Brazilian film posters from the National Film Agency website, alleging they were "immoral" and "anti-patriotic," and also refused to recognize the conferral of the Prêmio Camões—the most important literary prize in the Portuguese-speaking world and one recognized by the presidents of all Portuguese-speaking countries—upon writer and musician Chico Buarque, on account of Buarque's disapproval of the president's political ideas. In a related development, the government did away with the Ministry of Culture and transformed it into a secretariat with limited funding under the Ministry of Tourism.

On January 17, 2020, the then special secretary of culture Roberto Alvim plagiarized Nazi general propaganda minister Joseph Goebbels—in a speech that lifted entire sections from speeches made by his "mentor," complete with Wagner playing in the background, and even the minister's own vocal imitation of Goebbels—during his announcement of a new national artistic prize, when he also held forth on "conservative expectations" for Brazilian art. The secretary was dismissed after public outcry, but this government could not care less about freedom of expression and opinion—despite constantly invoking both, particularly when justifying its own acts of censorship or antidemocratic speech. The truth is, the former secretary too is a "symptom" of this authoritarian process, not its "cause." The day before Alvim's unfortunate speech, in a Facebook Live broadcast with the president, the two men praised the country's "swing to the right" and the resulting "cultural reboot," completely ignoring the rich cultural production to be found in Brazil today.

This is but one example of a project that is well under way, and which is empowering and incentivizing regional actors—such as the police in their respective states, school principals and professors, government officials, and even judicial officers—to censure that which makes them uncomfortable and which, because different and critical, offends them. The government has used the Special Secretariat for Social Communication to promote a battle of historical narratives, recommending a new pantheon of "true leaders and great national heroes" who have purportedly been passed over—all of them white men who are a part of a colonial history in itself characterized by more inclusive and pluralistic agendas. It has also promoted the dismantling of funding for film productions with LGBTQ themes, having asserted that "conservative artists" ought to unite to create a "cultural war machine," and appointed Sérgio Nascimento Camargo president of the Fundação Palmares, an important advocacy institution for Afro-Brazilian culture—despite the fact that Camargo, though Black, has attacked Black activists and expressed his belief that slavery benefited Africans. Meanwhile, in a country where structural racism is one of the most serious impediments to full democracy, the government has launched a veritable crusade, seeking to erase the memory of Afrodescendant populations. This erasure is a double death—physical and memorial—guided by a necropolitics, in the style of Achille Mbembe, that has been applied to wage a true genocide against the Black population and a massacre of the right to remember.

Throughout history, there are many examples of authoritarian and fascist governments that overhaul the State via tight controls of culture and education. In the case of Brazil, such changes seek, via a moral and ideological agenda, to alter the content of educational texts, films, and public museum programming, interfere in the granting of scholarships and research grants, or intimidate professors and scientists. Ricardo Galvão, former director of the National Institute for Space Research, who was dismissed for releasing data on deforestation in Brazil, has just received a prize from science magazine *Nature*, having been chosen from among the ten specialists nominated by the publication. The marketing director of Banco do Brasil, Delano Valentim, was dismissed, and had one of his commercials censored by the government, for no other reason than the inclusion of Black, LGBTQ, and other individuals from a variety of age groups and social classes.

As we have seen, there is a historical revisionism under way that seeks to return to a nostalgic and authoritarian version of a Brazil that never existed—a cultural demolition that parallels the educational destruction sought by a government that privileges ideology over quality information. By sidelining journalistic, scientific, cultural, and academic output, the current Brazilian administration seeks to push a conservative project predicated on a fundamentalist Christian and heteronormative moral vision, representing a regression from various advances made in Brazil since the end of the 1970s that resulted in a more diverse, plural, inclusive, and secular country. As this book shows, it is no accident that racial, gender, and religious intolerance in Brazil increased significantly in 2019.

With its efforts to erase differences, the Bolsonaro government is answerable for crimes against the Brazilian people. Its political agenda seeks to turn back numerous advances, such as the establishment of affirmative action policies, which is responsible, among other reasons, for the fact that in 2019 Black students accounted for 51 percent of the public university population, for the first time in history. There is a lot of work still to be done; but what Brazilians are witnessing at the moment is a movement in the opposite direction: a reversal of their most fundamental rights.

This is, besides, a government predicated on conspiracy theories: it creates, consumes, and promotes fake news; governs in the name of the few; and casts political opponents as enemies of the State. It is a government that surrounds itself with people of the same religion, race, social class, age, and gender identification, yet claims to represent all Brazilians. A government that believes in flat earth theory and denies climate change. A government that brooks no disagreement, and, at the first sign of it, issues threats of a coup, a return to dictatorship and AI 5—a 1968 decree that stripped Brazilians of their civil rights and gave birth to a repressive State machine. A patrimonialist government that doesn't hesitate to place its family, friends, and other relatives in positions of power. A government led by a president who seeks to undo attempts to stem and punish corruption, a practice common to members of his own immediate family. A government that selects ill-prepared ministers on the basis of their ratings potential, rather than confronting the country's longstanding inequality problem. A government with no concern for public policy, but an obsession with scapegoats. A government that attacks minorities and seeks to neutralize movements in support of the rights of women, Black people, the Indigenous, and the LGBTQ population, and fails to combat the slaughter of the Black population scattered across the country's urban slums, or of Indigenous peoples on their own reservations. A government that denies the fact of deforestation in the Amazon and treats environmental leaders with scorn and distrust. A government that defends and participates in antidemocratic protests, and that fails to confront urban and rural militias that strike at the heart of the country. A government that attacks scientists, academics, and journalists whenever it feels threatened. Moreover, a government that patterns itself on the model of Donald Trump and his way of governing.

Incidentally, Brazil shares the leaders' podium with the US when it comes to deaths provoked by COVID-19. Despite this, the Bolsonaro government named a general, Eduardo Pazuello, to lead the Health Ministry in May 2020—first as interim and later permanent minister—having previously overruled and then "scorched" two previous ministers who at least had technical expertise. By April 2021, Brazil was on its fourth health minister since the start of the pandemic. The president's preferred approach to the pandemic is denial, playing down its lethal effects, and even the deaths of over six hundred thousand Brazilians. He prefers to promote hydroxychloroquine's potential as a miracle cure, apparently believing that medical treatments, too, work by executive order, and to conceal the true number of sick and dying.

————

Epicurus posited a close relationship between "the art of living well and art of dying well." French historian Philippe Ariès, developing upon the Greek philosopher's teachings, explained that, at its core, philosophy has always been and always will be a meditation on death—on the relationship between life and death. Despite this, psychologists, sociologists, historians, and anthropologists have noted a recent paradox: the "invisibility of death."

According to Ariès, "the death of death" came about at the beginning of the twentieth century, in particular the period following the First World War (1914–18).[2] A sort of prohibition on death—a refusal to face it—was most clearly evident in the United States and northwestern Europe, as both began to glorify longevity and eternal youth. At the same time, the "Spanish flu" epidemic of 1918 led to a sort of medical and healthcare engineering that sought to overcome the "accident" of death. This resulted in the implementation of a highly adaptable technology capable of protecting individuals, with the aim of saving lives, seeking to set their bodies free so they might continue their daily tasks, free of the specter of death lurking just around corner, ready to pounce when one least expected it.

The silencing of death is of a piece with the arrival of modernity, which brought urbanization, industrialization, and a certain scientific reason aimed at cheating human mortality. Three different social and medical phenomena were set on a collision course. The first was the broader concealment of death, which came to be bestowed as a spectacle upon a few select losses only—those of celebrities. This process involved a sort of hyperexposure to the passing of certain individuals in the media and among a public that treats such a loss as its own, and silence before the deaths of the vast majority: the deaths of ordinary people in general; the perishing of older individuals; and the killing of young Black men across Brazil's urban slums, which largely goes unacknowledged. The second phenomenon was the transfer of the sick to hospitals, where the battle against death is waged, certainly, but where it is also hidden away, far from the eyes of the healthy. The third step was the extinction of mourning as a social phenomenon, especially in the case of collective loss on account of wars, natural disasters, or pandemics.

Walter Benjamin wrote sensitively of soldiers' return home from the First World War. According to Benjamin, they returned silent, with little desire to tell of their experiences. The death of friends and fellow soldiers had rendered them mute.[3] It was as if they were unable and unwilling to speak of death. It appears no coincidence that this moment marks a fundamental change in society's view of this stage of life.

Thus death became unmentionable. In practice, we recognize that we might die at any moment. However, we behave as if we were immortal and deny the natural aging process. According to Ariès, before the Great War, death profoundly modified a social group's place and time:

> The shutters were closed in the bedroom of the dying man, candles were lit, the house filled with grave and whispering neighbors, relatives, and friends. At the church, the bell tolled. . . . After death, a notice of bereavement was posted on the door (in lieu of the abandoned custom of exhibiting the body or the coffin by the door of the house). All the doors and windows of the house were closed except the front door, which was left ajar to admit everyone who was obliged by friendship or good manners to make a final visit. The service at the church brought the whole community together, and after the long line of people had expressed their sympathy to the family, a slow procession, saluted by passersby, accompanied the coffin to the cemetery. The period of mourning was filled with visits: visits of the family to the cemetery and visits of relatives and friends

to the family. Then, little by little, life returned to normal. The social group had been stricken by death, and it had reacted collectively, starting with the immediate family and extending to a wider circle of relatives and acquaintances. Not only did everyone die in public like Louis XIV, but the death of each person was a public event that moved, literally and figuratively, society as a whole. It was not only an individual who was disappearing but society itself that had been wounded and that had to be healed.[4]

Over time, however, society has expelled death. An episode that was once visible and intended to arouse emotion is now supposed to pass as quickly as possible, and increasingly without notice. The neglect with which we have seen certain governments treat death seems no coincidence. In the case of Brazil, the government has tried to sequester death and hinder the realization that Brazil is, in fact and in principle, a nation in mourning. In a display of blatant disrespect for both the living and the dead, the Brazilian president continues, in the mold of Trump, to promote the effectiveness of hydroxychloroquine and to question the number of registered deaths. Turning death into a political wedge, Bolsonaro has gone so far as to accuse state governors of "seeking to benefit" from the pandemic.

This is not the first nor will it be the last occasion that public health emergencies like that we are experiencing at time of writing become the target of political manipulation. However, in this specific case, in this crisis we are living through, the Brazilian government made a clear choice to engage in denial, along with a heavy dose of magical thinking. Disavowing the science, the press, and the academy, the current occupant of the Planalto Palace has thrown his weight behind a chimera. He chooses to deny his own age, to boast about his "athletic career," and in so doing send the message that those who die of COVID are "weak"—and, by comparison, people like himself who, in his own words, "prefer to fight back" against the coronavirus are "strong." It is but one more example of a State policy announcing "the death of death" and seeking to celebrate life as though it were endless, despite the contradiction with the reality of our times.

A great many Brazilian deaths could have been avoided by a sensible and essential policy of social distancing, better education and implementation on the part of the government around preventive measures, the use of masks, or even aggressive testing efforts; without these, it is impossible to implement strategies to protect the population. But what has been the reaction of Bolsonaro and his government? The exact opposite, and the cruelty of urging groups to boycott preventive efforts, of making light of the virus, and of disregarding the impact of this highly contagious disease corresponds precisely to a denial of death, in the form of its silencing.

The anthropologist Judith Butler has said that

> learning to mourn mass death means marking the loss of someone whose name you do not know, whose language you may not speak, who lives at an unbridgeable distance from where you live. One does not have to know the person lost to affirm that this was a life. What one grieves is the life cut short, the life that should have had a chance to live more, the value that person has carried now in the lives of others, the wound that permanently transforms those who live on.[5]

In 1919, those who had survived the "Spanish flu" the year before took to the streets in celebration: it was a lively Carnival. Nonetheless, among the throngs of people, there was no shortage of floats and songs referring to "the Spanish lady" who had disappeared but taken with her the lives of so many Brazilians. Now, for us, is not yet the moment to celebrate. Rather, this is a moment at which to step back and allow the time for our collective grief. Frequently, we process our deepest suffering through the suffering of others.

The suffering of others, certainly, is not our own. However, awareness of death, the civic and republican awareness of the loss another is experiencing, is common to us all. In some ways, it brings grieving strangers together.

———

When launching his 1936 book *Raízes do Brasil* (The roots of Brazil), Sérgio Buarque de Holanda said that democracy in Brazil was nothing more than one big "misunderstanding." At that time, he was experiencing at first hand the dilemmas of Getúlio Vargas's Estado Novo (New State) and claimed to fear authoritarian regimes of all stripes, referring both to Nazism and Stalinism—the clearest dangers at that time. Little did the historian know that with this declaration he would become a sort of national oracle: to this day, democracy in Brazil remains a misunderstanding, since it does not apply equally to everyone.

Democracy was invented in Athens around 510 BCE. *Demokratia* then referred to "the capacity for self-government among equals." In modern times, democracy has come to mean "power of the people," whereby common citizens relinquish limited parts of this sovereignty to the elected individual or party in power, but retain and do not forgo their remaining rights. As a result, notions such as equality and freedom allow us to distinguish between democratic and nondemocratic governments and are the two pillars of this form of government.

Democracy depends, above all, on institutions and the democratic process: free elections, political parties, constitutions, parliaments, justice. It is also based on checks and balances among the three branches—legislative, executive, and judicial—and relies on these checks and balances to drive the transformation of modern society, demanding and providing transparency and visibility in the workings of government.

But democracy is more than a system based on institutions. It is also a way of life and a societal practice. It is no accident that the founding values of democratic regimes are civil rights and freedom of movement, expression, assembly, and the press. These characteristics in turn are tied to the rights to self-determination, to vote and run for office, to the presumption of innocence until proven guilty beyond a reasonable doubt, and to justice for all. Democracy also brings with it the ideal of continuous expansion: a kind of enfranchisement guided by the concept of inclusion. For this reason, citizenship in a democracy ought to extend to a great number of people who maintain the differences that exist between them, whether in status, social class, race, ethnicity, gender, sex, religion, location, or generation.

Considered in these terms, then, democracy is the opposite of authoritarianism and totalitarianism; and yet it is also claimed that democracy, republicanism, and full citizenship exist in a country as racist, sexist, misogynistic, and unequal as Brazil. The Brazilian republic, as the historian José Murilo de Carvalho asserts, is hardly a democratic one.[6]

According to the Brazilian Institute of Geography and Statistics (IBGE), in 2020 Black people accounted for 56.1 percent of the Brazilian population; they do not, however, share in a democracy wherein equality dictates principles and guides policy. According the Municipal Human Development Index, which measures income nationwide, White Brazilians earn about twice as much as Black Brazilians. A study from the Institute for Applied Economic Research, in partnerships with the Fundação João Pinheiro and the UN Development Program, indicates that social inequality still profoundly affects the Black population. According to the 2018 National Household Sample Survey, the proportion of Black Brazilians living below the poverty line as stipulated by the World Bank is more than double that of Whites. In 2018, when this threshold was defined as living on less than $5.50 a day, the poverty rate in Brazil among White people was 15.4 percent, and among Black people 32.9 percent. According to the same survey, color and racial inequality can also be seen at the household level, whether in terms of the size of one's home, access to essential services, or other individual characteristics of each residence.

In a country where 43 percent of wealth is concentrated in the hands of only 10 percent of the population, reversing this trend is as necessary as it is pressing. While many advances have been made—such as, for the first time, a greater proportion of Black students earning advanced degrees at public institutions than Whites (50.3 percent vs. 49.7 percent in 2019, according to the IBGE)—there is still much to do in terms of making the university more diverse and inclusive.

It is the Black population, too, that most frequently falls victim to violence. According to the IBGE, the homicide rate among Black men aged fifteen to eighteen is 98.5 per hundred thousand; among Whites in the same age group, the number falls to 34. Inequality is not merely racial but ethnic in nature—Brazil's Indigenous people still face a double death: either by extermination or by "incorporation," which, more often than not, means the death of their culture. Inequality is also a question of gender and sexual identification, if we take into consideration the high rate of femicide and Brazil's shameful fifth-place ranking worldwide when it comes to killing of LGBTQ people, at a rate of more than one per day.

So, in Brazil, equality of rights—not to speak of representation— simply does not exist. In fact, it could be said that the Black community, women, Indigenous groups, and LGBTQ people together are not a minority: they constitute a majority, who have been made into a minority in terms of representation and in practice.

Brazil will be a democracy on the day that it can truly boast a plurality of voices; when it allows for alternative histories; when it engages in a genuine struggle against racism and other forms of discrimination; when more minorities are included in representative posts and deliberative bodies; when the environmental question is part of the national agenda. In this sense, the country has recently logged an initial victory: in a historic session on August 25, 2020, the Superior Electoral Court determined that political parties must allocate an equal sum of public campaign financing dollars to the campaigns of Black candidates for office. This stipulation will take effect as of the 2022 election, as a majority of justices determined that the measure must respect the constitutional norm whereby authorities must have at least a year to implement changes to the electoral process. Let us see what the future brings.

The measure aims to correct the inequality and disproportionality that can also be seen in the electoral process—in terms of who has access to the vote and who runs for office—and to make public reparations via this process. The structure of Brazilian political parties still very much centralizes power in a way that prohibits the advancement of social minorities in terms of representation. The advance is thus one that seeks to combat exclusion, recognize existing inequalities, and, to some extent, make reparations. Strengthening democracy in Brazil is a responsibility that falls upon all of us. As the Black Rights Coalition wrote in its 2020 manifesto, "Practice is the criterion of truth."

In the absence of progress in this area, Brazil's democratic institutions will continue to function, but they are regularly put to the test and have suffered under the initiatives of an authoritarian populist government of technocrats that daily launches attacks on democracy. The theories initially advanced in *Brazilian Authoritarianism* have been borne out, in spite of the fact that it was written at a moment when political tempers were running high, placing Jair Bolsonaro in the highest office in the land as head of the executive. Never has the present so closely resembled the past.

São Paulo, November 10, 2021

BRAZILIAN AUTHORITARIANISM

Introduction

HISTORY PROVIDES NO VACCINES

BRAZIL HAS A MOST PARTICULAR HISTORY, at least when compared to its Latin American neighbors. Nearly half of all enslaved Africans violently forced from their lands ended up in Brazil; and after gaining independence, Brazil, though surrounded by republics, formed a monarchy that enjoyed wide support for more than sixty years, thanks to which the country—the enormous size of which more closely approximates that of a continent—kept its borders intact. On top of this, because Brazil was a Portuguese colony, its inhabitants speak a different language from their neighbors.

Brazilian Authoritarianism dialogues, in part, with data and conclusions that appear in *Brasil: Uma Biografia* (2015; published in English as *Brazil: A Biography*, 2018), which I wrote with Heloisa Starling. I also make selective use of columns I have published since 2014 in the newspaper *Nexo*. As my aim is to give a general, not an exhaustive, view on a series of subjects that explain authoritarian practices characteristic of the country, some of which are not strictly part of my professional and academic specializations, I was only able to write this book thanks to the excellent books, reports, and articles written by academics, activists, and journalists on the subjects contained herein. As the circumstances of publication of the original (Portuguese) edition of this book did not allow for systematic use of footnotes or endnotes, a bibliography has been included at the end, in which I list details of works cited in the main text. (Bibliographical endnotes are instead provided, however, for the preface and afterword added for this English-language edition.)

Brazil is also a very young and original country when it comes to a regular institutional life. A good number of its national establishments were created when the Portuguese royal family arrived in 1808, at which time the first schools of surgery and anatomy were founded in the cities of Salvador and Rio de Janeiro. In Spanish colonies, by contrast, the university system dates back much further, to the sixteenth, seventeenth, and eighteenth centuries: the universities of Santo Domingo (1538), Lima (1551), Mexico City (1551), Bogotá (1580), Quito (1586), Santiago (1621), Guatemala (1676), Havana (1721), Caracas (1721), and Asunción (1733).

It was only with the arrival of the Portuguese court,[1] and the doubling of the population in some Brazilian cities, that the country would no longer rely exclusively on graduates of the University of Coimbra (in Portugal). The first Brazilian higher schools were the Royal Military Academy (founded in 1810), the Agriculture Course (1814), and the Royal Academy of Painting and Sculpture (1820), offering courses that earned one a professional diploma: one's ticket to privileged government posts and a highly restricted job market with its attendant social prestige. At the same time, the Royal Botanic Garden, the Royal School of the Sciences, Arts, and Crafts, the Royal Museum, the Royal Library, the Royal Press, and the Banco do Brasil were also founded— this last, according to witnesses, having been "bankrupt from the outset."

The Portuguese Crown also sought to transplant from Lisbon its enormous bureaucracy, a hierarchical structure that had previously been located at the Paço in the Portuguese capital, and which included the Government-General of Brazil, the captaincies, and the municipal assemblies. The judiciary had already established a presence in Brazil with the Tribunal da Relação (an appeals court), tied to the Casa da Suplicação—a royal higher court of appeals in the Portuguese capital; but this higher court also came in the prince regent's "baggage," along with other older Portuguese tribunals: the Desembargo do Paço, the highest court in this structure, and the Mesa da Consciência e Ordens (Board of the King's Conscience and of the Military Orders), linked to the archbishop of Brazil.

Political independence in 1822 brought few changes in institutional terms, but it established a clear objective: to build and provide the justification for a new nation that would also, as we have seen, be unique in the American context—a monarchy surrounded by republics on all sides.

It was no small task. There was the need to draft a new constitution, see to the health of the sick population, which had grown considerably, train engineers to secure the borders and plan new cities, bring proceedings that had previous been decided according to custom and regional power balances under the auspices of the judiciary, and, not least, invent a new history for Brazil, since until then the country's history was still largely that of Portugal. It is no wonder, then, that among the first institutions founded upon independence was the Brazilian Historical and Geographical Institute (IHGB), in 1838. Located in Rio de Janeiro, this center's purpose was clear: to create a history that could glorify the past and to promote patriotism through its various activities and productions. To identify the philosophy that led to the creation of the IHGB, one need only pay attention to the first civil service exam to be held there. In 1844, the doors were opened to candidates who were willing to hold forth on a thorny question: "How should the history of Brazil be written?" The prompt was clear; it left no room for doubt. It was a matter of inventing a new history *of* and *for* Brazil.

This was the first fundamental step taken toward establishment of the discipline that would come to be called, years later and without much thought, "History of Brazil," as though the narratives it contained had come ready-made or been the exclusive result of will or so-called destiny. We know, however, that in the vast majority of cases the opposite happens: founding moments seek to privilege a certain historical narrative to the detriment of others, and initiate a true rhetorical battle—inventing rituals of memory and classifying their own models as authentic (and any others as false); privileging certain events and obliterating others; endorsing certain interpretations and discrediting others. Such episodes are, therefore, useful for shedding light on the political artifice involved and its motivations. In other words, they help us to understand how, when, and why, at certain moments, history becomes an object of political dispute.

In the case just cited, the intention of the exam was to create a *single* history that was (of course) European in its argument, imperial in its justification, and centered around events that took place in Rio de Janeiro. Unseating Salvador, Rio de Janeiro had become the capital of Brazil in 1763—it would remain so until 1960—and needed, accordingly, to assert its political and historical centrality. Further, "the establishment" needed to reinforce the notion of its august origins, and to defend the composition of its membership, which consisted basically of local agrarian elites.

In this sense, nothing could have been more appropriate than the invention of an official history that could buttress what, at that time, appeared artificial and, furthermore, inchoate: an independent state in the Americas, but one whose conservative bent led to the formation of an empire (under a Portuguese monarch, Dom Pedro I) and not a republic. Further, there was a need to extol an emancipation process that had generated considerable distrust and to confer legitimacy upon it. After all, in contrast to its Latin American neighbors, the head of the Brazilian State was a monarch, the direct descendant of three of the longest established royal families in Europe: the Braganzas, the Bourbons, and the Hapsburgs.

The unusual nature of the IHGB competition was also reflected in its result and the announcement of the winner. First place in this historic dispute went to a foreigner—the well-known Bavarian naturalist Karl von Martius (1794–1868), a scientist of unquestioned importance who, nonetheless, was a novice when it came to history in general and that of Brazil in particular—who offered the theory that the country was defined by its unrivaled mixture of peoples and races. He wrote, "The focal point for the historian ought to be to show how, in the development of Brazil, established conditions are to be found for the perfecting of the three human races, placed here side by side in a manner hitherto unknown." Drawing upon the metaphor of the country's Portuguese heritage as a powerful river which would "cleanse" and "absorb the streams of the races India and Ethiopica," von Martius represented the country in terms of the singularity and scale of the mixture between people living there.

At that point, however, and after so many centuries of a violent slaveholding system—which took for granted the ownership of one person by another and created a rigid hierarchy between Whites who held power and Blacks who ought to submit, but not infrequently rebelled—it was, to say the least, complicated to flatly extol harmony. Further, Indigenous peoples were still being decimated along the coastline and deep in the heart of the country, their lands invaded and their cultures defiled. But this did not stop the Empire from seizing the opportunity to select a proposal that reconciled Brazil's past with its present and that, instead of introducing historical facts and thus demonstrating the prevailing cruelty in the country, presented a nation whose "happiness" was measured by its capacity to bring various nations and cultures together as one: a text, that, at its core, invoked an Edenic and tropical Brazilian "nature," exempt from all suspicion or denial.

Von Martius, who in 1832 had published an essay entitled "The Rule of Law among the Aborigines in Brazil," condemning Indigenous peoples to extinction, now opted to define the country according to a redemptive fluvial metaphor. Three long rivers would define a nation: one broad and roaring, made up of White populations; another, smaller, representing the Indigenous; and yet another, smaller still, pertaining to Black Brazilians. In the rush to write his work, the naturalist appears not to have had the time (or interest), however, to inform himself in equal measure of the history of the three peoples who were at the origins of the young autonomous nation. The section concerning the "White river" was the most complete, reassuring, and extensive. The remaining two sections were virtually figurative, demonstrating a clear lack of knowledge, though this shortcoming applied to what was anyway in truth "expendable," as the text had already accounted for everything that was really of interest: to tell *a* national history—the European—and show how it had "naturally" and without bloodshed imposed itself upon the rest.

And so we had the three peoples who together had formed Brazil—three peoples who were one but (also) distinct and separate. Commixture was not (and never had been) synonymous with equality. In fact, it was in this commixture that a "self-evident" hierarchy took root, propped up—as exemplified in von Martius's article—by appeal to an immortal past lost to time. This narrative provided an ideal vehicle for inventing a history that was as peculiar (a tropical monarchy defined by commixture) as it was optimistic: the flowing waters represented the future of a country being molded by a great roaring river into which all small tributaries emptied.

It was at this time that the common refrain regarding Brazil's three foundational races, a concept that would continue to resonate as time wore on, gained traction. Several authors repeated, with minor variations, the same argument: Sílvio Romero in *Introdução à história da literatura brasileira* (Introduction to Brazilian literary history) (1882), Oliveira Viana in *Raça e assimilação* (Race and assimilation) (1932), and Artur Ramos in *Os horizontes místicos do negro da Bahia* (The mystical horizons of the Black man in Bahia) (1932). Later, in an ironic and critical idiom that nonetheless demonstrates the narrative's staying power, the modernist Mário de Andrade, in his 1928 work *Macunaíma*, would recite the formula in a well-known allegorical passage in which the hero Macunaíma and his two brothers decide to bathe in magical waters that had settled in the footprint of the Indigenous spirit Sumé, after which each emerges a different color: one white, one black, and the other "the new bronze."

It was Gilberto Freyre more than anyone who ensured this interpretation took hold, not only in his classic *Casa-grande &*

senzala (*The Masters and the Slaves*) (1933) but, years later, in books on Lusotropicalism such as *O mundo que o português criou* (The world forged by the Portuguese) (1940). While anthropologist Artur Ramos (1903–49) might have been the one to coin the term "racial democracy" and apply it to Brazil, it was Freyre's role to be the great promoter of this expression, even beyond the country's borders.

The international resonance of Freyre's theory was such that it was not long before UNESCO came knocking. At the end of the 1940s, the institution was still reeling from the opening of Nazi concentration camps, which revealed the methods of state-sponsored violence and genocide and imparted a warning about the consequences of racism as practiced during the Second World War. It was also very much aware of apartheid in South Africa and the politics of hate that took root during Second World War and the Cold War. Buoyed, then, by the theories of the anthropologist from Recife, and certain that Brazil was an example of racial harmony for the world, the organization financed, in the 1950s, a broad survey with the intent to prove the absence of racial and ethnic discrimination in the country. However, the result was at the very least paradoxical. While the research in the Brazilian Northeast led by Americans Donald Pierson (1900–1995) and Charles Wagley (1913–91) sought to corroborate Freyre's theories, the São Paulo group, led by Florestan Fernandes (1920–95) came to exactly the opposite conclusion. For the sociologist from São Paulo, the greatest legacy of slavery—practiced in Brazil for more than three centuries—was not a unifying commixture but the re-inforcement of a deeply embedded social inequality.

In the words of Fernandes, Brazilians have "a sort of reactive prejudice: prejudice against prejudice," since they prefer denial to recognizing and remedying the situation. It was also Fernandes who called the already traditional story of the three races the "myth of racial democracy," nonetheless giving renewed life to the narrative and the fallacies that led to it. It took Black activists to finally administer the *coup de grâce* when, starting at the end of the

1970s, they began to show the perversion behind this type of official discourse, which threatened to outlast social movements struggling for true equality and inclusion. Despite their efforts, the image of the confluence of three rivers retained its impact across Brazil and maintained the ring of truth more than a century after its creation.

As we have seen, the history that Karl von Martius told in the early years of the nineteenth century had the features and form of myth: a national myth. It took the country's fundamental problems, such as an all-pervasive system of slavery, and recast them as harmonizing and positive attributes. For this very reason, the Martius text did not make reference to dates, specific locations, or well-known events; since it was crucial that the text make sense well beyond the time it was written, the absence of geographical and, above all, temporal specifics would confer immortality upon it and instill confidence in a grandiose version of the country's past and a still more promising future. It was the myth of "the golden age," which served to sustain certainty about the present and guarantee the continuation of the same order and hierarchy—as though these were eternal, because preordained.

Further, there was a certain rhetorical indeterminacy to the text that ensured it a prolonged reception: history becoming myth, and vice versa—the social myth transformed into history. An important detail is that myths do not necessarily work as "lies." As the ethnologist Claude Lévi-Strauss showed, because myths are concerned with deep contradictions within a society, they retain their power insofar as they operate beyond rational arguments or data and documents that seek to deny their veracity. After all, it often is easier to live with a false truth than to face reality.

During the nineteenth century, the IHGB would fulfill its mission, advancing the project that von Martius had begun. Well financed by the Empire, the center sought to popularize a grandiloquent and patriotic history, even if, at times, it had to sacrifice more impartial research in favor of texts that served as State propaganda. The metaphor of the three races would define, for a long time, the essence and the foundation of what it meant to write a history *of* and *about* Brazil; or, more precisely, of a given Brazil, a particular utopia, which remains with us to the present day, as though it were reality.

To grow accustomed to inequality, to run from the past, is characteristic of authoritarian governments, which not infrequently resort to "whitewashed" narratives as a way of promoting the State's power and their own. It is also a formula applied with relative success among ordinary Brazilians, however. Besides acquiescing in the fallacy of the three races, Brazilians are accustomed to shaking off the immense inequality in their country, and without much difficulty transforming a reality defined by the intense concentration of power in the hands of landowners into the ultimate proof of an aristocratic past.

As forms of understanding of the past, history and memory are not always aligned, or even complementary. History not only bears within it certain lacunae and misunderstandings vis-à-vis the past, but also frequently manifests as an arena for disagreement, debate, and dispute. For this reason, it is inconclusive. Memory, meanwhile, invariably brings a subjective dimension to its analysis as it translates the past into the first person and is devoted to the very act of remembrance that produces it. In so doing, memory recovers "the present from the past" and so ensures that the past, too, becomes present.

We will see that there is no way entirely to overcome the past, but the intention of this book is to "remember." Such is the best way to rethink the present while not forgetting to imagine the future.

———

Every nation constructs for itself certain basic myths, which together have the ability to evoke in its citizens a sense of belonging to a single community that will remain unchanged—"forever lying in splendid cradle," as Brazil's national anthem proclaims. Stories with a clear impact and importance within context take on a whole new meaning when they break free from the moment at which they were born and are filtered through the logic of common sense or transformed into national rhetoric.

By becoming myth, these discourses are stripped of their critical potential, to instead be subjected to a single reading or interpretation—that which exalts a glorious past and a single ennobling history. Such a form of State utopia tends to envisage, besides the misleading representation of Brazilian racial commixture that we have explored up to this point, an idyllic patriarchal society, with a hierarchy as deeply rooted as it is virtuous. This is a form of narrative that fails strictly to adhere to the facts, since it begins by choosing its overriding message, and only then conceives of a good argument to justify it.

Nor was von Martius alone in producing this type of narrative. It was a sanctified model of historical practice around the beginning of the nineteenth century, when a primary preoccupation of those in power was the aggrandizement of the past, and not so much the authentication of documents and the story that these had to tell. The historian's job, in fact, was to stitch together edifying examples from the past and thus confer dignity upon the present. This is also the concept of "true romance," as proposed by Paul Veyne to explain the role of the historian as a sort of orchestrator of events, in the sense that it is the historian who organizes them, chooses them, and endows them with meaning.

In one form or another, historical narrative always leads to battles over the monopoly on truth. However, history becomes particularly fertile not only during changes of government or regime, as in the case of the work of our German naturalist, but also at moments of economic crisis. In such cases, when a significant portion of the national population falls into poverty, inequality grows, and political polarization divides the public—encouraged by feelings of fear, insecurity, and resentment—it is not uncommon to go in search of faraway explanations for problems that impact us closely. Further, it is in such periods that the people become more vulnerable and predisposed to believe that their rights have been infringed, their jobs stolen, and finally, that their own history has been taken from them.

Such moments tend to dissolve into disputes over the best version of the past, which becomes something of a rigged competition whose outcome is determined by the present and its pressing questions. At this point, history is transformed into something of an exercise in justification—not unlike a chant sung by a sports team's most dedicated fans.

The construction of an official history is not, therefore, an innocuous or unimportant undertaking: it has a strategic role in State policy, exalting certain events and minimizing problems that the nation experienced in the past but prefers to forget, yet whose roots extend into the present. By the same token, the process permits only a single interpretation, focusing on certain specific actions and forms of socialization while obliterating others. The goal is, as the von Martius example demonstrated, to make peace with the past: to create a mythical past, lost to time, replete with harmony, and founded on the naturalization of frameworks of authority and obedience.

This kind of paradigm, which includes much imagination and projection, frequently functions as a sort of mortar for various "common sense" theories. In Brazil, everyday history tends to derive support from four assumptions, as pivotal as they are erroneous. The first is that Brazil is a uniquely harmonious country, free of conflict. The second, that Brazilians are impervious to any form of hierarchy, resolving conflicts, as a rule, with considerable ease and fairness. The third is that the country is a full democracy, free from racial, religious, or gender prejudices. The fourth, that the country's natural beauty is such that it guarantees Brazil's status as a paradise. After all, until proven otherwise, God (too) is Brazilian.

Far from being unimpeachable narratives, these are models resulting from agendas that are both deep-seated and deeply equivocal, and which, for this very reason, summon their strength from the absence of rebuttal and continued silence. When silence persists, it is undoubtedly because elsewhere there is too much noise. Noise, and social unease.

The problem is that this practice of history, reliant as it is on national myths, is so deeply ingrained that it tends to survive the most stubborn reality. How could one ever possibly assert that Brazil is a peaceful country, if for centuries enslaved men and women filled the land, and the country tolerated for more than three hundred years a system that presupposes the ownership of one person by another? Let us not forget that Brazil was the last country in the Americas to abolish such forms of forced labor—after the United States, Puerto Rico, and Cuba—having received 5.85 million Africans out of a total of 12.52 million who were forcibly removed from their own continent in this immense Atlantic diaspora, the largest in modern times. If we take into account only those who survived the journey, the total, according to the website Slave Voyages (https://www.slavevoyages.org), was still 10.7 million, of whom 4.8 million made it to Brazil. In place of an idyll, the enslaved experienced violence in its many forms and in a variety of contexts: while masters imposed control by force and cruelty, enslaved men and women themselves responded to this violence with all manner of rebellion.

Another question: How is it possible to describe a country in terms of an idea of purported amity, shared among its citizens, when it is still a world leader in social, racial, and gender inequality—a fact supported by research that demonstrates the routine practice of discrimination against women, Indigenous groups, and Black people, as well as lesbian, gay, bisexual, transgender, cross-dressing, and other queer individuals?

It is also worth asking why, at intervals, and especially at moments of political crisis, Brazilians fall prey to the delusion of the "serenity" of the military dictatorship, as though it had been a charmed period that brought with it the magical solution to our most fundamental problems. Why is it, moreover, that they refer continually to the lack of hierarchy in their social relationships when their past and present give the lie to this idea? It is not possible to gloss innocently over the fact that Brazil was an exploitation colony, or that its territory was almost entirely divided into vast single-crop estates where wealthy landowners deployed immense authority and violence while maintaining economic and political monopolies. Indeed, though Brazil is an increasingly urban country, a certain mindset stubbornly persists, one forged on the large estates, whose owners became the kingpins of the First Republic (1889–1930), and some of whom still hide behind their castle walls in their respective states, acting as political and electoral rainmakers. In the context of such regional and personalist forms of immense power, the country developed patrimonialist practices that imply the use of the State to personal ends. Granted, during the last thirty years Brazil has forged more robust institutions, but today these nevertheless show signs of weakness as they waver in the path of certain political winds. And this is not to mention the practice of corruption, which, as we shall see, whatever the various forms it has taken and the names used to designate it over time, was already common in the colonial and imperial eras and grew like a weed after the country adopted a republican form of government, devouring Brazilians' rights and privileges.

It is said that to question is a form of resistance. I am of the mind that a critical historical practice is one that knows how to "de-normalize" that which seems ordained by biology and is consequently presented as immutable. There is nothing in Brazilian blood or DNA to indicate that the problems outlined above are immune to humane and civic-minded action. Nor is it beneficial to adopt the alternative approach of relegating to the past and to "others" who came before them responsibility for everything that bothers Brazilians about their country today: "somebody else" is racist (not me); patrimonialism is a legacy of the country's prior history; inequality is a result of slavery—period. The blame for all of the country's current ills cannot be laid on a distant and inaccessible past. Ever since the colonial era, on through the Empire and later the republican era, Brazil has practiced an incomplete and failed form of citizenship, characterized by bossism, patrimonialism, diverse forms of racism, and sexism, discrimination, and violence. Though the country has experienced, since the ratification in 1988 of the People's Constitution, the most extensive period of rule of law and democracy since it became a republic in 1889, it has yet proved incapable of combating inequality or institutional racism against Black and Indigenous groups, or of eradicating gender violence. The present is full of a great deal of the past, and history is no consolation prize. It is crucial to face the present, not least because this is not the first time that Brazilians have returned to the past with questions forged in the present.

Therefore, for those who, to this day, cannot understand why we are living through such an intolerant and violent period; for those who express surprise at so many expressions of authoritarianism or the spread, unchecked, of discourses that openly undo a catalog of civil rights that until recently appeared guaranteed; for those who have watched from the stands the growth of a politics of hate that takes opponents and transforms them into enemies: I invite you all on a voyage through Brazil's history, past and present.

Currently, a conservative wave is sweeping through countries such as Hungary, Poland, the United States, Russia, Italy, and Israel, upending the international order and bringing with it new battles over the "true" story. There is nothing novel in this approach. In the former USSR, the Communist Party newspaper *Pravda*, whose name translates as "truth," was unequivocal: it defended authoritarianism as the only conceivable narrative. Even countries known for their liberal tradition tend to slide when they need to remember a past that they prefer to "forget." This was the case in France with regard to the Vichy regime (1940–44), during which local elites collaborated with Nazism, and currently is so in Spain, which has not managed to settle the score with the violent era of its Civil War (1936–39) that divided and still divides its population.

The elimination of "places of memory"—to use Pierre Nora's wonderful phrase—is, as a result, a widespread practice. However, this approach is still most common of all within societies where history plays a direct role in political struggle, becomes a form of nationalism, and soon glosses over or eliminates entirely the traumatic events of the past that it deems best forgotten. Brazil is "surfing" a conservative wave. Demonization of gender issues; attacks on minorities; a lack of trust in institutions and political parties; the adoption of dualities such as "us" (the righteous) versus "them" (the corrupt); campaigns against intellectuals and the press; the justification of order and violence, whatever the regime ultimately responsible for it; attacks against the constitution; and, finally, the insistence on a mythic past: these are all part of a longstanding narrative, but one that continues to exert an enormous impact on the country's current situation.

The aim of this short book is to identify some of the roots of authoritarianism in Brazil, which flourishes in the present but is nonetheless intimately tied to the country's five hundred years of history. The myths I have mentioned thus far amount to examples constituting a window that allows us to understand how authoritarian ideas and practices took hold there. Their examination also helps us to see how history and certain national myths are "weaponized": in these cases, unfortunately, they are often transformed into mere propaganda, or a crutch to support easy answers.

The influential myth of racial democracy affords us an opportunity to understand the process behind the emergence of authoritarian practices and ideas common to Brazil. But there are other important windows onto this issue, too: patriarchy, bossism, violence, inequality, patrimonialism, and social intolerance are stubbornly present throughout the country's history and continue to resonate in the present day. The purpose of this book is this: to build connections, often unexpressed, still less linear, between the past and the present.

History gives us no prescriptions for short- or long-term fixes. It can help us, however, to remove the veil of reverence and instigate a more critical discussion about Brazil's past, its present, and Brazilians' dreams for the future.

1

Slavery and Racism

IN BRAZIL, slavery became so ingrained in society that it ultimately metamorphosed into an idiom of its own, with dire consequences. From the sixteenth through the nineteenth centuries, a scandalous injustice, bolstered by legal subterfuge, took hold across the country. As there was no legislation to either prohibit or regulate this system, it extended throughout the national territory, becoming firmly established as "local custom." A bastardized version of a legal system prevailed, whereby some were granted no rights at all, while others wielded nearly unlimited power.

There was no escaping slavery. Indeed, in the case of Brazil, the institution was so widespread as to hardly be a privilege exclusive to plantation owners. Priests, military officials, government employees, artisans, tavern owners, tradesmen, small-time farmers, wealthy landowners, and even the very poor, including emancipated slaves themselves, owned human chattels. As a result, slavery was much more than an economic system: it governed conduct, reinforced social inequities, established race and color as fundamental boundary markers, sanctioned codes of authority and obedience, and gave birth to a society predicated on paternalism and the strictest of hierarchies.

Moreover, in direct contrast to official discourse, there is no evidence to support the notion that a "humane" form of slavery was practiced in Brazil. There is no room for benevolence in a system that prescribes the ownership of one person by another. Such a system implies the intense and extensive use of forced labor, un-relenting surveillance, and the absence of freedom and free will. In Brazil, slaves were worked so hard and subjected to such cruelty that the life expectancy for male field slaves—twenty-five years—was below even that of the United States, where it was thirty-five. The fate of women slaves was not much different. Forced into their owners' beds, their bodies bore the brunt of the system's vio-lence. They breastfed little masters and mistresses, often com-pelled to abandon their own children to the "foundling wheel" or "castoff wheel"—a mechanism put in place to give up newborns ("cast off foundlings" in the parlance of that time) who were then entrusted to the care of charitable organizations. These women were submitted to arduous work routines, tasked with a growing list of domestic responsibilities. The perverse representation of "mulatta" women as more "inclined" to sensuality and lust also dates from this period. These are nothing more than stereotypes, social and historical constructs that have no basis in reality. They carry with them, however, the power to construct realities and do enormous harm. Already in the early days of what would become Brazil, one could glimpse—as we shall see below—the contours of the "rape culture" so entrenched in the country today. With the disproportionate representation of the sexes among Africans forced onto slave ships, and the much higher number of male colo-nizers, as well as strictly maintained command hierarchies, slavery implied the establishment of equally hierarchical sexual relations, wherein consent was rare. One of the "daily activities" of enslaved women, therefore, involved their subjection to the caprices of their owners, which ultimately led to a contradictory representa-tion of the situation—as though the enslaved women were will-ingly "surrendering themselves."

There are two sides to every coin, however. In Brazil—in direct conflict with the refrain regarding Brazil's more "humane" form of slavery—enslaved men and women responded more aggressively than in other countries; rose up against masters and slave drivers; formed *quilombos*, or runaway slave communities; committed suicide; aborted; fled; and incited all manner of insurrection and rebellion. They also negotiated their roles and responsibilities, advocating for leisure hours, and to recreate their customs in a strange land, worship their gods and continue their religious practices, see to their plots of land, and keep their families and children together.

For their part, slave-owners invented veritable blueprints for punishment, ranging from whippings in the public square to the rod, just as they stayed abreast of abolitionist developments and laws in other slave societies, most particularly in Spanish America. With this knowledge, they delayed, as long as was possible, the end of the regime in Brazil, which adopted a gradual, plodding model of abolition.

A system such as this could not but lead to a society predicated on violence and institutionalized inequality. Enslaved men and women faced workdays as long as eighteen hours, received but one change of clothing per year, and had to settle for little food and water and a complete lack of possessions. If literacy was not formally outlawed, instances in which slave-masters allowed captives to attend school were nonetheless rare, thus creating a society divided by custom and in practice. In Western societies, there is no possibility of social change without access to formal schooling, with social classes otherwise acting like static castes deprived of the capacity to break poverty cycles passed down through the generations.

Slavery in Brazil came to a late end, and in a most conservative manner. Only after a series of incremental laws, such as the 1871 Law of the Free Womb (which provided for the freedom of children born after that date, but not their mothers, and still guaranteed a slave-owner's right to choose between keeping the emancipated until their twenty-first birthday and delivering them to government care), the Sexagenarian Law of 1885 (which emancipated enslaved individuals who had aged precociously and had often been rendered unfit for work, incurring expense rather than profit for their owners), and finally the Golden Law of May 13,

1888.[2] Eleven lines in length, this law represented a compromise solution. It did not compensate slave-owners, who had hoped to receive indemnifications from the State for their "losses." At the same time, it did not provide for any form of integration of the recently freed population, initiating a period called "post-emancipation," which had a fixed start date but no specified end.

It was precisely in this context that determinist theories, in the form of social Darwinism, sought to classify humanity into races, attributing to each distinct physical, intellectual, and moral characteristics. According to these "scientific" models, the Western White male should occupy the top of the social pyramid, while all others were considered inferior beings with limited potential. The worst fate was reserved for racially mixed groups, held to be "degenerate" due to their provenance in the commingling of essentially different races. This "racial knowledge" sought to justify, with the endorsement of the period's theories, the "natural" dominion of White slaveholders over other populations. It further sought to substitute the inequality fostered by slavery for another, this time warranted by biology.

And so, whereas the eighteenth-century Enlightenment and political liberalism had popularized the idea that all men were equal before the law, theories of social and racial determinism encouraged the opposite conclusion: that equality and free will were little more than a chimera, an Enlightenment ruse. Perhaps for this reason, in the period immediately following emancipation, a wise adage made its way through the streets of Rio de Janeiro: "Liberty is black, but equality is white." The phrase acknowledged the freedom Black Brazilians had only recently achieved with the abolition of slavery, but pointed in turn to the persistence of rigid patterns of inequality throughout the country: a problem that remains to this day.

Moreover, the result of these assumptions was to perpetuate structures of domination from the past, recasting them after new forms of racialization, which sought to use biology to justify distinctions that were historical and social. As the Black writer Lima

Barreto complained in his diary at the start of the twentieth century, "The intellectual capacity of Black people is discussed *a priori* and that of Whites, *a posteriori.*"

The emergence of racism is, therefore, a sort of "trophy of modernity." The presence of Black people in spaces of social prestige had already been almost forbidden, or made very difficult, by slavery; it remained uncommon during Brazil's early years as a republic. For this reason, slavery only *appeared* to have been relegated to the past. This social configuration, which led to the exclusion of a good part of the population from the principal institutions of Brazilian society, even resulted in the erasure of the few Black intellectuals who had succeeded in distinguishing themselves during the colonial period, and particularly during the imperial era. It also obscured the formation of a series of societies, associations, and Black community newspapers, founded during the First Republic, which aimed, in accordance with a principle of collectivism, to struggle for the necessary social inclusion of former slaves. As sociologist Mário Augusto Medeiros da Silva asserts, this represented a sort of "double death" for Black people: the memory of an individual was buried along with her body.

With the turn of the twentieth century, and in contrast with the republican government's official propaganda, social exclusion was once again on the rise in Brazil; Black people were being systematically excluded from State policies and assistance. This long history also explains the way in which, paradoxically, racism is the offspring of the sort of liberty that arises from republics founded by White men; to this day, an enormous taboo hovers over the guaranteeing of the rights of other populations, which face enormous obstacles in terms of access to healthcare, education, work, housing, transportation, and safety.

Moreover, if today racial theories are out of vogue—if a biological concept of race is recognized as fallacious and entirely misguided in terms of its moral consequences—we nevertheless still employ a notion of "social race," one that is reproduced daily by the culture and society. We also tend to perpetuate discrimination to a perverse degree, which leads to shorter life expectancy and infringement of the rights of the Black population in comparison to Brazilians at large. Our persistent racial narratives do not end with mere changes in regime. They become embedded in social practices, customs, and beliefs, producing new forms of racism and stratification. For example, to this day, inequality tends to fit a certain profile. Among those who express fear of the Polícia Militar (a heavily armed police force affiliated with the military but subordinate to state governments, whose actions have been the focus of numerous controversies), the majority are young people in the country's underdeveloped Northeast region who identify as Black. In 2009, Brazil's population surpassed 191 million, a 23 percent increase over 1995 figures. Among the more striking findings of the census, one demands particular attention: the size of the country's Black population (defined by the Brazilian census as both Black and Brown). In 1995, 44.9 percent of Brazilians identified as Black; in 2009, this percentage rose to 51.1 percent, while the White population fell from 54.5 to 48.2 percent.

Such an increase, however, did not proceed from an increase in the birth rate among the Black population, but rather from changes in behavior and the way in which Brazilians identify. Since the late 1970s—and particularly during the redemocratization of the 1980s, when a civil rights agenda emerged, characterized by the right to difference within a regime of purported universal equality—Brazilians have changed the way they define themselves and have increasingly claimed Black heritage.

Nonetheless, while this pattern allows us to glimpse a greater flexibility in the current models of classification, others signal a consistent and tenacious exclusion on the basis of race. According to a report from the Brazilian Institute of Applied Economic Research (IPEA), despite a general rise in life expectancy among Brazilians, figures spanning 1993–2006 show that the White population continues to live longer than the Black. During this period, the population of White men around age seventy increased from

8.2 percent to 11.1 percent, at the same time as the group of Black men in the same age range increased from 6.5 percent to 8 percent.

More worrisome still are the mortality rates for men in general and in particular for young Black men, the most frequent victims of urban violence and with limited access to medical care. In 2010, while the homicide rate for young White men was in the region of 28.3 per 100,000, it was 71.7 per 100,000 for young Black men—and even surpassed a rate of 100 per 100,000 in some states. Incidentally, according to Amnesty International, a young Black man in Brazil is, on average, two and a half times more likely to be killed than a young White man. In the Northeast—where homicide rates are the highest in the country—the difference is even starker: young Black men are at five times greater risk of death than their White counterparts.

If we look only at the year 2012, when just over fifty-six thousand people were murdered in Brazil, of this total, thirty thousand were young men between the ages of fifteen and twenty-nine, and of those, 77 percent were Black. Summing up, these figures are a numerical translation of extreme disparities in terms of rights and of elevated rates of violence within specific communities. They reveal more still: patterns of lethal violence tied to long-, medium-, and short-term problems of historic proportions.

To put these numbers in context, it is helpful to know that Brazilian homicide rates are comparable with those witnessed during several modern-day civil wars. During the Syrian conflict that has raged since 2011, the annual death rate has been sixty thousand per year; in Yemen, where war began in 2015, yearly homicides number close to twenty-five thousand; in Afghanistan, where conflict has raged since 1978, there are on average fifty thousand deaths per year. These figures point to the magnitude of Brazil's "war," permitting us to speak seriously of a "genocide" of young Black men.

It's of little use to, as it were, put a bandaid on the situation and buy into the belief that in order to put an end to the truly staggering death toll in Brazil—which, according to data kept by the

Brazilian Forum on Public Safety, reached nearly sixty-four thousand in 2017 alone—it would be sufficient to propose measures that encompass harsher sentences for juvenile offenders, in large part Black residents living in favelas, by making it possible to try them as adults. There is no proof that an increase in the incarceration rate leads to reduced rates of crime. On the contrary: Brazil already has the world's third largest number of incarcerated individuals, and yet continues to report record numbers of homicides. In contrast, countries like Denmark and Sweden, which have invested in alternatives, including rehabilitation, have experienced much better results.

The great paradox is that the Brazilian criminal justice system most closely resembles those of Europe when it comes to its treatment of juvenile offenders. Adolescents between twelve and eighteen years of age, perpetrators of less than 10 percent of serious crimes in the country, receive preferential treatment, on account of not yet having reached adulthood. The refining of the system has the capacity to reduce the rate of crimes committed by juvenile offenders, generally poor Black men, who find themselves in a vicious cycle that leads to recidivism and further incarceration.

It is a controversial subject, and the entire story cannot be told or resolved by crunching numbers. It is also clear, of course, that there is no such thing as a harmless racism: all are similarly freighted with trauma and suffering. At the current moment, with 55 percent of its population composed of Black people, Brazil is the nation with the second largest population of African descent, behind only Nigeria. If on the one hand this commixture has engendered a society characterized by the fusion of rhythms, arts, arms, cuisines, and sports, on the other it has produced a nation that has grown accustomed to racial inequality, as evidenced by the racial composition of domestic workers and manual laborers, and the absence of Black people in corporate and entrepreneurial environments, in the theater, in concert halls, in professional associations, and in certain social spheres. The country also engages in another routine form of racial exclusion, delegating to the police a role of performing discrimination through well-known "acts of intimidation": police batons that land more heavily upon Black heads than White and that humiliate them in a public show of power and hierarchy.

Carrying this burden on its shoulders, the country has become a profoundly inequitable and racist nation whose high crime rates have long outlasted the era of slavery and instead been reworked into a contemporary context: a demonstration of the ways in which racism works hand in glove with an ideology whose purpose is the guaranteed survival of privileges, deepening social divisions.

While racism has for some time now ceased to enjoy acceptance as scientific theory, it nonetheless lives on as an operative social ideology in the form of an all-powerful "common sense," whose perverse influence results in routine silence and complicity. Slavery bequeathed to us an authoritarian society, which we have now attempted to reproduce in modern terms—a society accustomed to command hierarchies, which appeals to a certain mythic narrative of its past to justify the present, and which takes very badly to the idea of equality in the division not only of responsibilities, but also of rights.

There is no ideology of "playing the victim" in Brazil, and especially where the question of racial exclusion is concerned. On the contrary, the victories secured by Black activists since at least the 1920s have shown that there cannot be so much as a trace of "racial democracy" in Brazil as long as current levels of social, economic, and racial inequality persist. On the other hand, as the sociologist Petrônio Domingues has conclusively shown, there has been no small number of initiatives by Black groups struggling for greater equality and inclusion. The Brazilian Black Front, for example, was active during Getúlio Vargas's government (1930–45), while during the Second Republic, the Union of Men of Color, the Black Experimental Theater, and the Black Cultural Association left their mark. In the context of the *abertura* (opening) beginning in 1978 that marked the slow transition to democracy from the dictatorship that had ruled Brazil from May 1964, the Unified Black

Movement assumed something of a leadership role in the country's antiracist struggle. Later, in the twenty-first century, it was the turn of Black feminists to put other forms of feminism in check, to produce their own theories, exposing as they did so the specificities and reality of Black women.

We know that social movements in general gain momentum and new life in the context of redemocratizations, and the Brazilian case further exemplifies this tendency. Indeed, with the passage of the Constitution of 1988 that gave form to the New Republic, new forms of Black activism flourished. Significant achievements include official recognition of Black communities' forms of knowledge, as laid out explicitly in Article 215 of the People's Constitution, and the designation of Afro-Brazilian cultural forms as "cultural heritage" in Article 216. Moreover, Article 68 of the Transitional Constitutional Provisions protects the right of "remaining members of escaped slave communities" to continue to live and survive in the small collective farming communities and agricultural properties they have occupied since the end of slavery. Lastly, Article 5 (Section XLII) finally recognized in the legal code the existence of discrimination in Brazil, rendering racist acts crimes subject neither to bail or the statute of limitations, and which can lead to prison sentences.

Following the establishment of this institutional landmark, the race question came to occupy attention at various levels of the State. One example of this was the creation, on the hundredth anniversary of the abolition of slavery, of the Fundação Cultural Palmares, at the time part of the Ministry of Culture and today, in the more conservative context occasioned by the current government, reallocated to the Special Secretariat of Culture within the Ministry of Civic Affairs. Other gains were soon made, and if these did not always represent a full evolution, they at least constituted steady progress. In 2002, the country engaged in a public debate around affirmative action when, for the first time, compensatory policies were implemented. The following year saw the creation of the Special Secretariat for Racial Equality Policy (SEPPIR). In 2010, Congress approved the Racial Equality Statute, a set of rules and judicial principles aimed at reining in discrimination and establishing policies to reduce inequality. In 2020, the country's supreme court ruled that racial quotas in University of Brasília admissions policy were constitutional, and that same year Law No. 12711 was sanctioned, mandating the application of such measures for at least 50 percent of admissions spots across federal universities.[3] Following these initiatives, racial quotas became part of a new reality for Brazilians in general and higher education in particular. The quota system consists of compensatory and temporary policies that seek to create temporary inequities in the interests of long-term equality. They seek to repair historical injustices that have had enormous impact on the education and social inclusion of populations that were shut out of formal schooling for a long period. They aspire, as well, to inject more diversity into Brazilian institutions and produce forms of coexistence and knowledge that are more dynamic on account of their plurality. In this regard, it is worth calling attention yet again to the way in which increased diversity generates an ever greater wealth of information and experience. As the renowned Africanist Alberto da Costa e Silva affirms in *A manilha e o libambo* (Manillas and shackles), "the slave trade peopled Brazil and inserted Africa into our veins."

Two other crucial advances had fundamental implications and repercussions for the education and the collective "imagination" of the Brazilian people. In 1997, quilombo leader Zumbi dos Palmares was finally recognized as a national hero, the first in line of a new genealogy of Black Brazilian leaders. The date of Zumbi's death—November 20—became a national holiday, the National Day of Black Consciousness, a break from the uniform Whiteness of all other celebrated national historical figures. In 2003, the National Educational Policy and Guidelines Statute was passed, which made obligatory in curricula across the country the teaching of "African and Afro-Brazilian History and Culture," an essential step toward finally creating alternative historical and cultural narratives, distinct from those that have traditionally privileged a colonialist gaze. These are, therefore, two measures of immense impact and relevance, as they seek to restore to the populations concerned the position that they have effectively occupied and continue to occupy and to advance the development of projects that validate their identity. They are also policies that stimulate pride in and understanding of a more pluralistic history, since they are not written exclusively by Whites of European origin who belong to a certain social class.

What this list of social advances proves is that Black citizens have slowly been making gains toward full citizenship, quadrupling their presence in the realm of higher education and significantly altering the way in which Brazilian history is made, as expressed in academic books and teaching materials that have begun to give space to the diversity at the core of Brazil's formation. In fact, Black activist movements have had a fundamental role in applying pressure for curricular change across higher education, generating recognition for the relevance of Black social leaders throughout Brazilian history and culture.

Meanwhile, where the racial question is concerned, Brazil remains a long way from "happily ever after," continuing to couple cultural inclusion with social exclusion—integration with segregation—and to tolerate heavy doses of silence and things left unsaid. For this very reason, it is not sufficient merely to blame the past and make peace with the present.

Since the return of democracy, Brazil has implemented an agenda that recognizes and values the ethnic and racial diversity to be found across the country, and legislative bodies have approved a plethora of measures aimed at reducing racial inequality. Yet, in contrast to this growing struggle for rights, Brazilians are at a moment in their history when the political, socio-cultural, and economic crisis foretold by the clamor of the streets in 2013 seems capable of turning back confirmed advances, in line with reactionary agendas with a questionable commitment to equality.[4] Indeed, these new movements are on the contrary more concerned with a return to authoritarian political models.

The struggle against racism and the advancement of racial equality are not themes that affect Black populations exclusively. All Brazilians lose something from populist discourses that seek to question the beauty and strength of the diversity that is part and parcel of the country's history. Democracy is diminished, too, in the process, as is the social pact constructed since 1988. In fact, as long as racism persists, Brazilians will be unable to lay claim to democratic consolidation.

The period following abolition in Brazil was not the prelude to a more egalitarian nation. Despite certain social advances, institutions and leadership positions remain dominated by White Brazilians, while Black Brazilians face systematic discrimination. In parallel, the population of Brazil's prisons and mental health facilities is still predominantly Black.

It is inherent to conservative discourses to ignore and discredit the demands of minorities struggling for their rights—rights inalienable from their condition as citizens. Among the political strategies of populist governments in recent years has been a disregard for data that reveal the societal factors that have divided and continue to divide Brazilians. Slavery, on the scale experienced in Brazil, was and continues to be an insurmountable feature of the Brazilian story. The country inherited a heavy burden, and the tendency is to perpetuate it in the present day: studies show the structural discrimination characterizing Brazilian society, which spans, as we shall see later on, the areas of education and health, and extends even to matters of housing, transportation, infant mortality, and risk of death. Various attempts to minimize the problem—to ignore reports and studies, characterizing them as *mimimi*, a pejorative allusion to those who do nothing but whine—provide insufficient support for claims that racism does not exist in Brazil; such efforts merely confirm its existence as a routine practice behind these acts of denial.

Of course racism in Brazil is not, as with the apartheid once in place in the United States and South Africa, codified in law. However, discrimination in the country operates through the social exclusion to be found in corporate environments, in newsrooms, in cultural enterprises, in the division of labor, and in many other environments that foster routine racial inequality. The potent myth of racial democracy, meanwhile, for a long time stood in the way of recognition of and respect for the claims of Black activists on the part of White elites, who seemed accustomed to a certain cultural and social myopia in this regard.

Authoritarian enterprises have the capacity to recreate the past and minimize the role played by those who lived and forged alternative histories—which depart, that is, from those of a European and colonial hue. Many histories existed simultaneously. Toni Morrison, in her novel *Beloved*, tells the story of 124 Bluestone Road, inhabited by two women and the ghosts of their pasts: the memory of violence, of the rapes, of the lost children, and of so many deaths during the days of slavery. Paradoxically, the ghosts that have insisted on returning are those with the closest ties to the present. In fact, the living and the dead share the same plane of existence. Brazilians, dogged by their past, are still engaged in the task of expelling ghosts that continue stubbornly to cast their shadows.

2

Bossism

SOMEWHERE AROUND 1630, at the time when he finished writing his *History of Brazil*, Brother Vicente do Salvador, a Franciscan friar who would become Brazil's first historian, concluded, "No man in this land is a true republican, nor does he watch over, or see to the common good, but rather each looks after his private good." Brother Vicente was not without his reasons. Five centuries later, the Brazilian republic remains unfinished: each person seeing to their own private interests above all and only later—much later—to those concerning the *res publica*.

The origins of this long history can be found in the sixteenth century, when the Portuguese metropole, facing the impossibility of populating such a vast territory as Brazil, opted to govern its American territory by delegating powers to a series of colonists, who transformed themselves into owners of vast dominions of their own. Such was the spirit and the foundation of colonization in Brazil: a small number of men accumulating latifundia, or enormous landed estates, which in general produced a single crop.

Latifundium is a term of Latin origin that condenses the notions of *latus* (broad, spacious, and extensive) and *fundus* (farm). "Plantation" was a term originally used to refer to English overseas estates and that later historiography put to general use across all colonies, but whose meaning was essentially the same: a rural property of considerable size, often made of lands that were fallow or little exploited due to the use of rudimentary techniques and poor land management.

Both during the era when sugarcane reigned supreme in the northeastern region of the country (the sixteenth, seventeenth, and eighteenth centuries) and at the height of coffee production, whose predominance in the export market dates back to the mid-1800s, "agroindustry" began to take new forms, and landowners not only inherited lands but acquired them. A landowner's control over his lands and those living on it remained more or less the same. It is true that, in parallel, a domestic economy based on small and medium-sized properties gathered strength in a few provinces as these centuries passed. At the same time, despite these developments, the growing power of local kingpins remained largely unchanged. In fact, so accustomed did society become to this system that it was transposed onto smaller operations, though on a limited scale.

The Brazilian colonial model relied overwhelmingly on slave labor and large swaths of single-crop agricultural estates and on the personalism of private influence combined with a near-total absence of a public sphere or State. It was in the eighteenth-century context that a new aristocracy was "invented"—because now transferred to the tropics—in the Americas. Epitomized in its infancy by extensive sugarcane plantations located along the coast of what are today the states of Pernambuco and Bahia, it was composed of new local chiefs who sought to transform themselves into icons of their economic, social, and political class.

This group composed a sort of "merit-aristocracy," newly formed rather than hereditary as in Europe, since their dominance derived from the concentration of wealth and power. In the case of the Portuguese colony, the titles conceded were not handed down from father to son; they represented an individual reward for services rendered or were obtained in exchange for payment. Thus, they constituted a sort of privilege: a privilege from the State, for personal ends.

What this amounted to in reality was a "pretense to nobility," which revolved around privileges acquired by this European minority that dominated a country whose majority population was enslaved, and gave them weight. In a landscape wrought compulsorily by slave labor, the mere fact of having skin of a color other than black already set one on the path to aristocracy. As the naturalist Alexander von Humboldt remarked, in the American colonies, "todo blanco es caballero" (every White man is a gentleman).

In fact, if we take a sample of the colonial-era landowning families in the sugar-producing Northeast, it becomes clear that very few were Portuguese nobility, and fewer still were Catholic. Many of them were "New Christians," merchants, immigrants of some means, who dedicated their time and capital to the production of and trade in sugarcane.[1] It was only with the evolution of the system, and with the perpetuation of marriage among themselves, that these landowners began to form a more homogeneous class of their own. From that point on, as Evaldo Cabral de Mello has shown us, they dedicated themselves to remaking and constructing mythical genealogies, seeking to establish in the distant past the purported aristocratic roots they had contrived. They also took great pains to construct an edifying history, fusing the figure of landowner with that of the father figure—gentle yet strict—and therefore etching a patriarchal society in which women fulfilled what was basically a secondary role and hierarchy was placed on a pedestal, never to be questioned. Therein lay the form of Brazil's patriarchal society; the (master's) family served as support and protection, literally and figuratively, for society at large.

If landowners were not noble by blood, they sought at any rate to reinvent themselves as such, and they put history, a certain history, to use as a way to flaunt their vaunted position. They likewise made use of a certain theatrics of power that allowed them to justify and underscore their eminent position in the social structure at the same time. There is no shortage of reports of masters atop chestnut horses leading processions of vast numbers of slaves while bedecked in full suits, wide-brimmed hats, and polished boots on even the hottest days in Brazil's sultry Northeast. Since to repeat something is to confer certainty upon it, they replicated this public ritual frequently.

This was, without a doubt, then, a peculiar aristocracy, but there was one aspect in which the members of this group mirrored their European counterparts. The aristocracy in Brazil was defined by what it *didn't* do: engage in physical labor, tend an establishment, work as artisans, till the earth, carry heavy loads, hawk wares, or sundry other manual tasks that fell to "savages" or the enslaved. In fact, the country's enduring prejudice against manual labor dates to this era, when such work was considered by the privileged "beneath them," if not outright "demeaning." And so, the new aristocrats sought to keep their distance from such forms of service, living off the profits generated by the cultivation of their lands, from the payment of rents or government posts, or from income from the State or the Church, achieved through considerable negotiation and godfatherism.

While there were several paths to aristocracy, the best, if capital was sufficient, was to be a landowner and to surround oneself with not only an abundance of slaves, but also numerous in-laws, extended relatives, and servants. This model gave birth to a patriarchal society founded on this pattern of extended family and allegiance beyond blood relations. To return to the example of the sugarcane plantations, it could be claimed that these provided the nucleus of what would develop into the Brazilian elite, until at least the end of the nineteenth century. The biological family in turn constituted the nucleus of the rural estate, and wealthy landowners generally brought up their male offspring with a view to perpetuating their family's dominance. There is no shortage of family tales of how, "with a bit of luck," one son would end up in business, another in the law, and yet another would enter the priesthood, thus guaranteeing influence in each of these areas. Daughters, meanwhile, were viewed as bargaining chips for use during negotiations and in alliances with other local powers. Marriage represented, then, a sort of strategy to guarantee good dividends if equally powerful suitors were to be found.

It also was part of "being a gentleman" for a landowner to look after all those around him and see to their needs; and in this way not only new duties but also privileges accrued to this class. A society characterized by the authority of powerful landowners thus became increasingly entrenched, as they exacted a steep price for "favors" performed, their dominance increasingly a foregone conclusion. Capital, authority, the possession of slaves, dedication to politics, command over an extensive kinship network, and control over poor free populations, Church offices, and government posts constituted the basic aims of this dazzling aristocracy, in whose shadow were obscured considerable inequality and the concentration of power.

In the countryside, above all, everything became a business: titles, protection, government posts, marriages. Landowners' dominion extended also to the surrounding area, the workers who lived in the vicinity, or the small-scale planters who were generally dependent on favors from these wealthy landowners to conduct their business, secure credit, and transport their goods. As a result, fealty to local chiefs, as a way to secure advantages, engendered rituals of submission in which the repetition of the most quotidian gestures revealed itself as crucial to the solidifying of certain hierarchies.

The populace would greet these landowners with deference, referring to them by nicknames, by first name, or even by affectionate variations on these. If such practices denoted proximity, they likewise underscored compliance with paternalistic mores that became increasingly fixed in rural areas. In other words, "proximity" merely disguised stable power hierarchies. Indeed, this very argument was made by historian Sérgio Buarque de Holanda, who in *Raízes do Brasil* remarks on the widespread use of such outlets as a way of conflating public and private relations, and disguising a real and strict social distance beneath a veneer of familiarity. The landowners may well have publicly responded to terms of endearment akin to "sah" and "massah," but they never relinquished their claim to social distinction or failed to be selective in deciding who gained entrée (and who didn't) to their private circle. For this reason they were considered the ultimate authorities on the plantation estates, which encompassed the big house, the slave quarters, the church, and neighboring small farms whose workers enjoyed and depended on the landowner's protection. In 1711, the Jesuit André João Antonil, known for his important documentation of the colonial-era economy in Brazil, defined the social status of local power brokers in this way: "'Plantation master' is a title to which many aspire, because it brings with it the right to be served, obeyed, and revered by multitudes."

Such a power-wielding position would scarcely change during the reign of another landowning aristocracy, this time located in southeastern Brazil during the era of the Brazilian Empire: a group made wealthy largely by the cultivation of coffee beans predominant in Brazil from the second half of the nineteenth century onward. Revolts and rebellions had always been a reality as long as Brazil had been Brazil, but the prevailing imagery of the country as promulgated by its various elites always sought to portray the instruments of control in a noble light. In the images left by travelers, or especially in the photographs commissioned from the 1850s onward, the representation of the elite social sphere—with its imposing dining rooms and sumptuous banquet tables, celebrations, pastimes, and evening strolls—was a constant. The powerful landowner was always to be found leading his legion of workers, hat on head, gaze resolute, pocket watch at his waist, ring on his little finger, and boots on his feet—thus distinguishing himself from the enslaved, who in general went barefoot and were to be found bent over the earth.

This reality and performance of power was also reflected in the attire of the landowning family, and in the hospitality and architectural luxury of their big houses, which ever since the seventeenth century had become increasingly eye-catching, taking on sumptuous dimensions in the mansions of the Vale do Paraíba during the reign of Dom Pedro II (1840–89).[2] Manor houses may have varied in size and proportions, but they all constituted material expressions of might and authority, intended to impress both outside visitors and those living nearby, and the workers who, catching sight of the edifice from a distance, recognized yet one more representation of control and compulsory subordination.

Incidentally, a landowner's power and influence could be measured by his income, the number of slaves he possessed and often flaunted, and his ability to extend credit to nearby residents, but also in terms of rituals that reinforced local power: customs, practices, and symbols that were transported to various areas throughout Brazil, above all those that featured extensive, single-crop plantations. This process became so prevalent that with the advent of coffee cultivation, first in the Vale do Paraíba region and later in western São Paulo state, new societies with landowning pretensions multiplied, soon sharing gestures, customs, and similar models of comportment.[3] Speaking of models, through the colonial and imperial periods a whole series of "manuals" was produced and disseminated, offering advice to plantation masters on how to discipline the enslaved, stamp out rebels, or increase reproduction among slaves. These slim volumes, which sometimes contained illustrations, circulated throughout the Americas and the Caribbean, constituting a sort of technical apparatus for the exercise of a master's authority. For example, in 1803, Dr. David Collins, an English physician who traveled throughout the American colonies, suggested a "bonus" for enslaved women who became pregnant. Collins recommended that, after the birth of her first child, a mother ought to be relieved from field work. After the second, she would gain two days of rest every fifteen days. A third child would earn her an additional day off each week; the fourth, two days of rest. By the fifth, a mother would receive three days, and so on.

Many of these manuals were dedicated to providing "counsel" on how to prevent slaves from escaping. "Moderate punishment" was the principal recommendation in terms of preventing "rebellion." On the other hand, these manuals suggested it was prudent to permit the enslaved to raise pigs or chickens, as well as to grow vegetables in patches next to the slave quarters. The idea was that the slaves would fill the hours not spent working with this small-scale farming, clearing the land of weeds, and, especially, "enjoying themselves," forgetting plans for escape or rebellion. Another theme that ran throughout these works was how to "employ and apportion punishment." It was suggested, openly and unabashedly, that women should never be whipped in public, so as not to provoke the ire of the men. But "males," according to documents from the period, ought to serve as an example, every last slave being assembled to witness the punishment of rebels, a scene that, generally speaking, involved both the master and a slave driver. Punishment was considered, then, an administrative act with the aim of maintaining order, but equally as yet another opportunity for a public display of the power by the master, who underscored his right of discretion and authority on these occasions.

The question of controlling food costs was another matter that required considerable attention. One manual maintained that starved slaves would steal in order to eat. Accordingly, it was better that the master set aside, weekly, two pounds of flour and a nearly equal portion of cured meat for the purpose of maintaining them "fed and obedient." It was also recommended that "feed" not be handed out on Sundays, in order that the food not be quickly squandered. It was more appropriate to "supply provisions" on Mondays or on workdays so that this "feed" should be conserved in such a way as to last for the entire week. In the case of children, it was prescribed that they be fed with rice, cream of wheat, and beef broth. From age five to ten, they ought only to be tasked with a light work load. The aim was to "strengthen their muscles and educate their spirits," since, upon turning twelve, they were considered apt for heavier work, and likewise capable of working so as to "provide a return" on the capital their owners had invested in them.

These manuals sought to share "management" solutions and aimed at the control of the enslaved and maintenance of "peace and harmony" on plantation estates across Brazil. However, rules only become necessary where there is fear that they might be contravened. That is to say, one only enacts laws imposing discipline and control when a society rebels with some frequency. What is clear is that workers did not conform to captivity, engaging in daily acts of insurrection, large and small. It is for this reason that the aforementioned manuals exude urgency: it was necessary to share forms of "training," to share experiences, and thus exert rigorous control over the enslaved, who, after all, accounted for the immense majority among colonial and even imperial populations. Fear and authority were, as a result, inseparable in these societies.

If insurrection was only ever hinted at in these documents, their central aims were nonetheless declared: they sought to attest to and reaffirm the rule of the master, who exercised control over the lives, fates, and even deaths of his ranks of slaves. The idea was to share knowledge, and consequently reign and rule more efficiently.

In photographs too, for which there was a veritable fever in Brazil from around the middle of the nineteenth century, the master made a point of immortalizing himself before his slaves. Visual documentation from the era of large coffee estates frequently captures a slaveholder flaunting his vast "slave holdings"—the master wearing shoes while the rest go barefoot, he in full formal attire and the enslaved wearing clothes often full of holes, his gaze resolute as his workers sought to evade the lens or betray the slightest of reactions.

In a photo taken by Militão Augusto de Azevedo (1837–1905) in his studio (fig. 1), despite the great pains taken by the photographer to demonstrate the control exercised by the owner (probably his client), and the pride of the same in exhibiting his stature, the result did not entirely correspond to the intention. At the exact moment the shutter clicked, the enslaved displayed all manner of reactions to the situation. Some did what was, most likely, demanded of them; others put their displeasure and vexation on display.

Marc Ferrez (1843–1923), one of the pioneers of Brazilian photography and a photographer of unusual skill and ability, developed a beautiful photo album to announce the arrival of estates

FIGURE 1. Militião Augusto de Azevedo, *Master and Slaves*, circa 1860,
6.3 × 8.3 cm. São Paulo, Museu Paulista at the University of São Paulo.

and coffee plantations in the Vale do Paraíba. The landscapes are
sweeping and orderly, and show workers in placid devotion to
their daily toils (fig. 2). The earnest slaves appear in geometric
harmony, with downcast gaze. These are gestures and attitudes, as
we shall see further below, specially orchestrated by the photographer, who sought not only to corroborate but to disseminate the
image of rigid hierarchy, in which workers were passive and conceal even the slightest hint of a reaction. Today we know, however,
that there is much intellectual and visual staging in these visual
records, since, in the given context, the region's situation was quite
the contrary. With the imminent end of the system, and the decline of the plantations of the Vale do Paraíba, masters became
increasingly demanding of their workers, who, for their part, reacted
in various ways to their oppressors.

FIGURE 2. Marc Ferrez, *Slaves on a Coffee Plantation in the Vale do Paraíba Region,*
30 × 40 cm. São Paulo, Archive of the Instituto Moreira Salles.

The ways in which Ferrez's iconographic representations uphold certain conventions, particularly in their effort to shore up forms of power, are noteworthy. One can see a world of reactions in these photos, taken during slavery's final days—featuring the enslaved whispering, wearing expressions of ire or vexation in response to the artificial and degrading exposition of their bodies. Their clothes are also often dirty and tattered, denoting the locale's decline. To obtain certainty as to the artifice and cunning behind the operation, we need only turn our attention to the left of the image at center. Instead of the plantation foreman, it is Ferrez's production chief who, signaling with his hands, positions the "models" in this imaginary scene with its distorted portrayal of the large property, of the master's dominance, and of slavery itself.

White women would figure much less frequently in the photographs of the nineteenth century. When they do appear, they are confined to the domestic sphere or concealed in sedan-chairs or by chaises-longues, denoting, through the fact of their rarely being observed in the streets, their position at once invisible—because obligatorily reserved and cloistered within this world of patriarchal bossism—and symbolically present in carriages-for-hire used only by those ascribed socially superior positions within the community. Enslaved women, by comparison, appeared much more often in photographs from the period. They were portrayed in turn as wet nurses—a traditional representation in the Afro-Atlantic axis that sought to confer "humanity" upon the institution—and in a sensual way, to an extent such that stereotypes then established persist in regard to Black women today.

Even with the end of the Empire, and the onset of the decline of this rural slave society that would ultimately crumble alongside the monarchy, the image of the master as provider, deserving of loyalty and submission, would live on. As a result, this masculine, patriarchal ethos was transplanted to the republican era, when the distribution of power continued to flow through the hierarchy and political might of wealthy landowners, who accumulated considerable political influence, not merely through representative positions but via electoral manipulation. A state's importance and political clout now relied upon the size of its electorate and the corresponding scale of its parliamentary representation, whose power continued to derive from regional bosses.

For its part, the new republic's political stability was secured by three fundamental procedures: the effort by state governments to keep political conflict confined to the regional sphere; the federal government's recognition of the full sovereignty of states when it came to local politics; and the persistence of an electoral process whereby, despite political mechanisms that sought to bring local disputes under control, fraud remained widespread.

Fraud featured throughout the electoral process, a form of interference by private interests within the public logic of the State, the vote viewed as a bargaining chip. "Yoke-and-oxen" voting, so termed on account of the tight control exercised by landowners over the electorate, became a political and cultural practice—an expression of the loyalty of the voter to the local chief. In a similar vein, the "electoral corral" alluded to a tent where voters were kept under close supervision and fed a square meal, leaving only when it was time to deliver their vote—which they received in a sealed envelope—directly to the urn.

We can be sure that power relations derived from the municipal level upward, and at the peak of this well-established system was the phenomenon of rural bossism, known as *coronelismo*. *Coronel*, or colonel, was the highest post within the hierarchy of the National Guard, an institution of the Brazilian Empire that tied rural property owners to the government. With the advent of the republic, however, the Guard lost its military significance; the so-called colonels no longer formed part of the military corps, but they did retain political influence in the municipalities where they lived, recreating the mystique surrounding local bosses under new circumstances.[4] Rural bossism then came to mean a complex system of negotiation between these local power brokers and state governors, and of state governors with the president of the republic. The colonel embodied one of the foundational elements of the traditional oligarchic structure based on individualized powers generally concentrated on large estates throughout Brazil.

Certain features consolidated over time survived, moreover, into the First Republic. One of these was, precisely, the nation's oligarchic profile, with limits on who was eligible to vote and run for office. In 1874, still under the Empire, only about 10 percent of the population could vote; but in 1910, for example, some twenty years after the proclamation of the republic, out of a population of twenty-two million, merely 627,000 had the right to vote. In the 1920s, the percentage of those eligible to vote oscillated between 2.3 and 3.4 percent of the total population.

The result was that the Brazilian republic was held together in the early years of the twentieth century by a system of bargaining chips, credit, favoritism, and negotiation. Now, however, the direct manipulation of votes is, for the most part, a thing of the past. Today, with 147.3 million eligible voters, distributed across 5,570 municipalities, and in 171 localities in 110 other countries throughout the world, Brazil is recognized as having the world's most expansive electronic voting system and a cutting-edge technological infrastructure that prevents interruptions in the transmission of voting data, guaranteeing a vote-tabulating process that is not only efficient, but secure and absolutely trustworthy. In a matter of hours after voting ends, Brazilians already know the names of their elected officials: an unprecedented feat in a country of continental proportions that boasts an enormous electorate.

And yet, even if the last thirty years of democracy have guaranteed such high levels of voter participation, the Brazilian republic nonetheless remains flawed—and characterized by the high concentration of power—when it comes to matters that frustrate social equality, as well as income and property equity. According to a December 6, 2016 story from Brazilian news portal G1 and data from the 2006 Agricultural Census (in the absence of more recent data), a report compiled by Oxfam Brazil reveals the persistence of inequality in Brazilian rural settings:

Large estates account for only 0.9 percent of all rural establish-ments in Brazil, yet compose 45 percent of all rural land area in the country. On the other hand, establishments under ten hect-ares represent more than 47 percent of the total in the country yet account for less than 2.3 percent of total land area. There is an enormous imbalance, as well, when analyzing the question of gender in rural settings. It is men who control the lion's share of rural land and the helm of properties with the largest land mass: they possess 87.3 recent of all the establishments, which represent 94.5% of all the rural lands throughout Brazil. At the other extreme, it is women who represent nearly double the number of farmers who do not own land when compared to men—8.1 percent and 4.5 percent, respectively.

The same report reveals that Brazil comes in an embarrassing fifth place in Latin America in terms of land use inequality, ranking behind Paraguay, Chile, Venezuela, and Colombia. Concentration has only increased over time: in 2003, there were 4.2 million prop-erties, a number that had grown to 5.16 by 2010. While small prop-erties, the *minifundia*, became still more scarce, properties with more than a thousand hectares grew in number. In 2003, 51.6 percent of all properties in Brazil boasted a land area of more than a thousand hectares; in 2010, this percentage had grown to 56.1 percent.

Put another way: the crisis of land inequality is not being ef-fectively tackled in Brazil. Nor does inequality derive from land ownership alone; it is also present in investments, technology, and worker gender. As we saw earlier, men dominate in these sectors, controlling 87.3 percent of all rural properties in the country.

In 2010, according to the program Repórter Brasil, income con-centration across Brazil's rural households was 0.727 by the Gini coefficient (a tool to measure income equality around the world). To give an idea of the gulf, the Gini for Brazil as a whole was, in this context, 0.53. Only Namibia, with 0.743, outstripped Brazil when it came to the rural divide. On the other hand, average monthly income from the principal income source for rural families represented 35 percent (R$360) of the average monthly income from the principal income source in cities (R$1,017).

It is possible to verify this level of inequality from yet another angle: data from 2016 pertaining to rural credit. Large rural properties—those larger than a thousand hectares—accounted for 43 percent of rural credit, while 80 percent of smaller establishments ranged between 13 and 23 percent. According to the National Institute for Land Settlement and Agrarian Reform (INCRA), there are 729 people or corporations registered as owners of rural holdings in Brazil who owe debts to the federal government exceeding R$50 million. In total, this group owes approximately R$200 billion, with land sufficient to accommodate 214,827 families.

The fact that Brazil continues to perpetuate inequality in rural areas is one of the great challenges the country has ahead of it. According to the Oxfam study cited above, it is in municipalities with increased concentration of land ownership, in those accounting for the highest levels of agricultural production, and also in those where big agribusiness has significant operations that we also find the highest levels of poverty and inequality. For example, Correntina, in Bahia state—a municipality with one of the largest agribusiness sectors in Brazil, and one that employs technologically advanced production methods—is among those with a considerable level of poverty, hardly in keeping with such modern advancement.

The flip-side of this coin is the accumulation of power in the hands of families that have long practiced political, cultural, and social bossism in their regions. It is true that in the latest election, in 2018, influential political bosses were unable to reaffirm their influence and dominance, as in the case with the Sarney dynasty, which suffered a resounding defeat in the state of Maranhão. Not even the return of patriarch and former president José Sarney at the age of eighty-eight could save his daughter Roseana Sarney from defeat in the first round of the election. Similarly, he was unable to prevent his son, Sarney Filho (of the PV/Green Party), from losing his run for office.

These losses aside, it is worth reinforcing the point that, after sixty-two years in power, José Sarney has been a deputy, a governor, a five-term senator—serving two terms during the dictatorship and three during democratic regimes—and president. Maranhão experienced fifty years of oligarchic dominance, during which the stain of being the poorest state in all of Brazil remained. According to the 2013 *Atlas of Human Development in Brazil*, the state led the list, with 63.6 percent of its population classified as "vulnerable to poverty," or in other words, "individuals with a household income per capita equal or inferior to R$255 per month [just over US $47, at time of writing], as of August 2010, equivalent to half the minimum wage at that date." Maranhão was followed by Alagoas (59.8%), Piauí (58.1%), Pará (56%), Ceará (54.8%), Paraíba (53.6%), Bahia (52.7%), and Sergipe (52.1%), each one of them dominated by its respective rural elite.

The association between local bossism and wealth concentration is also clear in Ceará, where the Ferreira Gomes clan could be classified as a political oligarchy. According to a story in the August 26, 2002 edition of the *Folha de S. Paulo*, Cid Gomes (Popular Socialist Party, now Cidadania) assumed the mayoralty of Sobral in 1997, breaking the power-alternating agreement established between the Prado and Barreto families, who had dominated city politics since 1963, "and re-established the Ferreira Gomes political dynasty. The Ferreira Gomes family was in power in the city's early days. Its first two mayors were forebears of contemporary political powerhouses Ciro and Cid: in 1890, Vicente César Ferreira Gomes, and in 1892, José Euclides Ferreira Gomes." The family returned to power in 1936, when another relative of Ciro, Vicente Antenor Ferreira Gomes, served as mayor for nine years, until 1944, a period when the federal government was under the control of Getúlio Vargas. From 1944 to 1977, the Ferreira Gomeses kept their distance from politics and the halls of power; until, that is, José Euclides Ferreira Gomes, a public defense attorney and father to Ciro and Cid, returned to head of the municipal government between 1977 and 1983—though still under the political tutelage of the Prado family. The *Folha de S. Paulo* article continues,

> Ciro entered politics at the age of twenty, when his father was mayor and appointed him city prosecutor. Aside from enjoying the support of the Prado family, José Euclides, affiliated with the conservative PDS [Democratic Social Party], counted on the support of César Cals, one of three local bosses who took turns as governor during the military regime (1964–1985). Following in his father's footsteps, the PDS was Ciro's first political party, via which he ran for election as state representative for the first time in 1982. In 1986, he ran for reelection as part of the PMDB, supporting the initiative by a group led by Tasso Jereissati, who was also a first-time candidate for the state governorship, to topple the colonels and establish what their adversaries call the "toucan oligarchy," in a reference to the party symbol of the PSDB.

The defeat of one oligarchy tended strengthen another—and one that traced a clear line from land ownership to political clout.

In Rio Grande do Norte, a small group of families dominates state politics; the same surnames take turns each election cycle, and the same politicians jump from office to office. The traditional clans in Rio Grande do Norte politics have a tendency to pin their hopes on the same pillars: organized campaigns, economic power, canvassing, and city governments. The Alves family is so famous in the region that its members can afford to skip debates and other hallmarks of participatory democracy. And yet local oligarchies suffered successive defeats in the elections of 2014 and 2018, and have been diminished as never before in the state's politics.

In Goiás too, an oligarchy of two families—the Caiados and the Bulhões—has divided power between them. Senator Ronaldo Caiado (of the center-right DEM) represents a family that has held power in Goiás since the nineteenth century. It is the oldest in the state and one of the most entrenched in the Senate. What few know is that the Caiado oligarchy got its start playing a supporting role to another oligarchy, which has long since disappeared: that of the Bulhões. Antônio José Caiado, one of Ronaldo's forebears, got his start in politics as the right-hand man to federal representative Leopoldo de Bulhões. Leopoldo sought Caiado's support because, by that time, the Caiados owned land throughout the state. The alliance with the Bulhões only made them more powerful. The break between the two oligarchic clans occurred during the political sunset of Leopoldo, who refused to share power with Antônio. Antônio's grandson, Totó Caiado, was the principal catalyst of the break. From then on "Caiadoism" took on a life of its own. Totó, Ronaldo's grandfather, was a federal representative and senator. For thirty-six years, Goiás was governed by oligarchies.

In Acre, another clan took its curtain call, for now, in the 2018 elections: the Vianas. The Workers' Party (PT) left command of the state after twenty years of dominance following the victory of Gladson Cameli of the PP, who for his part is nephew to the state's former governor Orleir Cameli.

Where they were not hit by accusations of corruption, other traditional Brazilian political clans faltered due to their association with bossism. Such is the case of the former governor of Paraná, Beto Richa, of the PSDB. He took leave from office to run for senator and managed only a sixth-place finish. On the eve of the election, he was arrested on corruption charges.

Though important figures in the politics of clientelism have taken hits recently, the apparatus as a living organism has escaped largely unscathed. One need only note that not all such families have seen themselves ejected from electoral politics. The family of Renan Calheiros were not owners of a large sugarcane tract, but his father was involved in city politics in Murici, in Alagoas state, for some time. To this day Renan is the state's senator, his son its governor, and his brother mayor of Murici. They also have relatives in the state assembly, such that the clan retains its grip on local power and federal resources. All the same, this longtime political boss suffered a setback in the Senate: having managed to win election as its president four times, he lost the post in 2019.

There is an unmistakable relationship between bossism and the accumulation of wealth and political power, and not just in rural areas. Though new forms of production and employment are taking shape even in the states mentioned above, it is clear that oligarchy still has the capacity to undermine the evolution of Brazilian democracy, shoring up the basest political practices. It is not the work of chance that in the regions cited above essential services for the people such as health, education, housing, and transportation remain extremely precarious, the State revealing its total failure and absence with regard to infrastructure. In these places, crime rates, too, are very high. According to the Program to Reduce Lethal Violence (PRVL/the Presidency of the Republic/UNICEF, 2016), when it comes to the rate of violent deaths, Sergipe occupies first place, followed by Rio Grande do Norte, Alagoas, Pará, Amapá, Pernambuco, Bahia, Goiás, Ceará, Rio de Janeiro, and Mato Grosso.

If the "neighborhood bullies," to borrow an expression from Brazilian sociologist Maria Isaura de Queiroz, were in some way weakened by the 2018 elections, the country is nonetheless yet to rid itself entirely of the authoritarian discourse that frequently surrounds them. In addition, election losses do not necessarily mean an end to the hegemony of regional family powerhouses, since they continue to exert control over state bureaucracy. In fact, one could say that it is a matter of trading six for half-a-dozen, their justifications being more or less the same. Public safety is an imperative in a country with epidemic-level violence, a designation the World Health Organization uses to define violence that surpasses ten homicides per hundred thousand residents; the problem has always been the increasingly close link between repressive authorities and certain regional elites, resulting in a police force for which impartiality is often not a defining characteristic. The preservation of hierarchy is another banner issue for conservatives and has always proven a powerful plank for electing politicians to various representative bodies across the country.

It is notable that the reforms undertaken during this era of redemocratization have, by and large, proven incapable of breaking free once and for all from certain issues that act as national fetters, continuing to come up against the limits of the low tolerance of several regional oligarchies. The well-known Grand Compromise, a pact between a small group of political and social elites dating to 1989, has to this day successfully deterred interventions, as it preserves the interests of wealthy agrarian landowners, the varied forms of violence practiced by certain agribusiness sectors, distrust of warnings from climate groups, and efforts to relax limits on gun ownership. An authoritarian model of politics, then, even having suffered bumps and bruises in recent elections, survives to this day—a model that is unable to extricate itself from traditional rural and, today, urban elites, and that does little to nurture a healthy and necessary itinerancy in power.

Historically democracy, from the Greeks up to our modern era, implies not only freedom of expression but justice in terms of the distribution of public offices and equality before the law. In the brief history of Brazilian democracy, the country has made several advances but has also suffered some obvious setbacks. There still exist, side by side, a model of "inclusive democracy," which has led to the growing inclusion of different groups of citizens, and, equally, an "exclusive democracy," which seeks to threaten, if not indeed obstruct outright, the rights of every citizen. With the preservation of political advantages vouchsafed by state-level oligarchies, the result is a sort of accommodation of political habits, of electoral procedures, which, not infrequently, converge to preserve power that has been inherited or constructed over a long period.

In addition, with the recent introduction of social media, a new phenomenon has materialized: if on the one hand such media have generated a certain democratization of information and plural environments for speech, on the other hand they have contributed to the emergence of a new brand of charismatic leader and a new way of doing politics, no less authoritarian. This is the digital political populist, who sows hate and intolerance, rails against the press and intellectuals, and claims the mantle of "modern" politician as he addresses the population without any mediation.

Meanwhile, even in the case of these new modes of communication (and with the spread of bossism to Brazilian cities), the image of president as father figure, a paterfamilias, authoritarian and strict in the face of those who defy him, just and "relatable" toward those who follow him and share his ideas, has never been as strong as now. Despite the fact, then, that digital speech theoretically provides a platform open to all, it continues to exploit exclusive models of authority and produce a segregationist dynamics, amplifying revamped systems of symbolic hierarchy and forms of authority.

There is no mechanical continuity—or historical determinism—between Brazil's past and present, but the country is at risk of giving new life to the authoritarian roots of its politics, in spite of new styles of governability. There are also fresh examples of the concentration of land and power in the Amazon, with a new elite destroying the land for timber, mineral extraction, cattle ranching, and soy farming. Yet again, equality and diversity, sentiments and values inherent to the expansion of democratic rights, are at risk as long as the country does not break with the myth of the politician-as-father-figure—now a sort of virtual chieftain, who speaks in the name and in the place of his children and dependents; of the outstanding and exceptional hero; of the idealized leader.

This is a language we inherited from the bossisms of the past, from the epoch defined by the exclusive dominion of wealthy rural property owners, but which survives and is recast in our era of digitized sensibilities, as authoritarian as they have always been.

3

Patrimonialism

FROM THE OUTSET of the brief five centuries of their history, it quickly became clear that Brazilians have considerable difficulty in constructing shared models of dedication to the common good. In place of these, several forms of political sponsorship, the currency of favor-trading, recourse to "big shots," the infamous habit of line jumping, of seeking undue advantage, or the use of corrupt intermediaries took root in this land where the mechanisms of State are abused for private ends. It is clear that as long as patrimonial and clientelistic practices continue to hold sway at the core of the political system and at the heart of public institutions, Brazil will continue to run a serious deficit in republican values.

"Republic" signifies "public thing"—common good—as opposed to private good: the *res privata*. Thinking in these terms, "[the Brazilian] Republic," as the historian José Murilo de Carvalho reasons, "was never republican." No matter how tautological it might appear to say so, there can be no republic without republican values, and in Brazil there has always been a lack of interest in the collective, in civic virtues, and in the principles necessary to the conduct of public life. Worse still is a failure to provide access to social rights, or, rather, to the full exercise of these rights to healthcare, education, employment, housing, transportation, and leisure—to a share, that is, in collective wealth.

In the face of these impediments, the precariousness of the citizenship of certain Brazilian social groups and the practices of segregation to which they continue to be subjected are laid bare. For the most vulnerable sectors of society in particular, democratic rule is many times suspended in the country, and the present is still very much defined by an authoritarian, slave-society past and its control in the hands of regional bosses.

As the Republic is fragile, it becomes particularly vulnerable to attack from its two principal enemies: patrimonialism and corruption. The first of these is the result of a perversion of the relationship between society and the State, whereby the public good is privately appropriated. To put it another way, patrimonialism consists in the understanding—misunderstanding—of the State as a private good, the "patrimony" of whoever holds power.

Though the concept of patrimonialism might appear dated and in disuse, even obsolete, it has in fact never been so applicable as to Brazil's present predicament. The practice spans different classes; it is not the monopoly of one social group or stratum. Used for the first time by the German sociologist Max Weber (1864–1920) at the end of the nineteenth century, the term is derived from Latin *pater*—father—while the term itself evokes a sense of private property. The concept also suggests the importance of patrimonial space—that is, an individual space that is constantly intruding upon the public and the collective.

Weber's theories were not limited, meanwhile, to the private and localized application of the concept. In his hands, the term gained a much wider meaning, referring to a form of power in which the frontiers between the private and public sphere become so nebulous as to blur. "Patrimonialism" came to designate the imposition of personal interests, without ethical or moral consideration, via public mechanisms. The opposite, however—the use of private goods in the service of the public will—does not apply. In this case, the order of factors changes, as well as, to a considerable degree, the result.

Weber argues that when the State resorts to this sort of patrimonial activity and is understood to be a mere extension of the will of the powerful, the machinery of government ultimately reveals itself to be inefficient. That is to say, the State loses rational/legal authority when the public interest no longer dictates the norms of government, and even more so when political personalism—the patchwork of personal arrangements that feeds the practice of collusion, political patronage, bossism, and clientelism, which together supersede popular rule—gains a foothold.

In the case of Brazil, there has been no shortage of writers who have invoked the concept of patrimonialism when summing up the country's backward political practices. As early as 1936, Sérgio Buarque de Holanda, in *Raízes do Brasil*, attacked the persistence of the country's "emotive ethics" and the national mania for evading the courts and the body of law. Terming this model "cordiality" (*cordialidade*), he sounded the alarm. *Cor* (Latin "heart," from which dervives the Portuguese word for heart, *coração*), he explains, serves to denote the manner in which Brazilians resort to sentiment instead of applying themselves to the exercise of reason. Such a habit had been part of their colonial past, but it would be expanded during the Empire and above all with the Republic, which, according to the historian, suffered from "weak institutions."

Responses to Holanda's work have, however, made shrewd use of the author's theories. Since the publication of the second edition of *Raízes*, he has had to defend himself against the misapplication of his interpretation and against misreadings of the book's most famous chapter, entitled—not for nothing—"The Cordial Man." What was intended as a critique and, according to Holanda, laid out one of the clearest obstacles to the country's aspirations to modernity, was soon understood as praise and a motive for rejoicing: as though Brazil's role in the concert of nations was to offer the world "a cordial man," or that Brazilians' very nature had been molded by a type of patrimonial practice. Certainly no remedy can be prescribed expressly for Brazilians, however much a series of social myths might seek to attribute to biology what pertains to logic and the political experience of citizens and social actors.

Attorney and historian Raymundo Faoro, in his 1958 work *Os donos do poder: Formação do patronato político brasileiro* (The owners of power: the rise of political patronage in Brazil), further explored patrimonialism by returning to the context of the sixteenth century. Specifically, he invested his energies in an analysis of Brazilian colonial development, heavily reliant on large latifundia, or estates, slave labor, and political and economic galvanization around wealthy landowners. It was this rural aristocracy that embodied the law and the very institutions of the land, and its members had not the slightest inclination to govern their territory by dipping into their own pockets.

Famed literary critic Antônio Cândido, too, in his 1970 essay "Dialética da malandragem" (Dialectic of malandroism)—which takes as its starting point Manuel Antônio de Almeida's 1854 novel *Memórias de um sargento de milícias* (*Memoirs of a Militia Sergeant*)—came to the conclusion that what would survive among Brazilians was a certain "dialectic of order and disorder," in which everything would become, at the same time, licit and illicit. In this complex structure, familiarity would become common currency, leading to a "vast wide-reaching arrangement," dissolving extremes and sapping any meaning from law and order.

The anthropologist Robert DaMatta, meanwhile, in his 1979 book *Carnavais, malandros e heróis* (*Carnivals, Rogues, and Heroes*), proposed a new interpretation of Brazil, based on a common expression: "Do you have any idea who you're talking to?" According to DaMatta, this expression captures the way in which Brazilians apply—de rigueur—individual standards in the preservation of social hierarchy and nepotist practices at the heart of the State. He further diagnosed the existence of a dual society wherein two parallel forms of conceiving of and being in the world coexist: a world of "individuals," subject to the law, and another of "people," for whom such codes were remote and even irrelevant formulations.

All told, despite the fact that Brazilians are in the midst of a long period of redemocratization, undertaken since the Constitution of 1988, which established more robust institutions, it is clear that the concept of the "cordial man" continues to represent a reality in Brazil, where political practice is still very much inured to the overlap between public and private will. This cross-contamination leads in turn to an increase in personalized forms of power both small and large, amplifying the power of certain individuals to promote their own interests through the workings of the State.

Incidentally, the persistence of local bossism leads to another form of patrimonialism, whereby regional and private interests begin directly to affect government behavior. Not that the State ought to be immune to the demands of specific sectors of society—the problem begins when a certain type of political corporatism favors the few to the detriment of the many.

Patrimonialist practices date far back in Brazilian history. Caio Prado Júnior, in his 1933 book *Evolução política do Brasil e outros estudos* (The political evolution of Brazil and other studies), demonstrated the way in which the Portuguese Crown's footprint in its American colony was small and merely residual during the first 150 years of colonization. Accordingly, it fell to the landowner, via municipal bodies, to exercise political power. Colonists and captains performed the role of "local delegates," since they were the depositaries of public authority, assigned to them by the motherland. Because they were "the State," all matters relative to the latter became, within these confines, private matters.

In this way, though different terms are often employed to describe this situation, their meaning and acceptation have remained fundamentally the same. As the colonizers centralized the exercise of power, and maintained considerable political autonomy for themselves, a series of consequences ensued. In the first place, these people came to believe that public institutions were irrelevant, in view of their enormous personal authority. They also assumed that they owed little loyalty to the Portuguese monarch, since overseas territories were administered in an inefficient and haphazard manner. Finally, they felt no obligation to account to the Crown for their actions, not least because the latter lacked the tools to keep them under supervision. For their part, the Lusitanian authorities' behavior was also patrimonialist, since they maintained ties to wealthy export estates; provided that they continued to receive their profits, they preferred not to push public intervention.

Until the middle of the seventeenth century, patrimonialism, whether we refer to it by this or other names, was the defining characteristic of the Brazilian colony's management; the Crown exercised its rights only within the narrow confines of the seat of the Government-General. Lisbon's oversight was rudimentary at best, involving only what was strictly necessary so as not to lose control over its rich overseas holdings. The Portuguese had no spare "hands" to export so as properly to oversee colonial administration. A sort of dependence was created between the Lusitanian government and the colonizers who in practice administered the Brazilian colony. This setup, for its part, was of a piece with the "passive" stance of the Lusitanian capital, which always preferred to live off the receipts accruing from the sugarcane plantations than to be obliged to itself manage the day-to-day operations of colonial enterprises.

On the other hand, Brazil's position as a Portuguese colony meant that a significant portion of the Lusitanian State and public administration was transferred there. Along with bureaucratic institutions came certain characteristics of this State apparatus; among them, precisely, patrimonialism. The king was surrounded by a royal court, "nobles of the robe" who occupied all public posts and roles but behaved as beneficiaries of dividends and proceeds. The aristocrats earned pensions and access to higher posts; navy and army officials were entrusted with public offices; civilians and ecclesiastical authorities could count on jobs and other benefits. The capital, meanwhile, faced with these concessions, reacted by raising taxes on the colony.

It is certainly the case that the class that entrenched itself in the administrative apparatus of the Portuguese Empire not only came at a high cost, but was lodged at the very heart of the colonial State machine. It was also closely associated with the sovereign and took advantage of this proximity, as well as the prestige issuing from the monarch, to benefit personally and, more often than not, to the detriment of the remaining segments of society.

Another factor attesting to the widespread patrimonialism operating during the colonial period is the model of the patriarchal family that prevailed in Brazil and led to the State being considered an extension and continuation of the domestic sphere. According to Buarque de Holanda, those holding positions of public responsibility, their worldview molded at the heart of this environment, soon learned to manipulate and merge the public and private domains. Since the administrative bureaucracy was under the direct control of the aristocracy, and part of a larger scheme of agrarian autarchy, this reinforced what we today refer to as the patrimonialist character of the State apparatus then existent in the country.

From the Crown's point of view, there was not, strictly speaking, any conflict in breaching the separation between the pubic and the private; after all, the exercise of virtues that allow a sovereign to know and guide his subjects in seeking to make manifest the fulfillment of the collective interest was ascribed to the role of king. In other words, the Crown was measured by its own yardstick; to advance the kingdom's patrimony was a way of exercising power that viewed the State as an enterprise subject to the king's control. Today we recognize this practice as blatant patrimonialism. At that time, however, and from the perspective of the king, there was nothing exceptional or immoral and unethical in the wielding of power.

The situation would become increasingly complicated, however, with the arrival of the Portuguese court in Rio de Janeiro in 1808. Along with the royal court, the entire administrative machine would disembark in the new seat of its power; indeed, it was now from the Brazilian colony that orders would be dispatched to all those places where Portuguese rule was in effect. From the moment his ship docked in Rio de Janeiro, the Portuguese king Dom João made clear his intention—conceived, suitably, before he departed from Lisbon—to oversee his empire from the colony. To that end, he left Dom Rodrigo de Sousa Coutinho in charge of the Ministry of War and Foreign Affairs. João Rodrigues de Sá e Meneses, the viscount of Anada, who had held the post in Portugal, was, upon arrival in Brazil, named secretary of the navy. To see to the internal affairs of the colony, he selected Fernando José de Portugal, later the Marquês de Aguiar, who had served as viceroy in Rio de Janeiro between 1801 and 1806.

So inefficient was this new ministerial trinity in the eyes of the local population that they were soon the butt of jokes that compared them to three different clocks: one that was slow (Dom Fernando de Portugal), another that had stopped (the viscount of Anadia), and a third that was always fast (Dom Rodrigo), all ticking around the monarch himself. In the lower rungs, meanwhile, the number of functionaries increased, simultaneously causing the administrative apparatus to swell and obstructing its performance, since many posts were created merely to cater to the recent arrivals, close friends of the king who, more often than not, were less an asset to the State than a drain on its resources. The majority of these emigrés—monsignors, judges, lawyers, doctors, employees of the royal household, those in the king's private service and his protegés—behaved like a horde of "hangers-on." Many of them were government parasites who would continue in Rio de Janeiro the role they had exercised in Lisbon: to fatten themselves at the State's expense and do little toward the good of the nation. The government apparatus ballooned, these familiar figures were rewarded, and to meet the new expenses, the only solution in sight was more taxes, such that the entirety of Brazil paid this steep bill.

The institutions that had existed in Portugal were also transplanted to Brazil, with the same spirit of bureaucratic routine. The idea was to mold the new government seat in the image of Lisbon, reproducing in Brazil the structures of Portuguese administration, but without neglecting to sustain the unemployed and close friends of the court who would arrive in the years subsequent to 1808. Accordingly, the government sought to establish its strategic areas of operation—security and policing, justice, the treasury, and the military. However, they would not be starting from scratch. The Crown always oversaw and maintained control of Brazil via the legal code that had been in effect in Portugal since the seventeenth century—the Philippine Ordinations of 1603. The metropole's administrative reach extended to the colony in a hierarchic structure whose center was the Paço in Lisbon, and which included the Government-General of Brazil, the government of the various captaincies, that of the municipal assemblies, and, as we have seen, the judicial apparatus that included the Casa da Suplicação (a sort of royal court), the Desembargo do Paço (a sort of royal supreme court), and the Mesa da Consciência e Ordens (Board of the King's Conscience and of the Military Orders). The intention was, therefore, to imbue the colony and, from 1815 onward, the United Kingdom of Portugal with new institutions, and also to satisfy the "friends" who passed through or remained at the king's side, bringing with them the heavy load of privileges to which they were accustomed in Portugal.

Expenses in Brazil soared as the state machine became bloated, growing alongside a patrimonialism of the State connected to the new Lusitanian emigrés, who arrived in the colony with the intention of remaining there, at least while war raged in Europe and in Portuguese territory. Existing private properties in Rio de Janeiro were famously acquired to accommodate the new members of the court. Once a handsome dwelling had been found, it was soon requisitioned either for members of the nobility or for Portuguese functionaries and military officials who were without a place to live. Witnesses said it was common to see the court lackeys painting on the doors of such dwellings the letters *PR*, signifying *Principe regente* (prince regent), and thereby putting the families living there out on the street. The only recourse left to the people in the face of this arbitrary act was to make light of the situation, suggesting *PR* instead stood for "Ponha-se na rua" (put out on the street). To prevent their homes from being confiscated, some local homeowners pretended to or did in fact perform perfectly unnecessary repairs, defending themselves from what they termed "the aristo-cratic invasion." Others simply feigned misunderstanding and failed to respond to the requisition order. Certainly the population turned its fury on these second-rung figures, swiftly denominated "court coolies."

The backscratching politics of favors and patrimonialism did not end there, however. For example, those merchants who were already living in Rio de Janeiro, the majority of them Portuguese, did not take kindly to the presence of compatriots who, with the help of the Crown, began to move in on their territory. The government realized that it needed to reduce tensions by appeasing both these aggrieved merchants and local landowners, who by that point were also displeased by the new turn that the government was taking. There is nothing like a good aristocratic title or other distinction to soothe tempers, and so the Honorifics Chamber and Registry was quickly established, as well as, in 1810, the Company of Arms, to properly attend to the birth of an aristocracy and the development of heraldry on Brazilian soil. By the time he returned to Portugal in 1821, Dom João had bestowed no fewer than 254 titles, naming eleven dukes, thirty-eight marquises, sixty-four counts, ninety-one viscounts, and thirty-one barons; and this is not to count the honors awarded under the Order of the Sword and the titles of "grand cross," commendatore, and knight. In these categories, the sovereign named 2,630 knights, commendatores, and grand crosses of the Order of Christ; 1,422 of the Order of Saint Benedict of Avis; and 590 of the Order of Santiago. The important point is that besides the aristocrats who had received their titles outside the country, there was an ever larger home-grown variety, eager to receive the same symbols of distinction.

It was only with independence and the formation of a national state that more autonomous institutions, in the sense of those that spoke to a reality more properly Brazilian, were created. The densification of urban populations gave rise to new economic agents connected to the services sector and a broader political representation of the interests of distinct social groups. With this, the bureaucracy of the State was no longer an extension almost exclusively of the traditional agrarian landowning class, or of established merchants and recently arrived Portuguese functionaries, but came to include certain sectors connected to urban services and the liberal professions.

Nonetheless, the social structure of patrimonialism remained basically the same: the State needed to respond to the interests of rural producers who, for their part, depended heavily upon slave labor. So great was this dependence that, beyond the national territory and neighboring countries, Brazilian emancipation provoked reactions in several African nations that were part of the Portuguese Empire. In Portuguese Guinea, Angola, and Mozambique, groups of slave traders proposed a pact with rebels from Rio de Janeiro. It is no coincidence, therefore, that the Kingdom of Daomé was the first to recognize the Brazilian Empire, before even Portugal. As the historian Luiz Felipe de Alencastro notes, in Angola, a handbill printed in Brazil invited Benguela to join the "Brazilian cause."

The emperors Dom Pedro I and Dom Pedro II would govern by manipulating and being manipulated by agrarian interests, the landowning gentry accumulating public and private offices and a great many titles.[1] The widespread distribution of titles and honorifics was an effective symbolic way to make allies, to the extent that, starting with the Constitution of 1824, one item nearly passed unnoticed amid other more polemic themes. This was Article 102, Clause XI of the Political Constitution of the Empire of Brazil. By this clause, the letter of the law guaranteed what until then had previously been merely customary—that is, that among the Emperor's powers as head of the executive was the right "to bestow titles, honors, military orders, and distinctions in recompense for services rendered to the state; pecuniary titles depending on approval of the General Assembly, when they were not previously assigned, and taxable by law."

This formalized the birth of an aristocracy whose emergence was umbilically linked to the figure of the emperor, given that he alone had the right to confer such privileges. This new aristocracy was, in some ways, quite original. In contrast to the European model, which rewarded service with titles that were valid not only for life but could be passed on, in Brazil the aristocracy "was born and never aged." Hereditary titles were guaranteed only for those of royal blood or those who arrived from Portugal boasting honorifics; titles conferred on Brazilian soil did not extend beyond their immediate owner. This was a unique way of tying the beneficiaries to the figure of the emperor, who held the exclusive right not only to "name aristocrats," but to "punish them" by refusing to extend the honor to an individual's descendants.

In the hands of Brazil's first monarch, the aristocracy grew significantly, constrained only by the fact that his reign would prove brief. From 1822 to 1830, Dom Pedro elevated 119 individuals to the aristocracy, among them two dukes, twenty-seven marquises, eight counts, thirty-eight titled and four untitled viscounts, and twenty barons, ten who were grandees and ten who were not. It was under the aegis of the second emperor that the monarchic project would become entrenched and put down roots as a sort of tropical court. During his long reign, which began in 1841 and came to an end in 1889, Dom Pedro II would govern with an element at his side that distinguished itself from the rest of society by boasting an aristocratic title and the use of a coat of arms, symbols of distinction and prestige. In the period between 1870 and 1888 alone, the monarch would award 570 new titles, each corresponding to a member of a new elite that accompanied the young emperor.

Over the course of the Empire, a total of 1,439 titles was bestowed (for a single beneficiary was eligible to receive more than one title)—a number that actually corresponded, as we have seen, to a sort of "meritocratic aristocracy," quite different from the aristocracy by birth typical of the European courts of the time. In Brazil, a good many of those with titles were ranchers from the Vale do Paraíba who were soon transformed into proud "non-grandee barons." And so, if many times it was a special moment, connected to the court calendar, that led to the bestowal of titles—"birthday of HM the Emperor," "the day of consecration and coronation of HM," "on the occasion of the arrival of the Empress," on account of a marriage, a baptism, or official anniversary— in several cases it was "good performance" that recommended one for such honors: "for services rendered," "acts of patriotism," "for fidelity and loyalty to HM the Emperor," "services against the cholera morbus," "service in the Paraguayan War," or even "works displayed at world exhibitions."

"Acts of patriotism" and "fidelity and loyalty to HM the Emperor" were pompous and vague references that, whatever their character, tied these new agrarian elites to their sovereign. Officially, the title holders formed the highest level of the imperial aristocracy. In practice, however, they composed an elite selected on the basis of economic, professional, or cultural merit, but also social influence, irrespective of privilege or presumption of material wealth or ties to the land. Merchants, professors, doctors, military men, politicians, ranchers, lawyers, diplomats, and functionaries were all represented, via their coats-of-arms, as the best in their field. For this reason, lacking the hereditary right that would guarantee the perpetuation of the title, it was necessary to "prove by actions" the importance of their achievement.

Among title-bearing Brazilians, other hierarchies too were established: while all were aristocrats, only some were "imperial magnates." Such a privilege, essentially honorific, was not conferred upon dukes, marquises, and counts but only upon viscounts- and barons-grandee. It was the members of this tiny subset of the elite that, according to the *Almanak Laemmert*, paraded at the front of royal processions, or closely accompanied their Imperial Highnesses, and were addressed as "Excellency."

Aside from those with titles and coats-of-arms coexisting in the daily routine of the royal palace, a select entourage was named to certain posts and offices, exchanging with the emperor not only formalities but intimacy, and so guaranteeing their own differentiated status. The counselors of state, aristocrats, and officials of the royal and imperial houses formed, alongside the titled aristocracy, this special group that during Dom Pedro II's reign was able to experience, in the Americas, a new iteration of a royal court, whose only drawback was the hundred-degree sun more typical of the tropics.

In Brazil, terminology served both to conflate and to distinguish. In theory, "aristocrats" were those who received titles conferred by the emperor. In practice, however, the term was more elastic. "The court" could refer to the group of people closest to the king, and also to the titled. It likewise designated "the court of Rio de Janeiro," whose focal point was the Paço de São Cristóvão. Accordingly, while to belong to "the court"—the court of Rio— was a relatively common honor, to be a title holder, an aristocrat, was a privilege assigned to the few. It was the monarch who maintained the balance, securing for himself a group of allies who, by necessity, orbited around him.

In this veritable crusade of aristocraticization, while the emperor bought the loyalty of Rio's coffee-plantation elite with titles and honors, the coffee growers for their part, above all those from the Vale do Paraíba, spared no effort to ingratiate themselves with the monarch and consequently to receive the favor of the State. This was, in effect, a model that placed a premium on titles and personal gifts as bargaining chips and means to public indulgences.

Such proximity to power also permitted rural entrepreneurs to wield great influence in the Senate. In the first place, given that the criterion for entry was pecuniary, it was necessary to have an annual income of 800 *mil-réis* to be eligible for a seat. Second, it appears to be no coincidence that the proportion of rural landowners in the institution reached its zenith in the 1840s, exactly at the apogee of illegal traffic in African slaves.

The proportion of bachelors of law in the Senate was always high, reaching nearly 40 percent by the end of the Empire, while competition with those in other liberal professions, such as doctors, grew stiffer during the republican era. Regardless of composition, for the length of the reign of Dom Pedro II the Senate remained an institution of the Crown, enacting its politics, as Raymundo

Faoro showed. It behaved, in fact, as an organ in the service of the "moderating power," exclusive to the sovereign, by which he made use of the institution to tame the House and his own ministers. Finally, to be named to the Council of State, it was necessary to maintain proximity to the monarch, given that its members were selected by him from a shortlist. Reaching such echelons was no easy feat, but those who managed it secured a lifetime term, were remunerated to the tune of one and a half times what representatives of the lower house received, and ran no risk of losing their posts.

Another way to understand how patrimonialist interests became insinuated into the State machine during Dom Pedro II's reign is to examine the radical dichotomy established between the provinces and the court, and how politics was practiced in these two distinct domains. Since no national representation existed, the easiest course—the surest way to satisfy regional interests—was to bet on local politics. As a result, though political parties operated at a national level, the variations in political positions between provinces were immense. And at the local level, the National Guard and police agents employed force against voters, to the extent that, from the October 13, 1840 poll onward, the democratic process became known as "election by cudgel."

The situation appears to change with the reform promoted by the conservative cabinet led by Honório Hermeto Carneiro Leão, the marquis of Paraná, in 1853, which favored a more equitable distribution of a deputy's "circles" or "districts." With this reform, Paraná sought a more just and faithful representation of the country in the Chamber of Deputies. In addition, the reform established the election of alternative (proxy) deputies and, above all, a more rigid system of "electoral incompatibilities." For the first time, the presidents of each province, their secretaries, armed forces commanders, the generals-in-chief, the inspectors-general of the Treasury, the police, the justices of the peace, municipal arbiters, and criminal magistrates were ineligible for candidature on account of their positions.

Conservative groups moved quickly to oppose the project, alleging that such a reform would do away with characteristics of an institution that, in their opinion, ought to be peopled by "notable personages" who were "recognized" in their respective provinces and not by "subaltern functionaries," amenable to "small-time local influences." And even with these changes—and the results of the 1856 election confirm this—suffrage in Brazil underwent very few demonstrable changes. After only one election cycle, regional powers learned how to react come election time, such that the law, though implemented, failed to achieve its objectives. The strength of these camps effectively permitted them in the end to leave their own imprimatur on the reform, which was then used to maintain privileges and prop up regional bosses. The State favored centralization, but the political force of the provinces was insurmountable.

Only in 1881, eight years before the regime came an end, did the imperial government actually change the format of its elections. The Saraiva Reform established direct elections, laying the groundwork for polls to be overseen by an electoral court; redrew congressional districts; regulated conflicts of interest; established penalties for fraud; expanded the vote to naturalized citizens, non-Catholics, and the emancipated; and also introduced voter identification cards, one of its most important innovations.

Meanwhile, it took no more than a single honestly conducted election for the country to wake up to the fact that Brazilian party politics was rife with division: the make-up of each chamber changed considerably, and they were much less homogeneous than in elections prior to 1881. Still, as members of the Senate were chosen from a shortlist by the emperor, that organ continued to function as a "governing party," and was broadly recognized as such. From whatever vantage point—the State's vis-à-vis regional elites, or vice-versa—the system was notable for a premeditated use of politics, marked by localized interests.

With the advent of the republic, the growing power of urban segments, the diversification of groups demanding their rights, and the increasingly normalized functioning of public institutions, this sort of political wheeling and dealing appeared, at times, to have been overcome. Patrimonialist practices continued, nevertheless, at the heart of the State, with politicians and heads of state accused of putting public funds to personal use.

In his book *Coronelismo, enxada e voto* (Coronelism, the plough, and the ballot box), Victor Nunes Leal explores the way in which public authority asserted itself in relation to the private in this context: the State relied on ample support from landowners, at the same time, and extrajudicially, permitting these individuals, at that time referred to as "colonels," an active role. In exchange for the votes that wealthy landowners commanded in their regions, known in that era as "moral force," the State conferred formal and informal powers upon these figures.

Even the process of urbanization that characterized the 1910s and 1920s in Brazil would prove incapable of breaking the dynamic created by the patrimonialist agro-exportation model. On the contrary, the First Republic saw an expansion of the phenomenon known as "the yoke-and-oxen vote" and of coronelism and its correlation with government, an arrangement that initially neutralized the influence of newly empowered groups, limiting their participation and the freedom of the vote.

The Republic's political stability, meanwhile, was secured by three main factors: the efforts of state governments to ensure that political conflict remained confined to the regional sphere; the federal government's recognition of the full sovereignty of the states in overseeing their internal political affairs; and the preservation of an electoral process in which, despite the political mechanisms that sought to control local disputes, fraud remained a common occurrence. In fact, fraud was a part of all phases of the electoral process, from voter registration to the validation of electoral returns. Some practices became notorious. The phrase "quill pen election" is familiar to us from the imperial era and refers to the many forms of manipulation committed at polling stations, such as the falsification of signatures and the adulteration of ballots. "Decapitation" referred to the refusal by the Verification

Commission of the Chamber of Deputies to recognize the elected—a practice that eliminated adversaries, annulling their election. The "voter corral," as already noted, became to all intents a politico-cultural practice—representing an act of loyalty on the part of the voter toward a local political chief. The phrase referred to large tents where voters were kept closely supervised and served a square meal, and which they were only permitted to leave when the time came for them to cast their vote.

It was difficult to exercise autonomy in this land of the favor and of public and private coercion. A far cry indeed from political liberalism—from the understanding that abolition was the result of a collective movement and that the First Republic was the result of a contract between citizens—the complicated game of personal relations, favor-trading, and debts-to-pay remained in force: a hallmark of personalism and clientelism.

Private use of the machinery of government would be heavily restricted by the 1934 Constitution, which not only expanded the federal government's power but made voting secret and mandatory from the age of eighteen. An Electoral Court and Labor Court were also created, institutions that sought to rein in the personal whims of wealthy landowners, as well as put a leash on their bargaining power with the State.

Since that time, when not only the secrecy of the ballot but also new workers' rights were established, the country has had various constitutions. In particular, the 1988 Constitution prescribed the reduction of the working week from forty-eight to forty-four hours, unemployment benefits, and paid vacation; all of these measures sought to secure the rights of individuals and citizens. The pillars of the Brazilian Federal Republic are: sovereignty, citizenship, human dignity, the social value of work and free enterprise, and a multiparty system.

Even so, the legacy of private power survives within the machinery of government. The Inter-Union Parliamentary Advisory Department (DIAP) presents some revealing data concerning the so-called family caucus, which continues to grow in the National

Congress. In the 2014 election, in the Chamber of Deputies, 113 elected deputies were related to established politicians from traditional oligarchical families. In the 2018 elections, the number of parliamentarians with family ties increased to 172. Paraíba is the state with the largest proportion of elected parliamentarians with family ties. Of the twelve deputies elected by the state in 2018, ten are related in some way to other politicians. In the Senate, the newcomers Veneziano do Rêgo (MDB) and Daniella Ribeiro (PP) came to power as a result of their family connections. The group was completed by José Maranhão (MDB), whose term lasts until 2023, and who is also a perfect example of the "family caucus."

The parties that have had the greatest number of relatives elected to the Chamber of Deputies are the Progressive Party (PP) and Social Democratic Party (PSD), each of them with eighteen such representatives in 2018, followed closely by the conservative Brazilian Democratic Movement (MDB) with seventeen, the Republican Party (PR) with sixteen, the Brazilian Social Democracy Party (PSDB) with thirteen, and Democrats (DEM) and Workers' Party (PT) with a dozen each. The Brazilian Socialist Party (PSB) has eleven such deputies, the Democratic Labor Party (PDT) and Brazilian Labor Party (PTB) nine, and the Republicans (PRB) eight. Solidarity (SD) has six, and the president's former party, the Social Liberal Party (PSL), has four. The Communist Party of Brazil (PCdoB) has four, and the Republican Party of the Social Order (PROS) and Popular Socialist Party (PPS) three each. Podemos (PODE), has two, while the Socialism and Liberty Party (PSOL), Social Christian Party (PSC), Avante, Christian Labor Party (PTC), Free Fatherland Party (PPL), Progressive Republican Party (PRP), and Patriota have one deputy apiece. The Senate's "family caucus" meanwhile shrank from thirty-nine to twenty-four members, including alternates—a nonetheless startling figure when one considers that the Federal Senate has only eighty-one seats. A preliminary study by DIAP identified 138 deputies and senators in all, among the 567 new parliamentarians, who belonged to political clans—an increase of 22 percent in relation to 2014. The full number of members of the "family caucus" is surely even higher, however, given that this study is still in progress and took only first-degree relatives into account.

The year 2018 saw "dynasties" that campaigned on an outsider platform, taking advantage of the current wave of antiestablishment sentiment. This is the case of Eduardo and Flávio Bolsonaro (both of the far-right Social Liberal Party, or PSL), elected to the lower and upper houses, respectively, who have long made careers in state-level and national politics. In the state of Pernambuco, according to an December 17, 2018 article published by Brasil Online, the deputy who garnered the highest number of votes, João Campos (of the centrist PSB), is the son of the former governor of Pernambuco Eduardo Campos, deceased in 2014.

> The politician's cousin, Marília Arraes (PT), who for her part is the niece of a former federal deputy and granddaughter of former governor Miguel Arraes, garnered the second most votes. In Bahia, the candidate with the second-highest vote count for the Chamber was the son of Senator Otto Alencar (PSD). In Piauí, Iracema Portella (PP), daughter of a former governor and former federal deputy, earned yet another term in the Chamber, while her husband, Ciro Nogueira (PP), was re-elected to the Senate. In Rio Grande do Norte, half of the open seats for the Chamber of Deputies were occupied by relatives—one is the son of a former governor.

Meanwhile, according to the same news story, in Ceará, one of the federal deputies who garnered the most votes is the son of the current president of the state assembly. In Pará, the Barbalho clan secured both the reelection of its leader, Senator Jader Barbalho (MDB), and that of two other members for the Chamber of Deputies—the senator's ex-wife and a cousin. For her part, Kátia Abreu (PDT), senator from Tocantins, now has the company in the Senate of her son Irajá Abreu (PSD), "[previously] federal deputy for Tocantins and who won one of two open seats in the state." In Paraíba, the deputy Veneziano Vital do Rêgo (MDB) won a seat in the Senate, where his brother was already serving and his mother served as an alternate. The other seat in the state belongs to Daniella Ribeiro (PP), sister to deputy Aguinaldo Ribeiro (PP–PB), who was also reelected to his post. In other words, Paraíba's representation in the Chamber of Deputies is in fact "a patent portrait of the persistent influence of political clans. Of twelve seats, ten will be occupied by deputies with family ties to someone else who already served in some elected office."

Another facet of the system that makes possible this practice of patrimonialism can be found in the federal budget, whereby the National Congress and the Planalto [Presidential] Palace determine how public monies will be spent. The government proposes a budget, and deputies and senators make modifications before approving it. There is, however, a kind of "tool" in the budget process that allows politicians access to part of these funds without obtaining the approval of their colleagues. This is known as "parliamentary amendments." Amendments correspond to requests made by deputies and senators to include specific expenses in the federal budget, such as those tied to healthcare and transportation. These tend to be earmarked for cities and other municipalities that fall within a parliamentarian's district; the parliamentarian uses them to strengthen political ties.

The inner workings of the government machinery are more insidious still. Though certain funds may be included in the budget, the effective disbursement of these resources depends on a government order. As a result, parliamentary amendments have become tools for political bargaining between the president of the republic and congresspeople.

According to the law, half of the value of individual amendments ought to be used for medical treatment or services. These amendments can likewise be directed toward public works, such as the construction of schools or community athletic centers, and to the purchase, for example, of medical equipment. It is also possible to redistribute funds to public or private organs, as long as they serve some recognized social purpose. For this reason, several congresspeople defend individual amendments as an efficient way to meet the populace's objective needs, given that a deputy or senator should have a better understanding than the federal government of his or her region's needs.

On the other hand, another way to view individual amendments is as a flaw in the current model of determining public spending, since, through their use, individuals appropriate parts of the budget without any scrutiny of their amendments by Congress or the federal government. A study published in 2014 by the Chamber of Deputies demonstrated that many public monies end up being used in exchange for the support of voters—for purely political purposes in relation to an official's efforts to remain in power. Amendments, then, facilitate voter corrals, enhancing clientelist and patrimonialist relations between a deputy and those he or she represents or whomsoever enjoys his or her favor. In this way, they take on a personal quality and can be used as an instrument for corrupt practices by conceding to fewer than six hundred congresspeople the power to decide how public monies will be spent. Numerous scandals involving the diversion of public funds indeed originate via individual amendments—such as the "Budget Midgets" scandal in 1993, in which congresspeople directed public money to organizations that were tied to family or that were fronts altogether, and the "Bloodsucker Mafia" scandal, whereby healthcare funds were used to buy equipment at a price well above market value.

There are several ways to employ the old "Brazilian way" when the majority of politicians view their public position as, in effect, private property—their own or their family's—to the detriment of those collective interests that enabled their election. And if such an attitude is generally agreed to constitute "patrimonialism," the practice, now routine, has—as sociologist André Botelho demonstrates so well—become its own "class of offense: it is a sin/crime which the 'other' brings upon himself, not the accused." Terms such as "patrimonialism" or "patrimonialist" have thus been used both to stigmatize political opponents and to undermine adversaries.

During the last thirty years, Brazil has not only sought to consolidate its democracy but has modernized social relations. The country has not yet managed, however, to root out deeply embedded patrimonialist practices, which helps to explain in part the crisis it is experiencing in the present day. For this and other reasons, patrimonialism remains one of the greatest enemies of the republic, having the potential to undermine and weaken State institutions. The health of a democracy is measured by the robustness of its institutions, and in Brazil's case, a substantial proportion of these has, since colonial times, been dominated by a selection of powerful interest groups, which make use of the workings of government for private ends. When practices like those described here result in the wellbeing of the few and the distress of the many, we might soon recognize the old notion, now merely in a novel guise, that Brazilians are averse to formality and "indifferent to bureaucracy."

The contamination of public spaces by private interests is a dark legacy of Brazil's past, but it is also a characteristic of the present. The concentration of wealth, the staying power of traditional regional chieftains, as well as the rise of "new colonels" in both the country and the city and the growing influence of corporatist politicians, make it clear that in Brazil it is still common to fight, first and foremost, for the private interest. This amounts to an authoritarian and personalist form of engagement with the State, as though the latter were nothing more than a generous family whose leader is a noble father-figure benevolently taking the reins of the law, magnanimous with his allies but severe toward his opponents, who are viewed as enemies.

As Max Weber wrote in his famous essay "Politics as a Vocation," "He who lives 'for' politics makes politics his life, its own internal reward." For all that Brazil seeks to strengthen its institutions, it still lacks a civic and civil commitment that might guarantee rigorous vigilance against a form of public malfeasance that remains a feature of the regular dealings of certain politicians, who make no distinction between the domestic sphere and the public sphere concerned with the interests of all Brazilians.

4

Corruption

IF THE BRAZILIAN republic's number one enemy is patrimonialism, its second principal adversary answers to the name of corruption. This is a practice that degrades the confidence we have in one another and leads to a crumbling of the public sphere, that diverts resources and erodes the rights of citizens. Not by coincidence, corruption is frequently linked to the poor use of public money, occasioning a loss of government control over policies.

Over time, corruption has earned various epithets, which lead, nevertheless, to a common understanding, as representing, according to historian José Murilo de Carvalho, the act of "transgression," in the sense of "disrespecting, violating, and infringing on many areas of activity." Etymologically, the word comes to us from the Latin *corruptio*, literally referring to a breaking into pieces; that is to say, "deterioration" or "decomposition." In the management of the state, corruption pertains to the act of conferring or receiving undue advantage, either on the part of public agents or the private sector, with the intent to profit. So widespread is corruption in Brazil that it has ended up taking on a fundamental role in the political world, but it is just as common in the sphere of personal relations.

History and time, meanwhile, have the power to transfer and accumulate meaning. The Portuguese term *propina*, for example, which today is used to refer to a sum offered illicitly to an individual or to an institution, was first associated with the world of libraries and essentially expressed an entirely different meaning.

In Portugal, which saw the creation of the Public Library in 1797, *propina* referred to the custom of acquiring a copy of every book published domestically for safekeeping in the institution. There was nothing illegal in this activity, which also did not aim to satisfy any individual interests. On the contrary, its objective was to safeguard editorial memory in such a way as to guarantee that public archives preserved copies of all books published in the country. It recalled, all the same, the act of receiving "contributions," in the form of copies of each book, from several publishing houses or booksellers.

Since then, however, the popular use of the term has led it to be increasingly associated with the act of gratifying someone in an additional and incorrect manner for a service that ought to be provided as a matter of course. For this reason, *propina* came to mean "bribe"—a sum paid or received to obtain or dole out privileges, most of them illegal, especially in the ambit of public administration. Corruption—the act of offering undue enrichment to a public agent—is the crime, while the *propina* corresponds to the advantage or payment offered or received. The bribery can be "active," such as when an individual offers money directly to an employee of a public institution to acquire benefits for himself or for others, or "passive," when a public agent requests money from someone in exchange for personal favors.

An act of corruption can also involve a variety of elements of society, since all those included in a criminal operation are considered equally culpable. The "corruptor" is the person who proposes an illegal act for his or her own benefit, or for that of friends or families, and commits the act fully aware that he or she is infringing upon the law. The "corrupted" or "corrupt" individual, meanwhile, is the person who accepts the execution of an illegal act in exchange for money, gifts, or other services that benefit him or her personally. Yet another actor is the "accomplice," who learns of the act of corruption but does nothing to counteract it.

Whatever form corruption might assume, what is certain is that it debases, rendering conduct immoral and unethical. The consequences go beyond the private sphere; they ultimately affect the wellbeing of the country's citizens in a direct way. This outcome is a matter of simple cause and effect: expenditure directed toward private enrichment subtracts from resources and public investment in health, education, public safety, housing, transportation, and social or infrastructure programs. Corruption also violates the constitution in another way: by amplifying economic inequality.

Corruption can occur at any point in history, but its meaning is broad, the details can vary widely, and there exists no unifying theme. Still, the corruption that ravages Brazil's national politics today, and which has left Brazilians outraged, has been, to a greater or lesser extent, a daily occurrence in the country since colonial times. In this way the cunning employed by colonial era elites is recalled, to varying degrees, in several illicit practices perpetrated by some current government officials.

Since the end of the sixteenth century, in satires, sermons, poems, and craftwork, Brazilian politicians have been accused of illicit self-enrichment and of engaging in a spoils system, influence trafficking, nepotism, and abuse of authority. Even in the letter that Pero Vaz de Caminha wrote when he landed in Brazilian territory in 1500, there are vestiges, if not of corruption, at least of patrimonialism.[1] At the end of his missive, considered the first written document about Brazil, the scribe takes the opportunity to appeal to the Portuguese king, Dom Manuel I, to give assistance to his son-in-law; specifically, Caminha asks that his relative be released from exile, in São Tomé, for "theft and armed extortion." Corruption, a spoils system, or patrimonialism: Caminha's missive resists strict classification but certainly indicates the application of personal advantage via his privileged position in the public sphere. There is also proof of conduct that we would term corrupt by today's standards in the Portuguese American colony from the outset of the period when Tomé de Sousa (1503–79) was Brazil's first governor-general and was authorized by the king Dom João II, in 1548, to make "make concessions to any persons" so long as these consolidated Portugal's hold on Brazilian territory.

Illicit enrichment was part and parcel of the personal trajectories of local authorities, and especially governors. Mem de Sá, who was governor-general of Brazil between 1558 and 1572, was accused of abusing his position. Slave traffickers who left the coast of Africa for the Rio de la Plata and were obliged to seek harbor in Rio de Janeiro to refuel their ships knew ahead of time that they would be coerced into offering up a certain percentage of their "goods" for delivery to the governor of the captaincy. On many occasions, the "toll" proved even more expensive: authorities demanded the right to board the ship and select for themselves the most prized slaves.

In the seventeenth century, travelers were fond of saying that it was preferable to be robbed by pirates on the high seas than to dock in Brazil, where they would be forced to pay a series of duties on their commercial goods, besides being obliged to render homage to authorities and wealthy landowners with all manner of gifts; and in traveler diaries from the eighteenth century, a certain "Brazilian way" had already caught the attention of those who traveled across Minas Gerais. In the letters they left behind, explorers tell of their astonishment at the "cunning of the Brazilians," who smuggled precious cargo and mixed dust with gold to give the impression that production levels were higher than in actuality and thus increase their profits. It is during this period that the expression "santo do pau oco" (cheat; lit. "hollow wood saint") comes into use: pilfered gold was hidden inside hollow wooden statues of Catholic saints so that merchants could evade the high taxes levied by the Portuguese Crown. In this case, the misdeeds consisted primarily of smuggling or tax evasion, since the goods were stolen from the motherland's treasury for private benefit. Yet again, while practices differed, they corresponded to terms and definitions familiar to us today.

Indeed, in the extraction of precious metals, where the possibilities for illicit enrichment were many, there are several familiar forms of bribery: bribes so as to avoid taxes, bribes to keep part of the gold assessed, and so on. One famous case, identified by the historian Adriana Romeiro, involves Dom Lourenço de Almeida, who governed Minas Gerais from 1721 to 1732. Rumors circulated that he had accumulated considerable wealth through the sale of gold, always by illicit means. So rapid was his ascent that in short order he held more than one hundred *contos de reis*, a veritable fortune by the era's standards. At a time when the motherland took a hands-off approach toward its overseas territories and control was exerted, as we have seen, through colonial administrators, there were two basic provisos that allowed a politician to thieve freely and unencumbered: it was necessary only to act with a measure of discretion and to respect limits. Dom Lourenço, however, broke both rules, going so far as to mine for diamonds, a commodity on which the Crown held a monopoly, without properly notifying his superiors in Lisbon.

Admittedly, this historical reality is far removed from the current one. That is to say, it was part of the Portuguese monarchy's own strategy to apportion lands and privileges in exchange for services rendered to the sovereign. The Crown simply looked the other way as its agents saw to their own enrichment, so long as their operations did not harm the royal receipts and were carried out, preferably, in a discreet manner, through carefully chosen frontmen, generally servants or local merchants. Be that as it may, however, by the eighteenth century, the term *corrupção* (corruption) was being used to indicate venality and disruption of the political conditions necessary for the exercise of virtue and liberty.

It is clear that corruption, whatever particular name, expression, or form it took, or whatever practices made it possible, though not a trait exclusive to Brazilians, has been present throughout Brazil's national history. The first explanation for the dissemination of corruption across the country, or at least a facilitating factor, was precisely the hands-off approach of the Lusitanian administration mentioned previously above. The second important element was the fact that the colony had invariably been understood to be a promised land of opportunities. After all, in early eighteenth-century Minas Gerais, it did not take much luck to find a substantial vein of gold and become rich overnight. In a span of only ten years, thousands of illiterate peasants were able to make a fortune, join the ranks of the local elite, and, if they were among the more daring, exert influence in the politics and economy of the captaincy.

Further, it should not be forgotten that Brazil financed a slave-holding system until only 130 years ago. Of course, to maintain such an institution, and for centuries—though the practice did not contravene the law—it was necessary to water down one's moral scruples in terms of relations to one's fellow man and instead think predominantly of one's own gain. Slavery hollowed out moral and ethical concepts; while commerce was conducted directly between owners and traffickers, its daily operations took place at the margins of the control of the Portuguese State, which owned the African trading posts but controlled neither slave traffic nor slave markets.

In fact, as we have seen, impunity in this context was, in some sense, usually to be expected. More precisely, impunity could be viewed as a privilege that the king conferred upon local elites and its agents. Insofar as these rendered services to the sovereign by taking part in the work of colonization—by opening up roads for the free flow of export goods, maintaining open ports, mining precious metals, cultivating agricultural products, and taking responsibility for the proper functioning of commerce—they earned in return a sort of right to impunity. Smuggling was thus by far the most common of illicit practices in colonial Brazil. While the Crown pretended to ignore these illegal activities, the local authorities involved in the repression of contraband were themselves active in this type of infraction. Consequently, the elites made vast profits, while the king turned a blind eye and then received his own share as well. Things were such that, in cases that required the investigation and punishment of someone who could put at risk the "common good" but who, at the same time, worked in service of the colonial enterprise and the interests of the Crown, the solution reached was, rather frequently, to reduce or dismiss the charge.

There was a separation, of course, between society and the State, whose presence was only effectively noted when the time came to pay taxes. Otherwise, the colonizers administered their goods without much external interference in their activities and decisions. In effect, they created a parallel government, under which illicit practices assumed a fundamental role in the smooth operation of the colony's business.

Corruption is certainly not an exclusively Brazilian problem. Nor does there exist some evolutionary and predetermined continuity between the past and the present; though the fact that Brazil was an exploitation colony dedicated to the export of material goods and agricultural products that complemented the European economies and, in addition, that it could count on only weak control from Lisbon, led Brazilians to develop a gamut of tricks and strategies to circumvent the colonial pact, with or without Lisbon's consent. It would be a mistake, however, to attribute complicity in corruption to Portuguese colonization alone. Ultimately, the colonial system itself stimulated such dealings, and societies colonized by other Western powers—such as the Netherlands, England, and France—adopted similar policies when the only interest was in "exploitation" of their territories.

That said, however, these practices persisted during the eras of the United Kingdom of Portugal, Brazil, and the Algarves and the Empire. On the day in 1808 that Dom João stepped off his ship in Rio de Janeiro, he received a generous "gift" from a local slave trafficker: the best house in the city, situated on a handsome and impressive plot of land. "Granting" the Quinta da Boa Vista to the royal family assured Elias Antônio Lopes the status of "friend of the king" and an entry into the world of privileges constituted by the royal court. In the years that followed, as a consequence of his "generous act," he not only grew very wealthy—and quickly—but collected various aristocratic titles.

The Lopes case was not an isolated one: many plantation owners, ranchers, and slave traffickers also established a regime of exchange and negotiation with the Portuguese prince, who arrived in his American colony with his coffers practically empty. Public and private business already mixed in colonial Brazil, but this relationship only grew with the arrival of the Lusitanian court, when, as we have seen, it became common custom to buy aristocratic titles in exchange for payment to the royals who had the power to distribute them. Anyone wanting to boast a title, or to engrave a coat-of-arms into the entrance of their home or imprint it on the house porcelain or on stationery, would have to pay the Crown a considerable sum, proportional to the degree of nobility bestowed: nongrandee barons paid half the amount a count paid, for example.

This process was stipulated by law, but the business that sprang up around it and the trading of favors and symbols of power that surrounded it were not. To give an idea of the scale involved: during his first eight years in Brazil, Dom João, in order to replenish the State coffers, distributed more titles of nobility than had been granted in the previous seven hundred years of the Portuguese monarchy. Portugal had up to that point created seventeen marquises, twenty-six counts, eight viscounts, and four barons. By 1816, the prince regent had already named, in Brazil alone, twenty-eight marquises, eight counts, sixteen viscounts, and twenty-one barons.

The popular refrain, "He who steals a little is a brigand / He who steals a lot is a baron / He who steals the most and makes not a sound / makes the leap from baron to viscount," signals the way in which, in the Brazil of that era, nearly everything was "up for sale"; but it takes on greater meaning still in this specific context in which the aristocracy was bargaining for place and position. It is said that the inspiration for the verse above was two important figures of the era, who successfully obtained the title of baron and, soon thereafter, that of viscount, thanks to significant tax evasion: Joaquim José de Azevedo, the viscount of Rio Seco, and Francisco Bento Maria Targini, viscount of São Lourenço, are considered by historians to be two of the principal exponents of corruption in the first half of the nineteenth century.

Excessive bureaucracy gave even the less wealthy an incentive to commit illicit acts. At the time of the Constitutional Convention of 1823, for example, a merchant sent a letter to the government affirming that he had managed to obtain a permit to sell food in his establishment. However, soon thereafter, public officials began to demand a new permit authorizing him to serve coffee. In the face of such a demand, inexplicable but also unavoidable, the way out was to bribe the authorities and join in the game.

During the period of the Brazilian Empire, the term "corruption" was rarely used or even alluded to. Every concept bears the mark of its time and subsequent transpositions from one era to the next bring with them changes in meaning. Our modern notion of corruption is tied to a concept of the State whose logic is founded upon the idea of equal rights for all, a model that played no part in the thinking of a government that, despite its more or less enlightened or constitutional nature, never relinquished its "moderating power": a fourth constitutional power—as we have seen, exclusive to the monarch—that could overrule the other three. In addition, thanks to rituals, official engravings, and documents widely disseminated at that time, the sovereign was increasingly associated with the image of the divine monarch; he was not judged for his acts among men but according to another kind of justice—God's. It is therefore necessary to "translate" the term, since in this context it has a different, even if often closely related, meaning from that we understand it to have today.

During the initial period of the Brazilian Empire (1822–31), the journalist Antônio Borges da Fonseca addressed Dom Pedro I as "Estimable Leader," and, as far as we can tell, not because he held him in high esteem. It was, instead, a reference to the enormous funds the imperial household might be estimated to consume from the public coffers and to the "emperor's habits," which came at great cost to the State. When Borges da Fonseca found himself in prison—more than once—as a result of criticisms he made in his commentaries, those he denounced continued to suckle at the public teat. Meanwhile Domitila de Castro, Dom Pedro I's mistress, whom he named marquise of Santos, facilitated a power-ful influence-trafficking scheme at court. In 1825, some ambassa-dors then passing through reported that anyone wanting to receive a special favor from the emperor—such as the easing of the politi-cal or economic life of a friend or even the frustration of that of an enemy—would have to pay the "toll" charged by Domitila and her brothers.

All told, during Dom Pedro I's reign, despite a political situa-tion that was itself turbulent—including the closing of the Con-stitutional Congress in 1823, or the crisis that would result in the emperor's departure for Portugal in 1831—in the newspapers and registers of the Chamber of Deputies the notion of corruption is rarely referenced directly, nor is any other term of similar meaning. Rather, having established a constitutional monarchy in the heart of the republican Americas, everyday questions were debated in the most heated terms, yet these debates often spared the State and its leader—outwardly, at least.

This tendency to spare the head of state becomes even more evident at the height of the Empire's popularity, with Dom Pedro II renowned not only as a constitutional monarch by divine right, but as a patron of the arts. Hand in hand with the economic pros-perity that took hold in the 1850s and 1870s—with the Brazilian monopoly on coffee on the international market—efforts were made, with great success, to convey the image of a political system above any such mundane concerns.

However, with the passage of time this would change. The emperor's image would remain unblemished until the end of the Paraguayan War (1864–70), when Dom Pedro II's Empire had reached its apogee but also, though no one yet sensed it, the begin-ning of its decline.[2] At that point, abolitionism was gaining steam, the Republican Party was founded, and the army asserted itself as an autonomous institution. The imperial government, meanwhile, found itself beset by issues that would give birth to a new order in which accusations were levied more freely, and in the firing line was the very standing of the system and its head of state.

It seems no coincidence that, at the same moment that the monarch and his government began to show signs of political fragility, several cases that linked the monarchy to corrupt practices—sometimes directly, sometimes indirectly—began to appear in the press, as a hapless Crown failed to quash them. Not that the population had previously been without reasons for ire; it is notable, however, that only at this point does such discontent break out into public view in the form of criticisms in the newspapers, and that it is directed squarely at officials of the Crown and at the sovereign, increasingly held responsible for the poor governance and shady dealings of officials.

There is no way to catalog all of the incidents that might, in this context, have been linked to the notion of a corrupt state. The most emblematic case of the blurring of public and private interests became known in the era as that of the "Emperor's little pocketbook." This referred to hefty funds from the Treasury allocated to the monarch, who could distribute them without explanation to other organs of the State. It is indisputable that he invested these resources, in particular, in support for artists, scientists, and musicians whose goal was to create and diffuse a national culture, but there was no accountability in such operations.

As the Empire waned, another iconic event became known as "the Theft of the Crown Jewels." The year was 1882, the time more precisely the early hours of March 17, when a thief was alleged to have gained entrance to the São Cristóvão Palace—private residence of the imperial family—and snatched from a closet all of the jewels belonging to the empress Teresa Cristina and Princess Isabel, her daughter. Up until this moment, the Empire was a victim, not the instigator, of the process that was under way. Nevertheless, as events unfolded, their political consequences would alter the scenario. The problem was not so much the monetary value of the stolen objects; rather, it was a matter of the political and symbolic nature of the episode.

In fact, the incident would play into the hands of the opposition, which began to accuse the imperial government of negligence in its handling of private affairs that had now become public. After all, if the palace grounds could be so easily breached, what hopes did its subjects have for their own safety? This was only the beginning of a complex story, which would ultimately develop into accusations of bribery and administrative incompetence, providing a field day for the era's tabloids. Internal affairs at the imperial palace, which until then had been home to an extremely discreet and guarded family, filled the front pages of all the newspapers. According to sensationalist publications from that time, the empress had worn the jewels at a ball, dropped them off at home, and then headed straight for the imperial residence in Petrópolis. The entire set of precious stones had been put away inside a box, which remained under the care of Francisco de Paula Lobo, a member of the court private staff. Documents from the era suggest that, unable to find the keys for the vault, the imperial official had opted to leave the box inside an armoire, whence it mysteriously disappeared.

The investigation of events up until that point concerned only the extent of the functionary's ineptitude; meanwhile, however, because the crown jewels were the property of the State, a conference of the court police and the minister of justice himself was called. In a long story, full of ins and outs, most important is that it quickly became clear that the theft had originated within the palace. Two functionaries were detained, as well as a former servant—suspected of having entered the building on the day the jewels disappeared. To further the mystery, and to begin to resolve it, some days later an anonymous letter arrived indicating the location of the stolen jewels: in a biscuit tin buried behind the house of the third suspect. Not only the jewels, but dozens of other items belonging to the Crown, were found there. And so the crime was solved, and fairly efficiently, but this marked the beginning of a much larger debate revolving around the government's moral failures.

It was not exactly the theft itself that led to the monarchy's downfall, but a certain complicity in it, and the fact that no punitive measures were taken. Manuel Paiva, the main suspect, had been formally removed from his duties at the palace, but he remained under the protection of the monarch; not only that, but he kept the keys to the palace. Moreover, the three individuals implicated in the theft were immediately freed with the prior consent of the emperor. To make matters even worse, while all this was going on, the two policemen who had worked on the case were rewarded for their work: the first with a commendation from the Order of the Rose, and the second with knighthood. Such gestures were quickly interpreted by the press as attempts to "silence" the police and "soften them up" by offering them titles generally reserved for the aristocracy. Other terms were used, but much reference was made to the notion of corruption or favoritism, and the muddle of terms in the official record is itself testament to the elevated political temperature.

Meanwhile, because the episode had been deemed a common theft, only the victim could initiate criminal proceedings—and the victim was none other than the emperor, who considered the case closed. The result was that Paiva was sent home, and press indignation spread like wildfire. The *Gazeta de Notícias* claimed that "in Brazil the law doesn't exist . . . it all amounts to organized crime." It was said that, along with the jewels, "justice" too had been "buried," and that the whole enterprise was nothing more than a "swamp." The events also drew in the legislature: the Chamber of Deputies and the Senate demanded a response from the justice minister and the emperor.

Once more, Dom Pedro sought to put a bandaid on the situation: via his majordomo, he delivered a declaration affirming that he would interfere no more in the course of the investigation. This new conciliatory gesture was not enough to contain an avalanche of criticism, however. To understand the impact of the event, we need only recall that at the time, three famous writers published serial novels inspired by it: Raul Pompeia, José do Patrocínio, and Artur Azevedo. All three were figures of significant public visibility and appeared to share a single objective: to lay bare the fragility of imperial institutions and sow doubts about the capabilities of Dom Pedro II's government.

The caricaturist and journalist Ângelo Agostini, a trenchant critic of the Empire, in particular from the 1870s onward, made history by dedicating an entire page in his newspaper *Revista Illustrada* to the subject (fig. 3), whose headline called the system into question: "The Theft, the Swamp, and the Mystery." Agostini belittled the police and the emperor, and concluded by saying that "sadly the veil of mystery is not thick enough that through it cannot be glimpsed an authority whom public opinion holds, justly or unjustly, to the involved in this sad affair." A refusal to enforce the law, a lack of order and hierarchy, a monarchy that was beginning to lose credibility, a police force dominated by base interests—these were accusations that would topple any system supposedly grounded in justice and ethics.

The episode might have been regarded as nothing more than a trifle, a passing affair, had it not borne the hallmarks of the notion of corruption as it was understood in imperial Brazil. In the first place, to attack the emperor became synonymous with directly criticizing the State, given that he was the State personified, and so, while the mere theft of the empress's jewels might be viewed as a personal matter, it resulted in a much greater furor. The making of representations of the emperor's character in the private sphere was in itself a sign of his political decline. As the French philosopher Étienne de La Boétie wrote regarding Louis XVI, "a monarch who flees—and is perceived to have done so—is less a king with each passing day." The same held for the Brazilian emperor. A sovereign who comes to understandings with his functionaries is less a sovereign with each passing day, for he is subject to the same temptations as his subjects.

In the end, the most decisive factor causing the case to take on the proportions that it did was not the criticisms of the monarch per se, but the political moment. Put another way: as long as the regime was strong, it escaped questioning. However, it required only a few defects to become public knowledge for certain episodes,

A gatunagem ja se estendeo ate' S. Christovão.
Roubaram a Coroa! Não serão republicanos?

FIGURE 3. "The thieving has even reached São Cristóvão. They've stolen the crown! Perhaps they're republicans?" *Revista Illustrada*, issue 291, p. 8, 1882. Rio de Janeiro, Archive of the Brazilian National Library.

generally swept under the rug, to become the subject of conversation in the nation's dining rooms.

Corruption is accordingly a notion that appears in this context, albeit by other names, as a form of accusation against the system, which, to justify its existence, ought to rise above such matters. In this particular case, criticizing the monarch amounted to a blow against trust in the fitness of the system. This was in 1882; the emperor had no way of knowing that the political situation would only grow more complicated from that point on. The monarchy would fall in 1889. We might be tempted to recall the ending of Hans Christian Andersen's famous tale: "The Emperor had no clothes"—and he hadn't even noticed.

Though there were very real personal consequences for the emperor, then, notable is the way in which, during the Empire and the First Republic (1889–1930), whenever anyone spoke of corruption it was in reference to governments and not to individuals. It was in this spirit that Alberto Sales, brother of Campos Sales (president from 1898 to 1902), regretting his support for a republic, groused in 1901 that the regime was "more corrupt than the monarchy." Alberto Torres, governor of Rio de Janeiro from 1897 to

1900, disenchanted with the new regime, sang to a similar tune: "This State is not a nation; this nation is not a society; these persons are not a people."

We mentioned above how the combination of the establishment of a federal republic and the ascendance of agrarian oligarchies led to a social and political phenomenon characteristic of the period: coronelism. This was an expression of the coexistence of new modern forms of political representation (universal suffrage) with an archaic agrarian model based on large rural estates. The right to the vote was now assured by the new republican constitution, certainly, but the fact that the majority of voters lived outside urban areas—and above all in the countryside—and participated very little in national politics led them to be controlled by agrarian landowners and vote according to the whims of these same. This was "yoke-and-oxen voting," by which local (municipal), regional (state), and federal (the central government) political chiefs were elected. Fraud, and also corruption, were rife. If landowners depended on the governor for the public works and improvements they required, the government itself depended on these landowners to deliver voters.

Everything was fair game. In some localities, the voter received a ballot and a number, which referred to his cemetery plot in the event he failed to follow the instructions of the regional boss. The landowners, meanwhile, agreed upon a sum among themselves and shared the burden, so as to secure the election of their candidate. In the middle of all this, the federal government, in line with the commitment made with those who held power, only certified such candidates, ensuring the continued power of the local groups already in command. And everything came with a price, which depended on rank and position within the government.

Another procedural maneuver during the First Republic, emblematic of the way in which the structure was overtaken by collusion and corruption, was known as "gubernatorial politics." This grew out of the commitment established between the federal government and the oligarchies governing the states—two groups whose principal objective was to avoid the instability and the political wayfaring that are a part of any federal system. An all-pervading form of institutional engineering during the First Republic allowed regional elites to exercise full control over the electoral process, with the federal government turning a blind eye to the plundering elites dedicated to the election of their own congressional caucuses and compliant state governments.

Nevertheless, the term "corruption" was still not widely used by major press organizations in the sense of "political malfeasance." Consulting the archives of newspapers such as *O Paiz* and *Correio da Manhã* between 1900 and 1930, one notes the more common usage of terms like "misappropriation," "inducement," "subornation," "compact," or "prevarication." In fact, the press seems not to have made much noise about or given much publicity to corruption on a grand scale (unless it was to attack momentary political enemies), opting instead to train its sights only on minor cases. As a rule, these vehicles published briefs about proceedings against minor officials, generally at the local or regional level. The following list is but an indicative sample. In 1901, while there is mention of "misappropriation" on the Brazilian Central Railway, the case of the Federal Asylum and that of the Lloyd Brasileiro grabbed the headlines. In 1910 and 1912, some members of the government were accused of "malversation of public money." In 1919, a group of judges was denounced, one by one, for corruption. In 1921, President Artur Bernardes was suspected of electoral bribes, and 1922, there appeared a list of bribes in the Congress. Incidentally, electoral fraud seems to have been the most significant form of corruption during the First Republic, also termed the "Old Republic" by the government that succeeded it: the idea was to associate these practices solely with, and thereby discredit, the First Republic while lauding its own performance. In the end, corruption assumed such proportions during the period, and has become so closely associated with it, that in 2017, in the state of Santa Catarina, a police operation to break up an electoral fraud scheme was named "Operation Old Republic."

History is not a long-jump competition, nor is it possible to build a linear narrative when the subject is corruption. What can be said is that it was only after 1945 that Brazil began to pass legislation against not only government corruption but also that committed individually by the head of state. Of this, many examples could be plucked from the still brief history of the Brazilian Republic; let us mention here only those that became, as it were, especially notorious.

In 1954, President Getúlio Vargas committed suicide. In the suicide note he left, he blamed the political crisis and the numerous accusations of corruption against himself and various members of his government. Besides the "Tonelero Street incident"—an assassination attempt perpetrated by aides close to the president against his greatest enemy, Carlos Lacerda—an even more serious case, which had shifted public opinion against Vargas, involved the news magazine *Última Hora*. At this point the only press organ to remain on the side of the president, the magazine was accused by a congressional commission of receiving money in exchange for its support of the government. Further, it was said that the magazine had managed to secure a loan from the Banco do Brasil thanks to Vargas's intervention. The scandal was so great that the expression "sea of mud," which remains (sadly) appropriate to our times, arose from this ordeal. To make the situation irrevocably worse, the owner of the periodical, Samuel Wainer, was a personal friend of Vargas. Getúlio's gesture represented, then, an extreme act by someone who is personally responsible for the State.

There are those who say that Vargas's suicide helped to prevent a military coup that was pending at the time, or, more precisely, delayed it for ten years, since in 1964 it would materialize, again following allegations of corruption at both the individual and State levels. In this connection, it is worth taking note of the terms employed by dictator Ernesto Geisel (1907–96) in explaining the coup: "What we had in 1964 was no revolution. Revolutions happen for an idea, in favor of a doctrine. We simply moved to depose

João Goulart. It was a movement 'against' and not 'for' something. It was against subversion . . . and corruption."

The construction of Brasília at the end of the 1950s was also the source of much suspicion of misuse of public funds. A congressional committee was established to investigate, seeking to verify the source of the bribes disbursed by the government to construction firms so that the immense project would be finished within the "proper timeline"—namely, by the end of the administration of Juscelino Kubitschek, who felt that he should be the one to reap the rewards of the feat.

It has never been clearly determined how much the new capital cost to build. Estimated at the time at 1.5 billion dollars, the sum spent on the construction of Brasília would be equivalent to 83 billion of today's dollars; this is equivalent to eight Rio Olympics, or nearly 10 percent of the Brazilian GDP in 1960, which then equated to 15 billion dollars. It is also unknown how many workers died as a result of haste, whether it is true that their bodies were buried, with the help of excavators, beneath the edifices rising up around them, whether corporal punishment of workers was actually practiced, and whether in truth they protested against their working and living conditions. All we do know is that thousands of laborers, coming mainly from the Northeast, from Goiás, and the north of Minas Gerais state—the *candangos* (deplorables)—only lived in Brasília while it was a worksite. Once the capital was finished and the government had moved in, workers had two options: either they were returned to their native states, or they went to live segregated in encampments similar to favelas, on the outskirts of the city.

There was never in fact any consensus around Brasília. The major news organizations were basically against the creation of the new capital. It was also unclear who paid the bill; so much so that Jânio Quadros was able to assume the presidency in 1961 by talking tough: he accused the previous government of elevating the cost of living, increasing inflation, and wasting public money on monumental works like Brasília, as well as insinuating that it was corruption that had made such sprawling projects viable in the first place.

Just as his rise to power had been meteoric, Jânio's fall too was swift. His vice president, João Goulart, better known as Jango, was already aware of Jânio's resignation as he returned from a diplomatic trip to China and made a long trip back via Montevideo, where he met with the Brazilian ambassador, Valder Sarmanho, brother-in-law to Getúlio Vargas, and accepted the instauration of a parliamentary system. He then stepped off a plane in Brazil, his prestige at a high, his hands waving, and a long list of problems awaiting him. Some, such as inflation and the drying up of a series of investments from the Targeted Plan,[3] were inherited from previous administrations; others, however—such as the agrarian question—had their origins in the historically and profoundly unequal structure of Brazilian society.

According to the constitution at that time, in the event of an elected president being unable to fulfill his term, the vice president assumed his place. However, since Jango was traveling on official business, the post was temporarily occupied by the president of the Chamber of Deputies, Ranieiri Mazzili. The military did everything it could to prevent the investiture of the vice president for what it believed were Jango's ties to "communism." Still, and because of political pressure and the reaction of civil society, Jango assumed the presidency, though under a new, parliamentary system. In 1963, when voters opted for a presidential system of government, the powers of head of government were finally returned to Jango, who would not, however, last long in power.

All this jockeying sounded a second alarm: organized efforts toward a coup continued. The common denominator here was the involvement of nonparty organs in the financing of campaigns, and the most radical of these, the Brazilian Institute for Democratic Action (IBAD), had been active in Rio de Janeiro from 1959 onward, in coordination with the CIA. IBAD unleashed a large-scale illegal operation, pouring an avalanche of money into the campaigns of 250 candidates for the Chamber of Deputies and six hundred for state Houses, plus those of eight gubernatorial candidates—a flagrantly illegal act, according to electoral law at the time, which prohibited outside financing of campaigns. The funds came from multinational firms and others tied to foreign capital, as well as from US government sources responsible for investing in the conspiracy against Goulart as, years later, the American ambassador at the time would confirm. The aim of this broad-based sponsorship was strategic: to construct an opposition front in the Congress, stymieing the government and opening the door to a coup. All such activity came under the heading of the crime termed in that context "electoral corruption." IBAD was shut down by Jango in 1963, after a congressional investigation confirmed accusations of illegal activities.

Corrupt practices were deeply entrenched in the country, so much so that in 1964 the military used corruption and the specter of international communism as the principal bogeymen to unleash a coup and install a dictatorship. At the same time, the censorship put in place from the outset of the new regime kept several accusations against the military cadre responsible from being investigated. Political propaganda notwithstanding, however, it was impossible to shield the government from a number of scandals. The Caixa de Pecúlio dos Militares (Capemi, a sort of military credit union) won a suspicious bidding process for logging in the northern state of Pará, in which ten million dollars were embezzled. General Electric went so far as to admit to having paid a bribe to public officials to win a bid to sell locomotives to the federal railroad network. There was also the suspicion of corruption regarding the construction of the Rio–Niterói bridge and the Trans-Amazonian highway, a gigantic road project, projected at 4,997 kilometers, of which 4,222 kilometers were (poorly) built, with the ambition of crossing the Amazon Basin from east to west and connecting the Northeast to Peru and Ecuador.

The Trans-Amazonian project served as a bridgehead and a symbol for an ambitious expansion and colonization program that involved the displacement of nearly one million people, with the idea of strategically occupying the region so as not to leave any stretch of national territory unpopulated and to tap the potential of the border areas. On September 27, 1972, the dictator Emílio Garrastazu Médici cut the ribbon on the project, which was used to bolster a wildly optimistic image of Brazil, spread the feeling that an impressive modernization process was under way in the country, and thus promote a certain identity around which Brazilians would coalesce. Things did not work out quite as intended.

The construction of the road led to the massacre of the forest and required billions of dollars, and to this day there are impassable stretches, due to rains, mudslides, and river flooding. The Trans-Amazonian consumed a sum of money that never existed in the first place, but it took some time for Brazilians to understand just how big a hole the government had dug. They only realized it when the so-called "Miracle" had ended and inflation was in the region of three digits—in 1980, it hit 110 percent. When the military government came to an end in 1985, the country was morally and economically bankrupt: many Brazilians and been tortured and killed, public debt was enormous, and inflation had hit a mind-boggling 253 percent.

Brazil had become a carbon copy of the Kingdom of Belíndia, situated in a faraway land between the West and the East, and dating to 1974: a product of the imagination of economist Edmar Bacha, who in "The Economist and the King of Belíndia: A Fable for Technocrats" sought to provide a warning about the crisis but needed to circumvent government censors. In Bacha's fictional kingdom, the ways in which national prosperity was measured served to hide a brutal concentration of wealth that divided the country between advanced regions—"Belgium"—and underdeveloped regions—"India"—where there was famine, stark poverty, low life expectancy, and a high infant mortality rate.

Corruption took other forms during the military dictatorship. From 1970 onward, sergeants, captains, and corporals from the First Company of the Second Battalion of the Army Police, in Rio de Janeiro, established a steady relationship with operators from the city's black market. According to a February 14, 2019 story on Brasil Online, Captain Aílton Guimarães Jorge—who had gone out of his way to earn the "Pacification Medal" he received for service in the Araguaia Guerrilla War—was part of a cartel that traded illegally in "crates of whiskey, perfumes, and luxury clothing, even stealing the goods off other smugglers. The military not only provided cover, but had a direct hand in shady dealings. They were arrested by the National Information Services and tortured, but were later cleared because their testimony was obtained through the use of force."

Another important case is that involving São Paulo police figure Sérgio Fernandes Paranhos Fleury, who was as widely known as he was feared in his time. He was implicated in incidents involving the capture, torture, and assassination of political prisoners. In addition, as revealed by the Brasil Online article cited above, the officer found himself accused by prosecutors of ties to drug traffickers and executions. Identified as the leader of the Death Squadron, a paramilitary group that took it upon themselves to execute left-wingers, Fleury also found himself accused of ties to common criminals, providing protection services, according to prosecutors, to drug trafficker José Iglesias, known as Juco, in the war between São Paulo cartels. Despite all this, his actions during the repression of opposition to the dictatorship earned him a Pacification Medal that, in addition to shielding him inside the armed forces, gave him cover when it came to the accusations against him. (Any similarity to the current situation is not merely coincidental.) At the end of 1973, Fleury was held in police custody for the assassination of a trafficker. However, around this time the penal code was rewritten, establishing that first-time defendants with "clean backgrounds" had the right to release while they awaited trial. Fleury died in 1979, while his case was still making its way through the courts.

In the 1970s, a scandal exploded surrounding so-called bionic governors—officeholders put in place by the military regime, at a time when universal suffrage did not exist. Consequently, the nomination depended on the sanction of authorities in Brasília.

For example, the dictator Médici (president from 1969 to 1974) had a role in selecting state governors, choosing them according to their "good conduct" in relation to the regime. Even this could not bring many to abandon their shady practices, however. Haroldo Leon Peres was chosen as governor of Paraná by virtue of his public support for the government, but he was later forced to resign after he was caught extorting money from a government contractor. In Bahia, in 1971, Antônio Carlos Magalhães was serving his first gubernatorial term when he was accused of favoring Magnesita, a company in which he held stock, granting it a 50 percent abatement on its debt. Finally, São Paulo governor Paulo Maluf was accused of corruption in 1979, after two years in his post, in a case that became known as "Lutfalla"—the name of a textile firm that belonged to his wife, Sylvia, which had obtained a large loan from the National Economic Development Bank at a time the company was already subject to bankruptcy proceedings.

In 1976, meanwhile, at a moment when newspaper offices remained under the observation of censors but were beginning to find some breathing space, Ricardo Kotscho published a series of articles in the *Estado de S. Paulo* that detailed the perks enjoyed by ministers and public servants in Brasília. According to the story, at the home of the Minister of Mines and Energy, the yard was adorned with a flashy heated pool. The Labor Minister proved worthy of his title, employing twenty-eight servants. The governor of the Federal District ordered 6,800 bread rolls for his household in one day alone.

As we know, dictatorships do not permit the scrutiny of facts or the control and punishment of corruption. By the era of the Third Republic, public institutions had begun to work better, such that scandals earned headlines. Perhaps the first case to galvanize public opinion against corruption was the impeachment process of Fernando Collor de Mello, president from 1990 until forced to resign on December 29, 1992. He was accused by his own brother of leading a broad corruption scheme that generated close to R$15 million (US$84 million in today's dollars) and moved R$1 billion

(US$ 5.6 billion today) from state coffers, with the businessman Paulo César Farias as his front man. During the *caras pintadas* (painted faces) protests, as the massive demonstrations organized by students that year became known,[4] the calls to order from the streets referred directly to Collor, portrayed as just another "maharajah"—the label given to those who got rich quickly and illicitly, and whom he had himself in fact promised during his election campaign to curb. His vice president, Itamar Franco, who would temporarily assume the presidency in September 1992, later served out Collor's term. Yet again, we find the past being echoed in the present, despite the change in circumstances.

We can thus cite many and varied examples of corruption. Taken as a whole, they reveal a practice that is old and deeply ingrained among Brazilians, even if the term carries with it a certain ambiguity and fluidity. What we are dealing with in all cases are "transgressions of the law," whether by the political class, its principal exponents, or ordinary citizens. No matter the period, past or present, corruption can only persist to such an extent if it is widespread throughout the society that, in one form or another, provides cover or reward for it.

This is not a story of continuities alone, however: there are also important ruptures when it comes to public sanction of the corrupted and their corruptors. Once again, there are several illustrative cases, but we will confine attention to a few contemporary examples that have had a significant impact in the media and among Brazilians.

On May 14, 2005, the newsmagazine *Veja* published a video in which Maurício Marinho, former head of the national postal service's department of contracting (DECAM/ECT), requested certain financial benefits for Joel Santos Filho, posing as a businessman from Curitiba, who had been hired for five thousand *reais* a month by then-businessman and postal service supplier Arthur Wascheck Neto with the aim of obtaining material proof of Marinho's illegal activities. A duped Marinho would describe in detail an active corruption scheme among public agents. In its May 18 issue, the same magazine published a scandalous story under the title "The Labor Party's Point Man," which revealed the name of former federal deputy Roberto Jefferson, then leader of the Brazilian Labor Party (PTB), as the leader of the operation. His back against the wall, Jefferson divulged yet more details of the activities inside the postal service, revealing an widespread corruption scheme among congressmen, in which he himself was involved. He further clarified that the so-called congressional base of the Workers' Party (PT) had been receiving monies from the PT to ensure the PTB remained allied with the federal government.

It was these events that gave us the term *mensalão* (monthlies), a neologism created by Jefferson to denote the monthly sum paid to congresspeople who voted in favor of the executive branch's legislative priorities. It would seem that the term was used widely in the Congress and in the backrooms of Brasília to designate this type of illegal practice. The expression had also been used by federal deputy Miro Teixeira, in September 2004, to label a similar scheme. If at that time accusations went nowhere, in 2005 they generated a scandal of enormous proportions. José Dirceu, then chief of staff to President Luiz Inácio Lula da Silva, was immediately incriminated and identified as the scheme's mentor. Meanwhile, only in August 2007 did Brazil's supreme court begin proceedings against a list of forty defendants, identified by the country's attorney general in April 2006. The defendants were accused of forming a cartel, money laundering, embezzlement, active corruption, government fraud, and tax evasion. All those incriminated were formally indicted and barred from holding public office.

By a sort of domino effect, other scandals soon came to light. Daniel Dantas, of the bank Opportunity, was singled out as one of the principal financiers of the monthlies. Dantas managed Brasil Telecom and Amazônia Celular. After investigators were given access to bank records, it was confirmed that these businesses, along with Telemig Celular, had injected R$127 million into accounts tied to DNA Propaganda, an advertising firm run by Marcos

Valério, a businessman from Minas Gerais, soon accused of supplying what became known at the time as the Valério-duct, another large-scale scheme of illegal payments to congresspeople.

In 2011, a 332-page report produced by the Federal Police not only confirmed the existence of the monthlies scheme, but revealed how this scheme, which redirected public money to buy congressional support, in fact worked. The crisis occasioned by the so-called Mensalão led to further accusations (the Bingos Scandal in 2004, and the Postal Scandal in 2005), all involving the Workers' Party.

This was not the first time that a government or political party in Brazil had adopted illegal tactics to secure votes in Congress, even if we limit ourselves to the Third Republic, which began with the promulgation of the People's Constitution of 1988. In any event, criminal case no. 470 was the biggest case ever heard before Brazil's supreme court, with more than six hundred witnesses between the prosecution and the defense, spanning several Brazilian states and even abroad. The transcripts run to more than fifty thousand pages and include more than eight years of proceedings.

Though such tactics had also been adopted on previous occasions, this was the first opportunity to witness the result of a longer-term policy of increasing resources and training for the Federal Police (one implemented, in fact, primarily during the Workers' Party's years in the presidency), working jointly with the Office of the Public Prosecutor; this made an enormous difference to the way the investigation was carried out. Up until that point, it was basically the poor alone, most of them Black, who went to prison. This time, influential politicians, not small fry, and even the economic elite, were prosecuted and brought to justice.

The politics of state-sponsored corruption did not begin with the monthlies, however, and nor did it end there. In 2014, Operation Car Wash would grab headlines across the nation. In March of that year, the Federal Police got hold of the bank records of a Brasília gas station. It was the discovery of this gas station and car wash, and—especially—the money laundering scheme based there, that inspired the name of this joint operation between Federal Police and the Federal Prosecution Office. While the money had ended up in Brasília, its trail began in the city of Londrina, in Paraná state, for which reason the operation fell to the Thirteenth Federal District Court in Curitiba—one of many across the country specialized in dealing with the crime of money laundering, thanks to an initiative of the National Justice Council dating to 2003—then led by judge Sérgio Moro. Once again, this was no small-time operation. The investigation blew wide open a rampant corruption scheme inside the state oil company Petrobras, involving a cartel formed by members of its top management, Brazil's sixteen largest contractors, and the country's major political parties—the Brazilian Democratic Movement (PMDB), the Progressive Party (PP), the Social Democracts (PSD), the Brazilian Social Democracy Party (PSDB), and, above all, the Workers' Party (PT). The scheme had been in operation for the previous thirty years and was complex, involving various offshoots and players, contracts, and bribes for politicians, parties, and public servants, as well as money launderers and businessmen. The contractors would meet periodically to determine how the Petrobras bidding process might be defrauded: prices were fixed ahead of time, and the percentage of costs destined for bribes was agreed.

The truth is that, so ingrained is corruption in Brazilian society, it had created a "political machine," which extended throughout all levels of government—federal, state, and municipal. Once again, but on an even larger scale than previously, several high-level executives and businessmen were arrested, across the country. The list included the CEOs of Andrade Gutierrez, Camargo Corrêa, OAS, Queiroz Galvão, and UTC Engenharia, as well as vice presidents of Engevix and Mendes Júnior. The case with the greatest symbolic value, and the one that stirred the strongest public reaction on account of the sums and the number of politicians involved, saw the arrest of the engineer Marcelo Odebrecht, CEO of the largest contractor and second-largest private corporation in Brazil. He was held without bail at first, then later he accepted a plea deal. All told, Odebrecht spent two years in prison, and in 2017 he was transferred to house arrest.

This was but a tiny thread in a much larger ball of yarn; testimony resulting from a series of plea agreements unmasked the high degree of collusion between big business and the Brazilian political system. Corporations, individually or acting as a cartel, purchased privileges from state companies and agencies. In exchange for a certain "latitude" and access to the State, they delivered large sums of money to individual politicians and financed the party system. The tip that hinted at the size of the iceberg was in the form of the depositions three money launderers—Alberto Youssef, Carlos Habib Chater, and Nelma Kodamaa—and Paulo Roberto da Costa, former director of Petrobras, gave to the Federal Police in Paraná. To this day, in addition to many businessmen, several political heavyweights remain in prison or under house arrest, among them the former federal deputy and speaker of Brazil's lower house Eduardo Cunha (MDB—Rio de Janeiro), the former minister Antonio Palocci, former state and federal deputy and presidential chief of staff José Dirceu, and Luiz Inácio Lula da Silva, president of Brazil between 2003 and 2011, who in July 2017 was sentenced to nine years and six months in prison for corruption and money laundering. After he lost his appeal, an order went out for Lula's arrest and he turned himself in to the Federal Police in April 2018. (In early 2021, the supreme court threw out the former president's convictions.[5])

The corruption scheme operated by the Workers' Party was not exactly new, but it had reached a scale and scope never seen before. The party, in alliance with other members of the governing coalition, was not engaged in building a "Gramscian hegemony" of the State to spread socialism, as politicians directly tied to the current Bolsonaro administration claim. Still, the stolen funds financed electoral campaigns and support in the Congress, and were used in efforts to maintain the party's hold on power. They also served to personally enrich some party members. Corruption is corruption, however, no matter the motive or excuse. It is a process that ultimately eats up state financial resources, leading indirectly to a lack of resources for the infrastructure of a society, such as education, healthcare, housing, and transportation.

The other scandal that caused a deep commotion among Brazilians, in this case involving verifiable illicit personal enrichment, resulted from Operation Car Wash's Rio de Janeiro operations. In 2016, Sérgio de Oliveira Cabral Santos Filho, of the Brazilian Democratic Movement (MDB), was arrested and indicted for passive corruption, money laundering, and tax evasion. He had been governor of Rio from January 1, 2007 to April 3, 2014, when he resigned. Cabral later found himself a target in several other operations—Calicut, Efficiency, Open Invoice, Street Peddler, Unfair Play—and is currently in prison. Altogether, his sentences add up to more than a hundred years of prison time.

The scheme set up by the then-governor of Rio was so entrenched that, before he left his post, during the transition to his successor, Luiz Fernando Pezão, also of the MDB, an attempt was made to keep the arrangement going indefinitely. Cabral went so far as to organize a meeting with contractors, asking them to maintain the bribery scheme in operation. The results of the investigation made clear that corruption had already become state policy in Rio. Former governor Pezão was also arrested, in November 2018, accused of taking over leadership of the scheme he inherited from his political mentor. The result is that in recent years, voters in the state of Rio de Janeiro have looked on as a former governor, a sitting governor, the president of the state assembly, ten federal deputies, a former attorney general, and five of seven councillors from the General Accounting Office have been thrown in jail.

One of the most frequently cited names in accusations of corruption is that of Aécio Neves of the PSDB, who has been a federal deputy, a senator (2011–19), and governor of the state of Minas Gerais (2003–10), and is serving again in the Chamber of Deputies. Neves, at the time of writing, is a defendant in a case before the supreme court of passive corruption and obstruction of justice. He stands accused of soliciting a bribe of R$2 million from billionaire businessman Joesley Batista, as substantiated by video evidence, in exchange for influence over political appointees and obstructing the Car Wash investigations. The politician from Minas is also a suspect in eight other cases, of which seven involve corruption; yet he continues to hold office unimpeded.

Many of these cases, indeed a majority, have yet to be concluded, and of course, much may still happen. Still, in spite of all of the aforementioned operations, which have resulted either in the imprisonment or the indictment of politicians and businessmen, the perception of rising corruption in the country only intensified in 2017 and 2018. This, at least, is the conclusion of a study conducted by Transparency International. Brazil lost seventeen spots in the report's ranking of countries worldwide, falling from seventy-ninth to ninety-sixth place, alongside countries such as Zambia, Colombia, and Panama, and behind Rwanda, Burkina Faso, Timor Leste, and Saudi Arabia. The TI study, called the Corruption Perceptions Index, revealed that, in 2014, when Operation Car Wash began, Brazil occupied sixty-ninth position. The deterioration of Brazil's image internationally is also a source of complaint from Brazilians themselves who, in the same study, lament the absence of effective measures to combat corruption.

This is not an exclusively Brazilian problem, however. At the moment of writing, several Latin American countries have undergone a process whereby the judiciary has taken on an unprecedented role. Courts in countries as diverse as Brazil, Peru, Chile, Colombia, and Guatemala are convicting, and even sending to prison, high-profile politicians and businessmen, demonstrating a degree of independence unseen in the past. Operation Car Wash in Brazil served as a model for other countries, and the international repercussions of bribery schemes involving Odebrecht lit a fuse for several investigations abroad. Presidents and former presidents have been targets of investigations, leading some to resign or be impeached; recent examples include Pedro Pablo Kuczynski (Peru), Otto Pérez Molina (Guatemala), and Dilma Rousseff

(Brazil). Numerous others have been denounced and charged, including Michel Temer (Brazil), Daniel Ortega (Nicaragua), and Danilo Medina (Dominican Republic). Peru proved a particularly egregious case, as all five living former presidents fell foul of the law in 2017. In Brazil, former president Lula was arrested. A former president of Argentina, Cristina Kirchner, faced legal problems over corruption, a first for that country. The vice president of Ecuador, Jorge Glas, was sentenced to six years in prison in December 2017, for his participation in the Odebrecht corruption scheme. The former president of Ecuador, Rafael Correa, is facing investigation for corruption. The list is a long one, and many other countries are engaged in the fight against impunity.

It is important to state that corruption—that of both the corruptor and the corrupt—is intolerable in all its forms, whatever its supposed goals. It does not become less deserving of our condemnation when it favors a given party, person, or business. It is a crime and ought to be punished to the full extent of the law. The fight against corruption, as currently being realized across Latin America, is significant. In a region long accustomed to the impunity of political and economic elites, this represents a considerable change. Improvement in education is one of the principal factors that can be expected to result in greater constancy in this fight.

The battle against corruption cannot be reduced to a moral crusade; the phenomenon will only effectively come to an end with long-term plans to break up schemes and convict those involved, not to mention considerable political will on the part of the State. To train the entire artillery on a single person, on the other hand—thus making the issue personal—or to transform a single party into a scapegoat when the problem is so widespread, and thus claim to be "vaccinated against the disease," is a fix that cannot account for a problem of this magnitude. Since 2021, Brazil has seen how single-minded Operation Car Wash was in its campaign to punish the Workers' Party and Lula. Unfortunately, corruption schemes are not only an old ploy, but also a deep-rooted one, giving rise, as researcher Célia Regina Jardim Pinto suggests, to an "approach to governing." The fight against corruption cannot be limited to a campaign pledge; it needs to reach every citizen and politician to whom past and present criminal activities can be imputed, whatever his or her political party.

It was Brazil's period of democratic stability itself that permitted the whistle to be blown on a fraudulent scheme being conducted at the heart of the national political machine. It should always be remembered that where there are corrupt individuals, there are corruptors, and businesses most certainly received their share in these complex plots to defraud the organs of state. To break open the implicit pact that is established by the practice of corruption is one of the enormous challenges Brazilians have ahead of them. It is an urgent priority of Brazil's democratic agenda, which calls for equality before the law. As supreme court justice Luís Roberto Barroso said, "Corruption is a violent crime practiced by dangerous individuals. . . . Corruption kills those waiting in line at public hospitals due to a lack of beds, . . . of medication, on roads that are not safe to travel." It also results in the dissemination of authoritarian governing practices, which have sought throughout history both to prolong a group's time in power with the help of illegal procedures and to make an illicit profit.

Apropos of this discussion, studies by the Fundação Getúlio Vargas (FGV) in 2009 estimated that the Brazilian economy loses from 1 to 4 percent of its gross domestic product, or more than R$30 billion, annually to corruption. In 2010, research by the São Paulo Federation of Industries (FIESP) put the annual figure at 1.38 to 2.3 percent of GDP. In 2013, a survey released by the National Industry Confederation showed that every Brazilian real lost to corruption represents damage of three reais to the economy and to society.

Brazil bears the burden of a sad tradition of scandals involving politicians who put public money to fraudulent uses, bringing personal benefit to those operating the schemes. The factors that explain the persistence of corrupt practices are tied—but not limited—to the country's past. First, the lack of secure audit mechanisms when it comes to national institutions and Brazilian politicians has tended to make a bad situation worse. Moreover, a lack of transparency in the handling of public resources works as a stimulus for authorities to be less stringent in their efforts to curb such practices.

The hostage-taking of the State by private interests and the consequent practice of corruption that takes hold with an eye to preserving this type of scheme is one of the main factors that explain the crisis Brazilians are now experiencing. Besides affecting the economy through inefficient allocation of resources, corruption has the power to establish an inept bureaucracy, to the extent that this bureaucracy's operation is fueled not by the needs of the State but by the extensive distribution of political appointments and public funds to "faithful friends," who trade favors and "interests." Finally, corruption flourishes when combined with a broader mentality that not only tolerates the practice but views its everyday occurrence as the natural course of things. Public corruption is sustained by individual practices that always seek to "find a way," "give a hand," "turn a blind eye." In this case, it is better to open our eyes wide.

The examples described above prove that, regardless of the different names and shapes the practice has taken throughout history, corruption has always been dangerously present within the Brazilian State. This more or less constant presence suggests that while history is not an antidote for present ailments, a knowledge of it can help prevent further politically opportunistic attacks.

The way past this national impediment, resistant as it is to time and changes in government, is not only through holding the guilty responsible or securing their resounding public humiliation. In fact, the identification and atonement of the accused in the media, before their day in court or the proof of their guilt, can lead to irreparable moral harm, without solving the problems we have discussed. While it is urgent to punish the corrupt and corruptors, it is equally necessary to ensure effective and equal justice for all, and in this chapter of their history, Brazilians remain some way from the last page and final period. Corruption becomes wide-spread when conditions are ripe, and it is a whole mentality of corruption that must be confronted in Brazil.

Corruption is so frequent and deep-rooted in the country that there is a serious risk of it *appearing* to be endemic. There is nothing to prove, however, that it is part of a "national character," and thus cannot be extirpated with the evolution of the country's democracy. Brazilians are not, therefore, plagued by an incurable "epidemic" or "virus" of corruption, and solving this problem that threatens the robustness of national institutions is the fundamental task of a true republic.

The prosecution of illegal practices at the heart of the Brazilian state, arresting the corrupt and corruptors, politicians and businessmen, intermediaries, and those who give the orders, is proof of a mature democracy. To engage in crowd-pleasing, however, to tie oneself in knots with speeches that promise more than they can deliver, is to create fertile ground for illicit practices to flourish. It is worth remembering—and history provides numerous examples of this—that governments with an authoritarian streak often take power or are elected using slogans that denounce the illicit practices of their predecessors, thus improving their own standing by comparison, but meanwhile, without a commitment to effective frameworks that apply equally to all, they find themselves, too, succumbing to corruption's siren call.

———

In 1904, the American William Sydney Porter ("O. Henry") coined the term "banana republic" in a short story entitled "The Admiral." The story takes place in the Republic of Anchuria, a fictional location that must have been inspired by Honduras, where Porter lived at the time. The joke stuck and became associated with Latin American nations more generally, its reference always derogatory.

In 1912, Brazilian writer Lima Barreto created *The Adventures of Dr. Bogóloff*. Russian anarchist Grégory Petróvitch Bogóloff, who gave his name to this novel composed of a series of mordant episodes and who reappears in the 1915 novel *Numa e a ninfa*, has decided to move to Brazil, a country specialized in the art of the swindle. Bogóloff relates how he had read "scandalously confessional brochures from the unknown South American republic." These contained descriptions of a country "where the weather was neither frigid nor sweltering; where everything came to pass with supreme speed; where you could find all the products of the globe; it was, in the end, paradise itself." A clever man, he suspected only "fifty percent" of what he read must be true, and even so decided to emigrate. In the event, he ended up cursing his adventure: "What a hellish trip!"

Not content to stop there, in 1918, during the First Republic, Barreto published in the Rio anarchist newspaper *A.B.C.* an article entitled "Republican Politics," describing the political context as follows:

> Republican government in Brazil is a corruption regime. All opinions are required, by one form of compensation or other, to be dictated by the period's powerful. No one is allowed to hold differing opinions, and, so that there will be no divergence of opinion, there is a "secret fund," funds allocated by this or that [government] ministry and the miserable little posts the mediocre are unable to earn for themselves, independently. . . . No one wants to discuss anything; no one wants to kick around ideas; no one wants to stir things up. . . . Everyone wants "a bite." The judges want "a bite," the philosophers want "a bite," the poets want "a bite," the novelists want "a bite," the engineers want "a bite," the journalists want "a bite": Brazil is one endless banquet.

Brazilians seem at last to have tired of seeing their image associated with such illegal trickery, which affects everyone, undermining both their self-esteem and the country's international reputation. It is more than a century since the above caricature was created. Sadly, however, in this regard the past is not yet a bygone era.

5

Social Inequality

A CRUCIAL PROBLEM facing Brazil's republican agenda is a persistent and shameful degree of social inequality, inherited from the past but also produced and reproduced in the present. According to a 2018 report by Oxfam Brazil, while in 2016 the country occupied the tenth position in a global ranking of income inequality, in 2017 it came in ninth, the problem growing increasingly critical rather than improving.

Inequality is so deeply ingrained in Brazil that it appears under various guises: economic and income equality, inequality of opportunity, racial inequality, regional inequality, gender inequality, age inequality, and social inequality, which appears in different levels of access to healthcare, education, housing, transportation, and leisure activities.

Social inequality is especially acute, and tends to increase, in countries that offer few employment opportunities, make only modest investments in social programs, and do not encourage the consumption of cultural goods. It is no coincidence that inequality is rampant in peripheral countries with colonial pasts, where a persistent social gap is evident in the lifestyles of their citizens.

Social inequality is present in the entire world; it only becomes a problem, however, when there is a yawning gap between the income earned by the majority of the population and that of a country's richest individuals. In other words, social inequality is the difference that either privileges or disadvantages a specific social group. The concept of poverty ought to be understood within a social, historical, and cultural context. In this sense, there is no single definition of poverty. The concept of poverty is frequently defined in purely monetary or financial terms, while concepts relating to the exercise of one's rights or access to services are placed under the umbrella of "social exclusion." In this regard, within the European Union, a formula was developed to calculate who is and is not at risk of poverty: the poverty line is defined as "60 percent of the average adult's income." Social inequality, meanwhile, is measured by the income gap within a single country.

We have already mentioned, but it is worth recalling here, that Brazil was forged through the practice of slavery, which is, by definition, an inequitable system in which a minority monopolize income and power, while the vast majority are denied access to remuneration for their work, freedom of movement, and education. The colonial-era landscape was dominated by large single-crop plantations where landowners had absolute authority and amassed all the wealth. Corruption and deeply rooted patrimonialist practices hardly helped, either, to make the country more inclusive. On the contrary, these practices were notable for placing private interests above public ones, cheating society's most vulnerable of benefits that the public sector ought to provide with greater parity.

Slave labor, the division of land into large estates, and substantial doses of corruption and patrimonialism explain the degree of Brazil's inequality. They also explain a sort of "idiom of social disparity," whereby society becomes accustomed to deep-rooted inequality. What they cannot account for, however, is why, despite the process of modernization and industrialization that the country experienced during the twentieth century, it has not managed to definitively break this vicious historical cycle. On the one hand, research has shown that some change for the better has been made when it comes to measures of inequality. According to records gathered by the Brazilian Geographical and Statistical Institute, via the National Household Sample Survey that analyzed the living conditions of Brazilians in 2018, the slice of national income belonging to the top 10 percent fell in recent years from 46 to 41 percent, while that of the poorest 50 percent rose from 14 to 18 percent. There are disagreements, however, about these results. Irish economist Marc Morgan Milá, a disciple of Thomas Piketty, signaled in research published in 2018 that Brazilian administrations, in practice, never made the choice to confront social inequality. In Morgan Milá's assessment, such inequality is worse than generally suspected, with an immense income concentration at the top of the social pyramid: the group that comprises the top 10 percent of income earners across the Brazilian population garners more than half of total income nationwide. Between 2001 and 2015, this slice of the population saw its portion of the national income grow from 54 to 55 percent. Morgan Milá's calculations further suggest that the income earned by the 50 percent poorest also rose in recent years, from 11 to 12 percent of the total. Meanwhile, 50 percent of the Brazilian population, the middle portion, saw its share of income shrink from 34 to 32 percent.

The same study revealed that the richest stratum of the population, which corresponds to a mere 1 percent of Brazilians, eats up 28 percent of national income. Comparing Brazil to other countries, the Irish researcher noted that, in the United States, the elite, the 1 percent, account for 20 percent of wealth, and in France, 11 percent. Moreover, while in France the average annual income of the richest is less than the equivalent of R$925,000, in Brazil the average annual income of this group comes to more than R$1 million.

In 2018, a report prepared by Oxfam Brasil, *País estagnado: Um retrato das desigualdades brasileiras* (*Stagnant Country: A Portrait of Brazilian Inequalities 2018*), presents a similarly pessimistic panorama. According to the institution, for the first time in twenty-three years Brazil had seen its income distribution stagnate and poverty worsen. The income gap between men and women had also grown, as had that between Black and White individuals. These results are alarming, to use the term employed by the authors of the report, even more so considering that the majority of the Brazilian population is composed precisely of women and people of color.

The same document explains that the period between 2013 and 2018 saw an increase in the proportion of the population living in poverty, growth in income disparity, and an uptick in the infant mortality rate. The index that measures income equality internationally, known as the Gini of household income per capita, which had registered decreases since 2002, stagnated between 2016 and 2017. According to the study's organizers, sustainable development "has taken enormous steps backwards." For example, between 2016 and 2017, the poorest 40 percent saw a fluctuation in income worse than the national average. In the same period, women and the Black population saw income performance inferior to that of men and the White population.

These results cannot, however, be understood in isolation. In some sense, they are the consequence of the economic, fiscal, and political crisis that has plagued Brazil since the end of 2013, which ended up generating a sharp decline in national income, in line with the recession experienced in the country, where unemployment rates practically doubled, going from 6.8 percent in 2014 to 12.7 percent in 2017. This process impacted the poor, women, and the Black population above all, and was also felt across the country: nine in every ten Brazilians today describe the country suffering from "major inequality."

Indeed, despite the relative improvement experienced between the end of the 1990s and 2012–13, a series of studies has confirmed not only the high income concentration existing in Brazil, but the fact that the country maintains some of the highest levels of inequality in the world. A study conducted by the Institute of Applied Economic Research (IPEA) and published in 2018 by the United Nations Development Program's International Policy Center for Inclusive Growth places Brazil among the five countries with the greatest inequality on the planet when considering the concentration and distribution of wealth.

Beyond this, a study released on December 5, 2018 by the Brazilian Institute of Geography and Statistics (IBGE) indicated that income inequality remains a serious problem, and that poverty and extreme poverty have increased in recent years. After the NGO Oxfam designated the situation as "stagnant," it was IBGE's turn to show how the crisis in the economy, the nation's finances, and the job market had a direct impact on the lives of the working population.

Another datum reveals that the most affected are, in descending order, people of color, children between zero and fourteen years of age, single mothers, women of color who are single mothers, and those aged seventy or older. Without a doubt, it is Black women who are their families' breadwinners who have been most affected by this crisis. While the number of White men in poverty rose by 7.8 percent, that of Black women also increased, but only 2.68 percent. Yet in absolute terms, the number of women of color in poverty reached 35 percent, while the percentage for White men is less than half of that: 16.6 percent. The scenario repeats itself for those in "extreme poverty."

The fact that the country faces a serious conflict in terms of the relative tax contributions of the various social classes is yet another defining feature of Brazilian inequality. According to the 2017 Oxfam report *A distância que nos une: um retrato das desigualdades brasileiras* (*The Distance That Unites Us: An Overview of Inequality in Brazil*), there is a true abyss when it comes to tax matters. The top 10 percent in terms of income pay 21 percent of their earnings in taxes, while the bottom 10 percent pay 32 percent. Indirect taxes consume 28 percent of the income of this bottom 10 percent of earners and only 10 percent of that of the wealthiest 10 percent. Inheritance taxes, for example, account for about 0.6 percent of national tax revenues, a figure based on low tax rates that at times are not even assessed.

To provide a comparative view, while in São Paulo the tax rate on inheritances is 4 percent, in the UK, it reaches 40 percent. In Brazil, moreover, "the revenue generated by taxes on estates represents only 4.5 percent of the total, while in countries belonging to the OECD, such as Japan, Great Britain, and Canada, this rate is higher than 10 percent." Additionally, those who make 320 times the minimum monthly wage in Brazil pay the same effective income tax rate (after discounts, deductions, and exemptions) as those who earn only five times the minimum wage. For those earning more than eighty times the minimum wage, 66 percent of their income is exempt from tax. For those earning 320 times that amount, this figure reaches 70 percent. On the other end of the spectrum, the middle class's average exemption is 17 percent of income, and this falls to 9 percent for those who earn between one and three times the minimum wage. Finally, only two member countries and partners of the OECD do not tax corporate profits and dividends: Estonia and Brazil.

When it comes to healthcare, statistics also reveal unmistakable disparities among Brazilians and between different regions of the country. As table 1 shows, the highest rates of lack of care are registered by the following groups: women (3.5 percent); individuals between twenty-five and forty-nine years of age (3.7 percent); people of color (4.3 percent); people with little or no schooling, or high school education only (3.3 percent and 4.1 percent, respectively); and those who lack health insurance (4.2 percent)—all this despite the crucial role of the Serviço Unificado de Saúde (SUS), a national public health system instituted under the 1988 Constitution. There are also stark geographical differences, with the highest rates of lack of care by health services afflicting the North and Northeast regions of the country. Differing levels of medical care are also to be found between urban and rural areas: studies conducted between 1998 and 2009 highlight elevated levels of inequality in access to healthcare in the latter.

A comparison of those formally employed and those participating in the informal job market reveal increased health risks for this second group. The criteria for comparison, according to an analysis of the 2008 National Household Sample Survey (PNAD) numbers, in line with a study conducted by Isabella O. C. Miquilin

TABLE 1. Percentage of those who did not receive care/were left untreated by the National Health Service, by sociodemographic characteristics, in Brazil and its regions, 2013

Characteristics	North	Northeast	Southeast	South	Midwest	Brazil
Total population	5.7	4.0	2.8	1.5	4.1	3.1
Sex						
Male	6.4	2.2	2.3	1.1	3.7	2.3
Female	5.4	5.0	3.0	1.7	4.3	3.5
Age (in years)						
18–24	7.3	3.1	3.2	0.1	1.7	2.8
25–49	5.5	5.1	3.3	1.3	5.0	3.7
60–64	8.8	2.4	3.1	3.2	3.8	3.3
65 or older	0.2	4.2	1.0	0.2	4.0	1.6
Race/Color*						
White	4.8	3.0	1.9	1.2	2.8	2.0
Black	5.7	4.5	4.0	2.6	4.8	4.3
Education Level						
No formal education, or primary education only	5.3	4.3	2.8	2.1	4.6	3.3
High school	8.3	4.8	4.3	0.9	3.5	4.1
University	1.4	1.7	0.2	0.4	3.7	0.8
Private Health Insurance						
Yes	0.2	1.7	1.3	0.3	1.8	1.2
No	7.2	4.7	3.9	2.3	5.5	4.2

Source: Brazilian Institute of Geography and Statistics—2013 National Health Survey

Note: Percentage of those who did not receive care in relation to the total number of individuals who sought care in the two weeks prior to the survey.

*Excludes Indigenous and "yellows" (a term 1 percent of the Brazilian population still uses to refer to itself as of Asian descent)

Letícia Marín-León, Maria Inês Monteiro, and Heleno Rodrigues Corrêa Filho, are: "has been bedridden in the last two weeks, lack of private health insurance, did not seek healthcare treatment in the last two weeks, and lack of care by health services when sought out, and lower level of doctor visits in the last twelve months." Finally, there is the no less revealing statistic published by the sociologist and researcher José Alcides Figueredo Santos, also based on the 2008 PNAD: people of color, as defined by the national census, have a 56.7 percent greater chance, in relation to White Brazilians, of having their overall health classified as "not good." The same inequality can be seen in relation to the number of COVID-related deaths, which have affected Black and poor Brazilians at higher rates. One hundred and thirty years after the abolition of slavery and thirty after the promulgation of the Constitution of 1988, which stipulated the distribution of wealth via education, healthcare, and sanitation, Brazil remains an unjust country, because unequal.

Education and Illiteracy

In Brazil, a country defined by its continental proportions, slave-society past, and institutionalized concentration of wealth, education has never been a right for all. Slavery, while it endured, created a country of disparate realities in this regard, too. Historians have shown that, although there was never a law against teaching slaves to read, for motives of security and with an eye to preventing rebellions, they were not in practice allowed to read or write. Still, documents show that former slaves created special schools for Black people around the country, preparing them for a life in freedom. Slaves arrived, of course, with broad knowledge they had brought from the African continent, but few were able to participate in any coherent way in schooling or formal education.

It is important to clarify that during the colonial period even the free population had limited access to formal education, something that was considered a matter for the privileged few. Starting with the 1824 Constitution, however, the imperial regime established free primary education for all citizens, meanwhile keeping the right to vote from the illiterate. This move was reinforced by the 1881 electoral reform, which abolished income requirements to vote but kept the literacy requirement for exercising one's full political rights. Education, therefore, meant an irrefutable leap in access to citizenship. Perhaps for this reason the Additional Act of 1834 assigned provinces the duty to legislate, organize, and monitor primary and secondary education.[1] As a consequence, public, private, and home schools sprouted up according to the conditions of each province, the budget being quite often insufficient to the task.

In 1854, through the Statute for the Reform of Primary and Secondary Education in the Municipality of the Court, access to schooling was made available to all free, vaccinated persons, so long as children did not suffer from "contagious maladies." Matriculation in public schools was, notwithstanding, expressly prohibited for the enslaved, codifying an existing division at the very heart of Brazilian society. In addition, the same statute made schooling obligatory for free persons between five and fifteen years of age, under penalty of a hundred-reis fine for "parents, tutors, curators or guardians." Boys under twelve, "in such a state of poverty that, beyond the lack of decent clothes to wear to school, [they] live from mendicancy," and who could be found wandering city streets, would be brought to foster homes and then sent to private workshops, in a sort of informal contract with the State, to learn a trade and thus develop working skills. Note, incidentally, that in the 1854 statute reference is made only to "poor young boys," never to "poor young girls."

The accepted thinking at the time was that a primary education would be more than sufficient for the poorest classes. Secondary education, meanwhile, was not mandatory and consequently remained limited to a select portion of the free population. Fundamental inequality was indisputable. Both secondary and post-secondary education, which made it possible to practice the most prestigious intellectual occupations and prepared people for much-coveted government positions, were the preserve of the landowning classes, while the rest of the population found itself consigned to manual labor.

Education was also considered the best way around the so-called work question. In 1867, the counsellor of state José Liberato Barros doggedly pursued educational initiatives as the most effective way to "conserve the hierarchy and civilization of the Empire."

There is a manifest relationship between the foundation of an establishment such as the Home for Abandoned Children and the Law of the Free Womb: the institution was to provide for the education of the "innocent"—those born free or who had acquired their freedom as of September 28, 1871—who were delivered by their owners to the government's care. Further, it was to attend to the "free boys" in a state of "mendicancy," as well as adopt solutions to instruct "the freed." A series of slave-owners, unhappy with the government measure, began to solicit the "enrollment of the innocent" in the Home, as a form of indemnity for the expense of feeding and clothing them. The assumption on the part of slaveholding elites was that they held no responsibility for these children; on the contrary, they required compensation for their expenses.

As the 1870s came to a close, the number of public schools founded throughout Rio de Janeiro grew from forty-five to ninety-five. In this period, the imperial government constructed the first school buildings, of a size and architectural layout suitable to accommodate five to six hundred children. Between 1870 and 1880, the so-called school palaces of the court in Rio de Janeiro were founded: the Glória Public School (currently the Amaro Cavalcanti State School, in the Largo do Machado) the São Sebastião and São José municipal schools, situated in the heavily populated parishes of Santana and São José and attended, basically, by the children of the coffee-growing elite. Important, nonetheless, is that education rapidly became a significant item on the imperial agenda. Politicians, lawyers, doctors, professors, and ranchers founded philanthropic associations and societies, both religious and secular, that sought to "protect," "accompany," educate, and instruct children.

Over time, schools became increasingly specialized, too. Primary schools, for example, divided students by gender—boys and girls studied in separate locations and buildings. Catholic doctrine, reading, writing, and the most rudimentary arithmetic were considered sufficient for girls who attended primary school, as long as they were accompanied by sewing and dressmaking classes. The curriculum devised for girls placed limitations on the teaching of algebra, geometry, grammar, and national history and geography. The instruction they received was geared toward home life and domesticity, since the public sphere was reserved for men. For this reason, too, from 1870 onward the few girls who made it to secondary education were generally destined for a career in education. The remainder—poor, Black, enslaved or free—were immediately put to work.

These fates of those who studied and those who went to work were a reflection of disparate worlds, wherein distinct roles were stipulated for the poor, women, and people of color. Still, education represented, for those who would secure a place in the new schools, an effort at social inclusion, no longer being limited to the elite but now possible for those who had so long been deprived of the benefits of citizenship, such that, at the margins of the system, and still in modest numbers, there could now be found—in politics, in law, in engineering—Black elites who had carved out a space for themselves in institutions and environments of great social prestige.

With the proclamation of the republic, a new constitution was promulgated in 1891. Article 25 established that "it likewise falls to the Congress, but not exclusively . . . to create institutions of secondary and postsecondary education across the states." In practice, the federal government took control over secondary and postsecondary education across the country, while the task of opening primary and trade schools fell to the states: "normal schools" (teacher training colleges) for women and technical schools for men. On the other hand, with the vogue for racial theories that, as we have seen, sought a "scientific" justification for inequality—which has nothing natural about it, given that it is the effect over years of a deeply entrenched slaveholding system and a concentration of wealth that saw little distribution of resources— these tiny openings for social ascent again became very restricted, indeed almost unattainable.

It was only from the 1920s onward that education-oriented initiatives were given a new lease on life. Indeed, these were so numerous and so varied that the period became known as a time of "pedagogic optimism." Primary school became, at that time, one of the more serious foci not only of educators, but of public officials. Notably at stake was a bid to demonstrate the profound democratic importance and necessity of primary education. These were the ideals of the New School, a project led by scholars of the caliber of Fernando de Azevedo (1894–1974), Anísio Teixeira (1900–71), and Lourenço Filho (1897–1970), who discovered ways to galvanize state governments across a significant portion of Brazil.

Some of the country's authoritarian structures survived basically untouched, however. Primary and professional school were directed toward the more humble, while secondary and postsecondary instruction remained closely guarded privileges of the elite. It is worth adding, too, that the proportion of the population that was illiterate in 1900 was nearly 75 percent, according to the Annual Brazilian Statistical Report published by the director general of statistics of the Ministry of Agriculture, Industry, and Commerce.

The history of education in Brazil does not, then, resemble an upward and progressive arc. With the Estado Novo (New State, 1937–45) of Getúlio Vargas, for example, the country took many steps backward. In its unmistakable zeal to centralize authority, the government interfered in the area of education via several legal decrees, between 1942 and 1946, that became known as the Capanema Reform, in a reference to the then-minister of education, Gustavo Capanema. Eight decrees set forth regulations for primary education, secondary education, and each area of vocational instruction (industrial, commercial, normal, and agricultural). The reform did not alter the prevailing dualism in education in Brazil, however. The Fundamental Law of Education provided for two "tracks" to be followed from primary school through professional training—a bifurcated system, with public secondary school destined for elite leaders and trade schools for lower classes.

Thus, while on the one hand the State under Vargas regulated the relationship between employer and employee via the Consolidation of Labor Laws Decree (CLT in Portuguese), on the other it imposed upon the public education system legislation that sought to separate those who could study to the fullest extent from those who ought to study less and more quickly enter the workforce. For students from the middle and upper echelons, school life entailed primary school, then two cycles of secondary (junior and high school), and finally professionalization in postsecondary school, which allowed one to pursue any course of university study. For the children of families from the lower rungs, meanwhile, school life meant something very different: finagle an opening in public school—which did not guarantee matriculation for all—and complete a primary education. The student would then go on to a secondary professional program, also divided into two cycles, before finally, when possible, starting a postsecondary course, in a spot related to his or her secondary-school specialization. Female students who had completed teacher training, for example, could only earn a postsecondary education in one of the disciplines to be found at the School of Philosophy.

The process of economic development itself eventually demanded greater diversification of occupational responsibilities and the expansion of educational opportunities. Nonetheless, since work, in the cultural universe that the slaveholding society had forged, comprised activity that was suitable only for the inferior classes, what happened in practice was the disorderly expansion of the education model in place up to that point. On account of the urgency of giving the working masses early job training before they left secondary school, SENAI (1942) and SENAC (1946) were set up, with the aim of training the labor force to provide services in industry and commerce, respectively.[2] Such professional training schools, under the direction of the National Industry Confederation and the National Commerce Confederation, offered, in those early days, financial aid to their students, which made this type of career more attractive to students who came from the lowest rungs of society.

For this reason, even taking into account the success of SENAI and SENAC, it is imperative to recognize how these two entities reinforced the dual education system, creating conditions such that society's demand for education would grow in only two ways: those belonging to the middle and upper strata continued to opt for schools that provided social distinction, and those belonging to the more humble strata began to attend institutions that prepared them earlier for the workforce. The educational system thus represented, in general, a system of social discrimination and division.

Beyond perpetuating this sort of dualism, the Brazilian education system, consonant with the context in which it operated, created a primary course geared toward a model of authoritarian nationalism, as was then in force. Elevating the figure of the president Getúlio Vargas as "father of the nation" and making school into an institution that demanded its students absorb information rather than think critically were the objectives. The era was host to grand *concertos orfeônicos* at which, under the baton of maestro and composer Heitor Villa-Lobos (1887–1959), students paraded, sang, or attended performances at enormous secondary schools, a photo of Getúlio always present for inspiration (fig. 4). Civic pride, in this case, seems to have been the same as patriotism, despite the fact they are not identical concepts. Education with the aim of liberation, of forming citizens with greater agency, is a project that carves out a role for schooling that it actually deserves. Memorizing anthems, marching in parades, and watching as others do the same hardly produces people who are better prepared to practice civic values and behaviors. Once again, any similarity to actual events or people is merely coincidence.

In figure 4, we see how the rituals of patriotism, enjoying ample support from Getúlio Vargas, dialogued with those of other populist and authoritarian regimes in power at the time, putting their

FIGURE 4. Photographer unknown, *First of May, 1942, at Campo do Vasco Stadium,*
Rio de Janeiro, 1942. Rio de Janeiro, Brazilian National Library,
Seção de Iconografia.

stamp on a model of education that prized the exaltation of a ficti-
tious past extolled via anthems sung by large groups of students.
It is indeed integral to the very symbolic effect of national anthems
to feature melodies so grandiose that they either overshadow or
emphasize certain nuances in the content of the lyrics. We merely
sing them as the ritual casts its spell: they bring us to tears without
ever giving us pause for a moment to think about what and why
we are singing. It is no accident that dictatorial governments dedi-
cate special attention to the moments when national anthems are
sung in unison: these are the moments at which the nation becomes palpable and recognizable to and for all. So it was in the
former Soviet Union under Joseph Stalin, which every year produced a festival to celebrate the nation, an event that began and
ended with young people singing anthems. So it was in Nazi Germany under Adolf Hitler, who called upon blond adolescents and
children who, overcome with emotion, would then sing hymns of
praise to the Fatherland in enormous stadiums or immense public
squares, joined by the rest of the population, singing loud and
clear. So it was in the Estado Novo of Getúlio Vargas, who also had
recourse to stadiums, conventionally assigned to football matches
but newly converted into exalted patriotic stages, where students,
roused by the tones of the national anthem, paraded with an image
of the president raised high.

As Benedict Anderson shows us, such circumstances soon take
on special meaning, since they have the capacity to create a sort of
"imagined community," making concrete concepts and values
that, on these occasions, are idealized projections. Patriotism and
civic pride may appear to be synonyms, but they are not. Civic
pride refers to attitudes and behaviors that inspire a citizen to
share and defend certain notions and practices as though they
were fundamental duties toward a country's collective life. There
is nothing reprehensible, therefore, in envisioning with our students unity in service of a more just, democratic, and inclusive
country. The problem is the political use of such strategic moments,
when patriotism becomes a form of pragmatic exaggeration of

civic pride, without any positive impact on the quality of the education on offer.

This is so much the case that, in yet another educational setback, the Estado Novo saw a decline of approximately one-third in education spending in relation to GDP. While in 1940 educational spending accounted for nearly 1.5 percent of GDP, it had fallen to less than 1 percent by 1945. During the Kubitschek years (1956–61), education spending practically stagnated, showing a slight increase only in 1957.

Several benchmarks, established by previous governments, would be taken up again as of the Congressional Bill on National Educational Policy and Standards, first proposed in 1948 and finally approved in 1961. In that year, the Federal Council on Education was created and several campaigns and measures were implemented to teach adults how to read, besides ensuring an unmistakable expansion of primary, fundamental, middle, and higher education. Still, in the Portuguese saying, "the sheets were too short for the bed": a much greater share of resources and effort were mobilized for the construction of a new capital, Brasília, than for education, and an enormous cohort of children remained out of school.

Quality, universal, free public education, the only kind with the power to reduce inequalities and promote effective social inclusion, much like the dedication of public resources to education, is still not a concrete reality in Brazil, especially if we compare the investment with that made in other Latin American countries. The portion of the GDP spent on education in nations such as Argentina, Chile, Bolivia, Colombia, Paraguay, Uruguay, Peru, and Ecuador is appreciably larger. In Brazil, there is no consistency or proportionality as regards investment in education, as figure 5, revealing fluctuations between 1933 and 2002, makes clear.

The Constitution of 1988, the result of a robust movement toward redemocratization, established a commitment to universal early education and the eradication of illiteracy. Despite this, Brazil is still a long way from meeting these benchmarks. The National

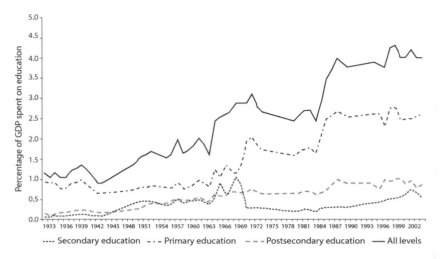

FIGURE 5. Percentage of GDP spent on education in Brazil, 1933–2002.
Source: Paulo Rogério Maduro Jr., "Taxas de matrícula e gastos em educação
no Brasil" (Enrollment fees and educational expenses in Brazil),
Master's thesis, Fundação Getulio Vargas, 2007, p. 25.

Education Plan of 2014 forecast a fall in the illiteracy rate to
6.5 percent in 2015 and total eradication by 2024. As the country
has yet to meet the specified interim goals, however, the project
becomes less viable with each passing year, at least in terms of the
original proposal.

Brazil has always had the highest illiteracy rate among Latin
American countries. The group of countries with the lowest rates,
each of them with similar figures, includes Argentina, Chile, and
Costa Rica. This situation is tied to historical patterns that have
resulted in differing contemporary outlooks. For example, at the
beginning of the twentieth century, illiteracy in Argentina was at
50 percent, while in Brazil it approached 80 percent. Today the rate
in Brazil is nearing 10 percent, while the Rio de la Plata region has
practically eradicated the problem altogether (fig. 6).

One of the objectives outlined by the National Education Plan
was, additionally, universal school attendance by 2016 among the

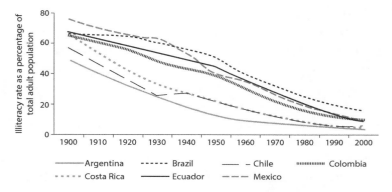

FIGURE 6. Illiteracy rates in seven Latin American countries, 1900–2000. Source: María Teresa Ramírez G. and Juana Patricia Téllez C., "La educación primaria y secundaria en Colombia en el siglo XX" (Primary and secondary education in Colombia in the twentieth century). Bogotà: Banco de la República de Colombia, 2006, p. 5.

population between fifteen and sixteen years of age. However, once again, the country found itself far from the stated goal, insofar as the rate of school attendance of that age group remained stuck at 87.2 percent of a total of 9.3 million students. On the other hand, in the same year, among those students who attended class, only 68 percent found themselves in the appropriate grade level for their age. Among this group, women were represented in larger numbers—73.3 percent—while men came in at only 63.1 percent. In addition, confirming the long-established practices of social exclusion, while the figure among White people was 75.7, among Black and Brown people it was 63 percent.

Criteria such as gender and race also point to the existence of distinct patterns among students aged over twenty-five who had studied for an average of eight years as of the year 2016. While women studied for approximately 8.2 years, men studied for an average of 7.8 years. As a counterpoint, while White Brazilians had studied for around nine years, that figure slid to 7.1 years for Black Brazilians, reinforcing, from another angle, the existence of racial discrimination in schools.

It should be noted that the current situation is still a far cry from the intentions of the 1920s. According to data collected by the Instituto Paulo Montenegro via the Functional Illiteracy Indicator (INAF), and included in a 2018 report, among a quantitative sample involving select interviews, 29 percent of participants were considered functionally illiterate (or, in other words, even if they were able to decode the combinations of letters composing short phrases and texts and to grasp simple numbers, they had not developed the ability to interpret those texts or perform mathematical operations). Of these, 8 percent were classified as illiterate— unable to complete simple tasks such as reading sentences or individual words—and 22 percent as "rudimentarily" illiterate— able to locate one or more pieces of basic information in very simple texts and to identify and determine the relative value of numbers. As for the rest of the participants, 34 percent were classified at an "elementary" level—able to pick out information, make basic observations and solve mathematical operations, and establish relationships between data expressed as graphics or tables—and 12 percent were at a "proficient" level, composing texts of some complexity and completing problem-solving questions involving relative values.

Meanwhile, the National Continual Household Sample Survey (PNAD Contínua), in data released in 2017, shows that Brazil is still home to 11.8 million illiterate citizens, a contingent that represents 7.2 percent of the population over the age of fifteen. The heaviest concentration of such individuals is to be found in the over-sixty population living in the country's Northeast. Such a finding highlights another chronic problem: the negative correlation between education in rural areas and wealth concentration. In the Northeast, the illiteracy rate reaches 14.8 percent, double the national average: of the 11.8 million illiterate individuals across the country, 6.5 million live in this region. Illiteracy rates become progressively worse, too, as one moves up the age scale and when filtered by race: among Brazilians of color, 9.2 percent are illiterate, and 20.4 percent of all illiterate individuals are sixty or older.

There have, however, been considerable advances in recent years, when public educational spending relative to national GDP was significantly higher than historical averages and closer to the investment of developed countries. Still, it must be acknowledged that, after a long history of neglecting education, Brazil continues to struggle with illiteracy, school attendance, and with the enormous age-to-grade imbalance that often creates a gulf between the schools and the reality of young people.

Much of the explanation for this predicament, or at least for the failure to meet established benchmarks, lies not only in the past but in the recession that hit the Brazilian economy in recent years. The recession affects all Brazilians, but its effects are much worse for the most vulnerable. Poor, young Black individuals, and those with erratic schooling, find themselves consigned to poorly remunerated temporary jobs. As a result, they only attend to their most pressing needs, unable to break the cycle of poverty in which they find themselves.

These young people have been defined as "neither-nor": they do not study, scarcely have work, and are also never taken into account by public policies whose objective is to build bridges between educational projects and the job market. Since schools remain alien to their universe, adolescents lose motivation, becoming more inclined to abandon their studies. On the other hand, on account of the recurring delay in learning and consequent age-to-grade imbalance, those who remain in educational institutions find themselves among classmates whose own realities are far from their own, not to mention the difficulty they experience in keeping up with the content being taught, carrying over from year to year problems that appear early in their education.

All the same, there have also been consistent advances in this area. As far as the programs that fall under the federal program Education of Youth and Adults (EJA) are concerned, and compared with the year 2016, there was 3.4 growth in the attendance of students across elementary school programs and 10.6 percent improvement in high school programs in 2017. Another promising statistic is that the proportion of those over twenty-five years of age who managed to complete basic mandatory education increased from 45 percent in 2016 to 46.1 percent in 2017. Lastly, the average number of years spent in school was greater across all regions of Brazil, reaching 9.1 years in 2017.

It is possible to claim, therefore, that the Brazilian educational system underwent significant changes in the last two decades, with a substantial fall in the illiteracy rate, an appreciable increase in the number of students enrolled across all levels of study, and growth in the average number of years spent in school. In recent years, after a long history of neglect, there has been an appreciable increase in public education spending. According to data from the federal government, between 2008 and 2017, the proportion of federal investment in education in relation to revenues accruing to central government nearly doubled. In relation to GDP, however, growth only kept pace: 1.8 percent in 2017 as opposed to 1.1 percent in 2008. Further, total public spending on education (comprised of investment by federal, state, and local governments) did not follow the consistent growth in federal expenditure.

At any rate, whether evaluated individually or against other countries with comparable colonial histories and geographies, the Brazilian educational panorama is revealed to be disappointing, whether in quantitative or qualitative terms; the most vulnerable populations (in terms of region, generation, gender, and race) suffer higher rates of illiteracy and inconsistent access to education. With the COVID-19 pandemic, this only worsened, as private schools held virtual lessons while public schools did not.

The factors that explain social inequality in Brazil are many, but among them, education policy continues to function as an important trigger for reproducing these circumstances. Currently, three in every ten children abandon school and, of those, nearly all come from economically disadvantaged regions, not to mention that more than half of the students in the third year of primary school exhibit inadequate reading and math skills, and the rate of dropouts across high schools is of the order of 11.2 percent.

This form of social inequality, made manifest by the inconsistency of educational opportunities, becomes even more acute when combined with the income dependency of an adult with low levels of education. According to specialists, each additional year of study leads to a 10–20 percent increase in income. The quality of education, as measured, for example, by the standard of teachers' training, can add nearly 50 percent to the income of people with the same ostensible level of education.

The provision of poor schooling to less privileged children and youth, by failing to enact more aggressive policies to reduce illiteracy, has contributed in Brazil to the preservation and even aggravation of economic, social, and cultural inequities. This education deficit is historical and structural, and continues to be one of the most crucial contributors to the perpetuation and expansion of social disparities across the country.

Only an intense and effective fight against structural inequalities will be capable of creating a more just society and more stable democracy. This type of inequality results in the unraveling of the social fabric and devalues public institutions. When we talk about taking on inequality, however, there is no easy way out or five-step program. Inequality is not just any accident or contingency. Nor is it a "natural" and "unchangeable" feature of a process over which we have little influence. On the contrary, it is a consequence of our choices—social, educational, political, cultural, and institutional—whose result is a clear and persistent concentration of public benefits among a tiny stratum of the population.

In these times when authoritarian discourses have gained ground in a number of countries, and most especially Brazil, where schools have been a particular battleground, the promotion of a more autonomous education system, which seeks to produce students who are critical of, but connected to, their realities, would be a beneficial approach, running counter to the latest trends that may be making waves in national politics but are having very little impact upon the structural problems facing Brazilian society.

What the country truly needs is more programs to train teachers and to buy books for teachers and students, who could then
have access to their own libraries and enter into the marvelous
world of reading, along with a much bigger budget for instruction
and resources toward a respectable education covering all areas of
knowledge. In the face of this most unequal Brazil, it is time for us
to pick one's battles. Mine is for a quality education that is independent, responsible, ethical, and secular. When crisis knocks,
many allow themselves to be swept up by polarization in the
search for a scapegoat. I prefer to place my bets on the full exercise
of citizenship, which only exists with a national plan for education
that embodies belief in the broadening of horizons, in democratic
schools—not in the rhetoric of bullying and threats.

Poet Carlos Drummond de Andrade, in "The Perfect School,"
from his 1985 book *Contos plausíveis* (Plausible stories), described
the form of his ideal school:

> It was a festive school, where monkeys, butterflies, the pebbles
> from the road not only formed part of our study materials but
> offered their opinions on each subject, according to the peculiar
> manner of each. Enthusiasm ran so high that parents and
> children came to the conclusion it would be better to transform
> the establishment, then without a fixed location or the need for
> one, into a school of natural affairs, where everything was an
> object of curiosity, free of curricula and diplomas, where every-
> one learns about everyone, their joy unbound and free of for-
> mality, until INCRA or some other civilizing organ remembers
> to divvy up the lands of Sambaíba into legal and bureaucratic
> tracts. Could this be the perfect school?

So far, the poet's question has gone unanswered; what remains is
the beautiful utopia of a country of readers that views school as a
"festive" and "natural" place, where "everyone learns about everyone," and (what's more) with their "joy unbound," and without
the many restraints and forms of censorship seen in Brazil in recent years.

6

Violence

THE DAILY NUMBER of homicides in Brazil is equal to the dead from the crash of a packed Boeing 737–800. This is one of the conclusions of the 2018 *Atlas of Violence*, produced by the Institute of Applied Economic Research and by the Brazilian Public Safety Forum. This places the country within a group deemed violent, with mortality rates thirty times greater than those seen on the European continent, for example. In Brazil, around 170 deaths by violence are recorded each day, or 62,500 per year, going by the statistics for 2016—and making for 553,000 murders over the last decade. The same report indeed confirms that in 2016, for the first time, the number of violent deaths in Brazil crossed the threshold of sixty thousand in a single year, the 62,517 homicides registered resulting in the country reaching a rate of thirty homicides for every hundred thousand people—another first.

The figures for Brazil are comparable to those for Colombia, and trail only that country, Belize, Honduras, and El Salvador. It is true that the World Health Organization has reliable data for only a few countries: the majority of African nations, for example, fall outside the list of countries with dependable record-keeping. Still, going by those numbers we can effectively trust, we can be confident that the rate of violent death is much higher in Latin America than in the rest of the world.

Though Brazil as a whole has some of the highest rates, in general there are significant discrepancies between the different states of the union. Sergipe and Alagoas, with rates of 64.7 and 53.4 homicides per hundred thousand residents, register numbers well above the national average of thirty per hundred thousand. Some states have lower rates—such as São Paulo, with 10.9, Santa Catarina with 14.2, and Piauí with 21.8. There are, however, other states whose numbers have grown significantly in the last ten years: Rio Grande do Norte, for example, registered the greatest increase, 256.9 percent above previous levels.

There are also notable discrepancies when we break down the data by generation. The homicide rate among young people is worse than that mentioned above: the 33,590 youths murdered in 2016 represent an increase of 7.4 percent in relation to the prior year. For males aged from fifteen to twenty-nine, the homicide rate nationally reaches 122.6 per hundred thousand. According to the *Atlas of Violence*, homicides account for 56.5 percent of all deaths among men between fifteen and twenty-nine years of age. In absolute numbers, from 2006 to 2016, or the space of ten years, 324,967 young men were killed in Brazil.

The *Atlas* shows that, in addition, between 1980 and 2016 close to 910,000 people across the country died in incidents involving a firearm. In 2016, for example, 71.1 percent of homicides were committed with this kind of weapon. According to the study, a veritable run on firearms, dating to the mid-1980s, only slowed in 2003, when the Disarmament Statute was passed into law. During the 1980s, the proportion of homicides by firearm was already around 40 percent, and this grew uninterruptedly until 2003, when it crested at 71.1 percent, remaining stable through 2016.

Despite the statute's limits, according to data from the army, obtained by the Instituto Sou da Paz via Brazil's Freedom of Information Act, nearly six guns are sold commercially every hour. Between January and August 2018 alone, 34,731 guns were sold. The number of new licenses issued to regular citizens also grew enormously, from 3,029 in 2004 to 33,031 in 2017. Following the same tendency, the roster of collectors, hunters, and recreational gun owners practically doubled. In 2012, they numbered 27,549; in

2017, 57,886. As a result, there are well over half a million guns in the hands of civilians: a total of 619,604.

Contrary to the opinions expressed by the Bolsonaro government, which has defended the relaxation of regulations on arms sales, the figures given in the *Atlas of Violence* reveal that, in a series of issues that need to be addressed together to ensure Brazil becomes a less violent country, gun control must remain a central strategy. The authors of the *Atlas* claim that, over the last decade, the states that saw the highest growth in lethal violence are also the states that saw concomitantly the highest growth in gun deaths.

The Disarmament Statute, which came into effect on December 22, 2003, prohibits the possession of firearms, making exceptions only for cases of demonstrable need, which are subject to a time limit determined at the outset. Even after a license is granted, it can be revoked at any moment, particularly if the bearer is found in a state of intoxication, or under the effect of drugs or medications that affect brain or motor function. Starting with the day the law came into effect, and translating the findings of the *Atlas* authors into raw numbers, it can be asserted that, between 2003 and 2012, nearly 120,000 firearm deaths were avoided in the country. This is equivalent to a packed Maracanã stadium, or nearly one Hiroshima or two Nagasakis—all in the space of a decade. The positive impact of the Disarmament Statute on Brazil's violence statistics is thus undeniable. Looking at it from another angle, in the years that preceded the law—1980 to 2003—the average increase in the number of homicides by firearm reached 8.36 percent per year, a percentage that fell to 0.52 percent after the statute went into effect.

Still, according to the World Health Organization, 123 people are victims of gun-related homicides every day in Brazil. According to data from the Latin American Faculty of Social Sciences, which conducts the studies for the annual *Violence Map*, in the year 2014 alone Brazil registered five deaths an hour, for a total of 44,861 victims. When it comes to violent deaths by firearm, the country registers 207 times the number of killings in Germany,

Austria, Denmark, and Poland combined. Moreover, according to the Health Ministry, between 2015 and 2018 there were 518 hospitalizations among children up to fourteen years of age due to firearms in the house.

Despite these alarming numbers, twenty-four thousand new guns were registered by citizens across the country in 2014 alone, revealing not a mere coincidence but rather a trend. The evidence suggests that Brazilians have begun once again to arm themselves, notwithstanding the screening required by the 2003 statute. This is a troubling phenomenon, because it demonstrates not only disdain for the spirit of the law, which sought to spur pacification throughout the country by reducing the factors leading to crime, but a liability at various levels of the State.

There is no shortage of reasons to limit gun ownership. One of them is that guns purchased legally end up replenishing the arsenals of criminal cartels: in 2014 alone, more than ten thousand legally registered guns were stolen, equivalent to 30 percent of the permits issued by the Federal Police. But there is another deleterious effect of the proliferation of gun-owners: the Congressional Commission to Investigate Arms Traffic estimated that, in the year 2006, for every 1 percent increase in the number of guns in the hands of ordinary citizens, there was a 2 percent increase in the homicide rate.

The subject remains controversial, since these arguments have no effect on certain sectors of Brazilian society, represented by a group of congresspeople known as the "Bullet Caucus," who continued to attack the Disarmament Statute and defend its further "relaxation." Their proposals include increasing the number of guns an individual citizen can own from six to nine, reducing the minimum age for carrying a gun, and doing away with the requirement to renew gun permits every three years. Some of these demands were met by the Bolsonaro government as soon as it took office in 2019.

What this approach fails to take into account, however, is that the escalation in arms ownership, though it might resolve internal problems, can provoke even greater violence. As Óscar Martinez, a journalist from the El Salvador site El Faro, explains, "those who promise bullets peddle demagoguery." That is, they assert that more guns would provide safety and put an end to violence, when what guns really have is the potential to increase it exponentially.

Even the arming of police units, where these are poorly trained and equipped, can have disastrous consequences. According to the United Nations, the Brazilian police are considered among the most violent in the world. Amnesty International, meanwhile, has revealed that in São Paulo state alone, there are at least a thousand deaths per year at the hands of the Polícia Militar. Research conducted by the Brazilian Public Safety Forum in 2018 shows, furthermore, that 62 percent of residents in cities with populations greater than a hundred thousand fear abuse at the hands of the police. The study interviewed 1,307 individuals from every corner of the country, and their responses echo and revive a certain image cemented during the military dictatorship, when amid the heavy atmosphere occasioned by the repression of the 1970s, musical artist Chico Buarque de Hollanda sang out "Call the crooks," inverting the image of the police as a force for good. Where they act violently, the police lose their standing as a force for the protection of citizens, tarnishing the very principles that ought to guide their conduct. Meanwhile, though the police are responsible for many deaths in Brazil, they also die at alarming rates. Once again, statistics from 2017 show Black victims among the police outnumber White by 56 to 43 percent.

Factors of a historical order are helpful to explain the current rates of violence in Brazil. An extensive slaveholding system was only sustained by a veritable repressive machine in the hands of landowners who themselves relied on the complicity of the State. Thus, while history cannot account entirely for our current predicament, it does reveal certain persistent patterns, and though the epidemic violence perpetrated in the country is not a recent problem, it also cannot be explained by any single episode. A reversal of expectations with regard to the health system, together with an increase in violence that led to an atmosphere of skepticism with regard to public safety, created fertile ground for increasingly hurried and radical fixes. Clearly, however, serious issues such as these arise neither all of the sudden, nor, still less, by the hand of history alone.

For this very reason, though violence and the demand for security were the issues with the greatest impact in the 2018 elections—representing legitimate demands by voters—the problem's true solution is a far cry from the most immediate formulas, such as doubling down on policing and arming the population. In times of crisis, it is easy to offer quick fixes wrapped in authoritarian clothing. As constitutional law expert Conrado Hübner Mendes notes, "the political placebo is . . . a magic trick. It leaves the underlying social condition untouched but momentarily reduces symptoms and generates the short-term sensation of having found a cure."

The problems that plague Brazilians are much more complex and are tied to the country's vicious social inequality. Tolerance of police brutality, a reduction in the age at which an individual can be tried as an adult, and efforts toward arming the population represent heavy doses of an elixir that no doctor would prescribe and that answers to the name of self-delusion.

Urban Violence and Insecurity

So widespread is violence that it assumes various guises and angles in Brazil. Theft and robbery occupy a privileged place among the infractions to which Brazilians are most frequently subjected. According to the National Information System on Public Safety, Prison, and Drugs (SINESP), the average number of deaths resulting each year from armed robbery comes to 1,700. Meanwhile, according the *11th Annual Report of the Brazilian Public Safety Forum*, there was a 57.8 percent rise in such incidents between 2010 and 2016. This means an average of 2,500 such crimes reported each year, or seven per day, producing a total of 13,800 murders in the course of robberies. The same survey showed that, between 2015 and 2017, armed robberies increased in nineteen states across the country. In 2014, a car was stolen every two and a half minutes in Brazil, making a total of 213,400 stolen cars for the year.

Brazil is among those countries with the highest individual rates of car ownership—a result of choices in the 1950s and 60s, when rail transport was practically discontinued altogether. The number of cars increases each year. In a 2017 study, it was noted that one in every 4.8 Brazilians has a car, for a total of 43.4 million vehicles circulating throughout the country. Consequently, it is little wonder that traffic accidents in Brazil have been classified by the WHO as one of the most common incidents leading to violence and death. According to the Ministry of Health, the country registers an average of forty-three thousand deaths of this kind each year.

Killings likewise account for a substantial share of violence nationwide. From January to May 2018, 21,305 people were killed. This number includes first-degree homicides, armed robberies, and physical assault resulting in death, which constitute the so-called premeditated lethal crimes.

Another significant trigger of urban violence levels is drug traffic. As political scientist Sergio Fausto reported in a January 2019 article in the magazine *piauí*, the homicide rate has practically tripled since record-keeping began in 1979. In 1980, there was an average of eleven deaths for every hundred thousand Brazilians, a number that, as noted above, surpassed thirty cases per hundred thousand by 2017. A significant portion of these incidents, much like the consequent deterioration in public safety, is a result of growth in drug trafficking and the control exerted by criminal factions and militias, both of which depend on the collusion of "bad apples" among the police. Brazil has turned into the main drug trafficking corridor serving North America and Central Europe, according to the United Nations Office on Drugs and Crime (UNODC). Internally, consumption is also at a high; the country is the second largest consumer of cocaine in the world.

Drug trafficking–related crimes account for 70 percent of all prison sentences. Organized crime factions exert control over eleven million people living in favelas, and have established a parallel state and illegal economy, besides generating a great deal of violence with their presence on the streets of cities large and small. The role of militias is not much different, as these, as we shall see, behave like criminal groups, coercing those living in suburban slums in exchange for protection.

The staggering rate of child abuse also stands out. According to an estimate by the Presidential Secretariat for Human Rights, in 2017, 84,049 incidents involving children and adolescents were recorded. The major perpetrators are family members, which also explains the high rate of unreported crimes, now estimated at 74 percent. In a country suffering from clear educational deficits, the high incidence of crimes against children, many of them deprived of the guidance provided by the school environment, appears to be less than mere chance.

In the end, the growth in criminality, lethal or otherwise, has generated an increased sense of impunity among Brazilians living in cities. It also explains, in part, the authoritarian turn the country has taken in recent years. To put an end to violence, voters are demanding measures that are equally violent.

Meanwhile, as we have seen, although the quickest and most visible fixes may have the ability to momentarily soothe the population, they are unable to address the challenges, systemic and structural in nature, contributing to the daily reality of violence: social inequality, inadequate schooling, economic crisis, recession, corruption, unemployment, and also police ineffectiveness, as well as the problems that have appeared in state-level programs to reduce crime—programs that, in absolute terms, have seen a reduction in funding. According to the WHO, Brazil is experiencing an "epidemic of violence," which in turn becomes an enormous obstacle to the country's economic development. Incidentally, the WHO has begun to classify this level of violence as a disease in itself, which can even be found in the International Classification of Illnesses (ICD).

The increase in armed robberies and crimes resulting in death has produced a widespread sense of vulnerability, which cuts down on individuals' freedom of movement in cities and leads to fear. Fear and a sense of vulnerability are valid reactions, and are reflected in data from national and international studies that point to Brazil as a worldwide leader in urban violence. These emotions are also reflected in the number of electors who in 2018 associated the issue of safety with candidates who promised immediate responses involving the use of greater force by state authorities.

While there is an urgent need for fixes capable of meeting voters' legitimate demands, there can be no doubt that such fundamental problems can only be combated with a combination of short-, medium-, and long-term measures. Without these, Brazil's national narrative will remain a far cry from that of "happily ever after." More often than not, authoritarian solutions that promise to rain down justice amount to little more than hot air.

Violence in the Countryside

Disputes over land ownership in rural areas is one of the greatest causes of death in Brazil, in particular when the victims are Indigenous groups, whose constitutional rights, which grant them ownership over lands that belonged to their ancestors, are repeatedly violated. This is not, however, anything new. Records of this practice date to the colonial period, when what was in truth an invasion of a densely populated area was termed "discovery."

Documents attesting to the utilization of Indigenous slave labor date to the early years of Portuguese colonization, when various native nations would complement or substitute for African labor. In other words, despite being considered "subjects of the Crown," native peoples could be legally enslaved. At the beginning of the sixteenth century, coastal tribes were exploited in the logging of brazilwood and were compensated via *escambo*, or bartering, involving various items such as machetes, mirrors, and even cane liquor. By the end of the 1500s, tribes living in what is currently the state of Amazonas were being captured and employed in the cultivation of "backcountry drugs," as spices native to Brazil were known.

It was only from the seventeenth century onward that legal impediments began to restrict the use of Indigenous labor. Still, there was never any lack of recourse to justify the enslavement of these peoples. Natives could be pressed into service for "just war"—when they displayed "hostility" toward colonizers—or could be bought as prisoners of intertribal wars, an activity designated by the expression "to purchase by the chain gang." The Indigenous also tended to lose the "biological battle" with the Europeans that arrived in Brazil. They might perish due to a simple cold or to the flu, measles, or smallpox, illnesses against which their bodies had no defenses. There can be no doubting that, throughout the nation's history, Indigenous peoples were decimated by the violence of White colonizers, expelled from their lands, and killed by nonnative diseases, aside from being subjected to practices that sought to impose their invisibility.

To represent Indigenous peoples as passive and weak, resigned to European dictates, is nonetheless to perpetrate a false image, created by European colonizers. Highly adapted to the territory where they were born, they formed, in the words of anthropologist Nádia Farage, a veritable "backcountry barricade," rebelling, fleeing, staging ambushes, and killing. At times, the Indigenous and Africans fought side by side; on other occasions those "natural to the land" were put to use by slave catchers during raids or the capture of runaway African slaves.

There was nothing idyllic, then, in this (mis)encounter between the Indigenous and the colonizers. According to the anthropologist Manuela Carneiro da Cunha, it is estimated that the Indigenous population of the South American lowlands was between one and 8.5 million at the time Europeans arrived. If this was indeed the case, it is possible to assert that a handful of colonizers accomplished the unenviable task of wiping out a densely populated continent. Historians do not differ in their assessment of the overall magnitude of the catastrophe; they vary, however, as to the proportion of losses. According to some, from 1492 to 1650, America lost a quarter of its population; for others, it was a loss of the order of 95 to 96 percent. In either case, it is clear that this was genocide.

Notwithstanding the elevated number of human losses and the tyranny inflicted against this population, whether during the colonial period or today, a common attitude toward the Indigenous seems to prevail: there is an attempt to render them basically invisible, stripping them of their right to property and self-affirmation. Treated alternately as "children" who have yet to reach legal age, or as political subjects predisposed to a "natural extinction," the result is the same: an effort to deny these people their own history, their customs, and the richness of their cosmologies.

A strong sign of the authoritarianism that governed the attitude toward these populations can identified in the figure of the *bandeirantes*, or explorers, who for a long time were understood only as national heroes, not only because they braved untamed jungles and forests, expanding the country's borders, but because they had "tamed" Indigenous peoples "savage and impervious to civilization."

Within a narrative that was notable for denying the validity of other histories and obliterating all that did not represent the razor's edge of colonization, there was no space for the inclusion of others' experiences and suffering. Nonetheless, more recently, a series of studies has revealed the fundamental role of the *bandeirantes* in the enslavement of Indigenous peoples, the bulk of whom were delivered to wealthy landowners, but some also to small and medium farmers or city-dwellers for use as cheap labor.

Thus, contradictory and exaggerated images were constructed of the Indigenous, as characterized either by extreme passivity or by an aggressiveness no less extreme. Both, however, led to extermination, as though Indigenous groups were ultimately captive to the past with no right to the present, much less the future.

As the reign of Dom Pedro II unfolded, the dominant model of behavior would not differ much from that adopted during the colonial period, no matter how much the government vaunted a policy of inclusion and study of native peoples. The emperor personally financed, in the areas of fine arts, literature, fiction, and history, the formation of a "Romantic Indianism" that idealized the image of a country composed of different races, whose fate was nevertheless to be overcome or to disappear, as in the case of native Brazilians, and according to the myth created by the naturalist Karl von Martius, in the face of European superiority.

Novels such as José de Alencar's *Iracema* (1865) or Gonçalves de Magalhães's epic poem *A Confedereração dos Tamoios* (The confederation of the Tamoios, 1856) represent the pinnacle of this model, which ultimately determined that it was the destiny of the Indigenous to perish so that civilization might prevail. It was not long before *Iracema* came to be understood as a national *Bildungsroman*, its very title an anagram of "America." In a book replete with symbolism, the name of the heroine, which in the language of the Tupi—the tribe chosen by the Romantics to embody the "noble savage"—meant "come forth from honey," was translated as "lips of honey," a reference to the "docility" and "languor" of native women, Brazil's ultimate "virgins." As the story unfolds, the protagonist falls for a European warrior, Martim, loses her virginity and gives birth to a boy—Moacir—whose name means "child of suffering." In an extended metaphor the Indigenous woman dies that her son might live, and with this a new nation is born, a melting pot, but one dominated by the European colonizer.

In a genuine rereading of the von Martius legend, here "the melting pot" is not only synonymous with "mixture." In the novel, which purposely eschews temporal markers or precise geographies, a basic injunction is issued, Iracema's death announcing the "civilized" destiny of a nation that will "naturally" take root in the Americas. Violence and the massacre of native Brazilians are sidelined in this ultimately Eurocentric vision, which seeks to mold political history into mere paean. The image of the Indigenous woman is also stereotyped in terms of the representation of native women "surrendering themselves" to male colonizers, as though the hierarchy among genders was not also a form of force and power in the hands of the colonizer.

A *Confedereração dos Tamoios* was entirely financed by the emperor with an eye to creating a national epic. Its title is, still, the name that is given to the final revolt of the Tupinambá (1554–67), a people who occupied the coast of Brazil between Bertioga, in São Paulo state, and Cabo Frio, in the state of Rio de Janeiro, and who steadfastly resisted colonizers. In Magalhães's work, the conquest is already recast as a defeat, or, put otherwise, as a symbolic moment that marks the point at which the Indigenous recognize conversion as the best and only way out of their predicament. Once again, the violence of men is recast as destiny, leading to a clear inversion: extermination becomes a choice, justified by the State and the Church.

In Rodolfo Amoedo's canvas entitled *O último tamoio* (The last Tamoio, 1883), also made possible by the patronage of Dom Pedro II, we see the Indigenous chieftain practically lifeless, being laid to rest by a Jesuit priest, José de Anchieta[1] himself (inexplicably in Franciscan attire), who looks on as the chief meets a slow and peaceful death (fig. 7). This death represents the final submission of a brave warrior and Jesuit efforts to catechize the "infidels" of the New World. The tropics are the setting, duly Edenic, and there are no signs of violence or force. On the contrary, America appears to bow before Europe, giving birth to a new nation, beginning with the "voluntary" and magnanimous "sacrifice" of its native-born.

Certainly the Empire, while it took great pride in fostering the study of native languages, did not let that stand in the way of the massacre of this population, and in fact created a sort of hierarchy between "good" and "bad" Indigenous tribes. The Tupi were considered the "natives of Romanticism" and a group that "cooperated," by their submission, in the happy conclusion of the national narrative. The Kaingang, meanwhile, who fought to hold on to

FIGURE 7. Rodolfo Amoedo, *The Last Tamoio*, 1883, oil on canvas,
180 × 260 cm. Rio de Janeiro, National Museum of Fine Arts.

their lands in western São Paulo state, were written into the history
books as "savages," not to mention "depraved."

And so, through stealth, the message spread that those who as-
similated to White supremacy could be regarded as "noble savages," while those who revolted appeared to be following a wrong
turn on the road to civilization. It is a specific and selective way of
viewing history, which values those who did not struggle for their
rights and discriminates against peoples who rebelled and did not
accept the invasion of their lands, their properties, and their
cultures.

The problem is that such a perspective, as romanticized as it is
violent, has been endlessly perpetuated in Brazil, to the extent that
the Indigenous were among those systematically excluded from
the First Republic beginning in 1889. Even if during the Empire
interest was more rhetorical than pragmatic, and if native peoples
figured more prominently in Romantic novels and historical

portraiture than in concrete policy decisions, with the advent of the Republic this erasure would become even more evident. A perfect example is the massacre of the Kaingang in 1905, to make way for the Northwest Railway of Brazil. At the time, the scientist Hermann von Ihering, then director of the Museu Paulista, went to the press to defend the extermination of this tribe. The advance toward civilization must not be derailed, he brayed, publicly explaining his vision that the Indigenous, never considered to be landowners or friendly neighbors, were a sort of human impediment.

The process of demarcation of Guarani, Xavante, and Kaingang land began while the country still found itself under Dom Pedro II's rule, more precisely in the year 1880. While the first two of these nations were "integrated," even at the cost of nearly being decimated, at least in their form at that time, the last fought valiantly against the invasion of its lands. The situation was not brought under control until 1911, and then thanks to the intervention of the Indian Protection Service, but only after the Kaingang had practically been wiped out. Heading up the Indian Protection Service was Cândido Mariano Rondon, a veteran of the military and the backcountry, who, starting in 1890, installed telegraph lines in the Midwest region of the country all the way up to the Amazon. Already in that era, the republican government paid close attention to the area, which remained isolated from the urban centers and was located in a strategic border zone. The solution was to seek the "integration" of Indigenous peoples, mapping the locale, domesticating their lands, and seeking to establish contact with them.

In each region the policy toward such lands was different, however, not least because, we may recall, there existed both areas considered "new"—such as the Amazon, "rediscovered" on account of the expansion of the rubber trade—and other areas, previously colonized. In either case, around the beginning of the twentieth century the "Indigenous question" was slowly moving on from being one of labor, only to soon be reconfigured as a land ownership problem. In the case of long-established villages, the order was to control their size. On the frontiers or river routes, despite the continued widespread use of Indigenous manpower, the fundamental goal was now territorial expansion, justified in terms of a need to guarantee the settlers' safety.

The policies were either the extermination of "valiant" native Brazilians or "civilization," which meant their inclusion, but also their subjugation. Moreover, at that moment in which Positivist and racial determinist theories were in vogue, the certainty of progress and exclusive evolution was used to justify a policy of extermination, as though the Indigenous populations had been preordained to disappear. Despite the express terms of the republican constitution, it would be some time until a more systematic policy of protection and inclusion was implemented, and even this, in our current times, requires considerable rectification so that Indigenous lands do not become subject to the constant risk of litigation and custody disputes.

The topic has been especially pertinent in recent years, during which politicians and sectors of agribusiness, construction firms, mining companies, and industry have questioned the right of the Indigenous to their reservations, merely bringing hackneyed arguments up to date. They have also sought to weaken institutions such as the National Indian Foundation (FUNAI), an organ created in 1967 and until recently under the ambit of the Ministry of Justice, whose mission, among others, is the execution of the federal government's Indigenous policies, protecting tribes' rights, and identifying, delimiting, and demarcating their lands. In one of the first acts of the new government elected in 2018, FUNAI was transferred to the authority of the Ministry of Agriculture, in an attempt to nullify its impact. This created an unquestionable conflict of interest. It is a challenge indeed to understand how the responsibility to demarcate Indigenous lands can be shifted to groups that seek their elimination.

Whatever the case, these are antiquated policies whose objective is to delegitimize rights holders and justify incursion onto reservations. Though Indigenous rights to land are guaranteed by Chapter VIII of Title VIII of the 1988 Constitution, according to the Missionary Council for Indigenous Peoples (CIMI), a minimum of sixty-eight Indigenous people have been killed every year since 2003 in the country, always in conflicts over land. In 2015 alone, 137 were eliminated. In 2017, 110 Indigenous people were killed, seventeen of them in the central state of Mato Grosso do Sul. The principal cause, CIMI coordinator Roberto Liebgott has asserted, is rural conflict: "Wherever there is Indigenous resistance, leaders are generally identified and from there experience every sort of repression, threats, and even assassinations."

Encroachment on Indigenous lands is another grave problem. These areas are increasingly coveted for their natural riches. The number of incursions has increased appreciably, from fifty-nine in 2016 to ninety-six in 2018, five of these in Mato Grosso do Sul. According to CIMI, this is a reflection of the failure to adequately demarcate lands and protect Indigenous communities.

The British NGO Global Witness concluded in 2017 that Brazil was the deadliest country for climate activists and defenders of Mother Earth. In its third annual report—spanning twenty-two countries—on the struggle for human rights in connection to natural resources, a text entitled "At What Price?" singles out agribusiness as the most violent of all industries, responsible for forty-six deaths during the period observed. It is impossible, of course, to generalize and suggest that every agribusiness firm practices violence, but it should be noted that the sector has unseated mining, which had headed the list in previous surveys.

On account of the rising number of Indigenous deaths, the result of historical disputes across the country, in the first semester of 2016, the UN served a warning on the Brazilian government, which nonetheless had little effect. The various governments of the so-called Third Republic (beginning in 1988) have continually failed to demarcate and protect Indigenous lands, an attitude that leads to intermittent conflicts among agriculture, native peoples, and activists. On account of this tension, a concomitant rise can be seen in the number of suicides among the Indigenous population, not to mention the infant mortality rate, nearly two times higher than the national average of 13.9 per thousand births: the figure for 2016 was 26.3 deaths per thousand. The CIMI report points out that such deaths are caused by diarrhea, malnutrition, and other problems that could be avoided with better healthcare. In 2017, 702 children under five years of age died in Brazil; of these, 107 lived on Indigenous lands in the state of Mato Grosso do Sul. The situation has only worsened since 2018, with the government providing cover for the illegal actions of landgrabbers.

Indigenous areas are always changing, given that the demarcation process is slow; many are the subject of court disputes or have yet to emerge from the phase of identification and delimitation. In the Amazon, there are 419, and another 279 are dispersed throughout the rest of the country. According to the National Indian Foundation, in 2010, there were 688 Indigenous territories and a few urban villages. According to the census that same year, the 240 native tribes scattered across Brazil had a total population of 896,917. Of these, 324,834 lived in cities and 572,083 in rural areas, corresponding in total to 0.47 percent of the total national population. Today, there are only thirteen certified territories with an area of 1.5 million hectares. The rest remain classified under the status "awaiting action," a clear sign of the provisional nature of these social policies.

Since the approval of the Indigenous Statute in 1973, this formal recognition process was stipulated by an administrative procedure specified in Article 19 of the same law. As a complement, the 1988 constitution dedicated a specific chapter—in Articles 231 and 232—to Indigenous rights. We are not, therefore, talking about an "ideological" question, to employ the terms of the current national debate, which has used and abused this concept. In reality, we are talking about hard-won rights, and rights that in truth have been upheld, since the existence of inalienable Indigenous lands is stipulated in the constitutions of 1834, 1937, 1946, and 1967.

These lands are, in the first place, fundamental for the physical and sociocultural perpetuation of Indigenous peoples. These groups and their way of life are likewise essential to the preservation and sustainable cultivation of Brazil's forests, which they have maintained, for centuries on end, through sustainable management. Finally, self-determination, equality, and the right to the preservation of their lands are internationally recognized in the United Nations Declaration on the Rights of Indigenous People, of which Brazil is a signatory.

As Manuela Carneiro da Cunha wrote in issue 148 of the magazine *piauí*, old habits die hard. The State has been preoccupied with "incorporating" Indigenous societies into society by doing away with all that is particular to them. In the terms employed by the anthropologist, however, "integration is no longer an attempt to eliminate differences but rather to do justice in articulating the differences that exist." Tearing down forests is not, and never was, a prerogative for the national wellbeing. Those who know the forest best are traditional populations, true specialists in Brazil's socio-environmental diversity. Only 10 percent of the estimated two million species of fauna, flora, and microorganisms that make up Brazil's biodiversity are known, and it is this diversity, human—305 ethnicities speaking 274 languages—and biological, that needs to be treated as a national asset. It should be remembered still that, since the pre-Columbian era, these peoples have been contributing to the enrichment of the soil and the forest cover, cultivating sweet potato, yam, peanuts, cacao, manioc, squash, and an immense variety of other agricultural species.

Even so, and despite the existing bevy of arguments and legal protections, the demarcation of Indigenous lands remains a chronic problem in Brazil, particularly at moments of polarization like the present, with its passions and hostilities. In a context in which a number of people feel exploited, what could be better than to deprive others of their most fundamental rights? Very similar problems face what remains of the country's quilombos, or runaway slave communities, whose establishment can be traced back to the colonial period but which still remain largely excluded from public policies, becoming targets for all sorts of conflict.

Since 1988, the Brazilian constitution has recognized the material and immaterial goods of different groups composing our society as national heritage; only with the Constitutional Transition Act, however, did the government acknowledge the right of descendants of quilombo communities still occupying their lands to have them recognized as property, requiring the State to supply the relevant land titles. Nonetheless, regulations governing the recognition, demarcation, and titling of these lands were only established in 2003. Currently, there are more than 3,200 quilombo communities scattered throughout the country, and more than 250 petitions in a phase of technical evaluation—a slew of groups fighting for the right to their properties, as guaranteed by the constitution.

According to the Agência Brasil public news agency, since 1988, the Brazilian state has officially recognized close to 3,200 quilombo communities. Nearly 80 percent of these have been identified since 2003, following the issue of Decree No. 4887. Between 2003 and 2018, 206 quilombos, home to nearly thirteen thousand families, received titles from the National Institute for Colonization and Agrarian Reform. In spite of this, up to 2019 fewer than 7 percent of these lands have been recognized as belonging to quilombo descendants or otherwise formalized.

Politics is the art of building consensus. On the other hand, the more conservative a political regime, the greater the risk of dismissing the histories of a country's minorities, transforming them into "foreigners in their own land" and systematically annulling their rights accordingly. A democratic republic can only be constructed when diverse groups are effectively included, their forms of knowledge recognized.

The recognition of these political stakeholders, until recently kept from full citizenship, is part of the expansion and distribution of democratic rights. Meanwhile, the lapse back into the favoring of private and sectoral interests, such as logging, agribusiness, and mining companies, and into the moralistic and normative discourses of those who recognize only a single community of origin (be it social, cultural, religious, or ethnic), is a clearly authoritarian development, claims to be respecting democracy notwithstanding. Once again, a certain mythology that fails to stand up to historical scrutiny seeks to impose invisibility on social groups who were present in Brazil before it became Brazil. Theirs, indeed, are stories of balanced, responsible management of the forest, but both the people and their practices run the risk of disappearing beneath the veil of social invisibility.

7

Race and Gender

EVERY SOCIETY DEVELOPS its own markers of difference. To put it another way, each society transforms physical differences into social stereotypes, in general attributing inferiority to these, and leading accordingly to prejudices, discrimination, and violence. For all that the concept of "difference" implies recognizing, as the philosopher Michel de Montaigne (1533–92) explained, that "man is indeed an object miraculously vain, various and wavering," meaning that human experience is rich and varied, the term has, in practice, been used to exclude. In the contemporary world, the word is also applied to justify the sort of behavior that favors the forming of groups isolated in their own digital media, separated by their distinct interests, and polarized in their identities, each individual becoming a prisoner absorbed in his or her own bubble.

On another front, the broadening of societal recognition of equality, due to the inclusion of new political constituents, often generates dissatisfaction among those sectors of society that tend to view the "Other" as less legitimate and therefore deny him or her the right to full citizenship, on account of the "difference" on display.

Social markers of difference are therefore, as the definition provided by the University of São Paulo's Research Group on Social Markers of Difference (NUMAS) suggests, "categories understood as social, local, historical, and cultural constructions that both belong to the class of social representations—not unlike the stories, myths, and the ideologies that we create—and exercise real influence in the world through the production and reproduction of collective identities and social hierarchies."

These categories do not produce meaning in isolation, however; their power derives above all from the intimate connections that they establish among themselves—which is not to say they can all be lumped together. On the list of social markers with an impact on everyday experience are categories such as race, age, region, gender, and sex, among other elements with the capacity to produce varied forms of hierarchy and subordination. In Brazilian society, the perverse use of these categories has led to all manner of expressions of racism, femicide, and a great deal of misogyny and homophobia, as well as justification for a wide-reaching "rape culture," the data around which are alarming despite the fact that reporting of crimes is most often silenced, as we shall see further below.

A stream of official statistics demonstrates that Afro-Brazilian populations are the preferred target of the "intersection" of a series of social difference markers that negatively impact their social inclusion, resulting in more precarious access to healthcare, employment, education, transport, and housing. For example, Black men and women face enormous salary disparities on the job market. Data published by the IBGE for 2016 reveal that they earn only 59 percent of the income of White Brazilians. Life expectancy among these groups is also inequitable: in 1993, the total percentage of White women who were over sixty years of age was 9.4; that of Black women was 7.3. In 2007, these proportions reached 13.2 and 9.5 percent, respectively. This is not to mention, moreover, that Black women are the most common victims of violent crimes motivated by sex and gender. Social markers function even more deceptively, then, when they intersect.

The same 2016 IBGE study indicates that young Black men tend to die earlier than others, due to reduced access to medical services. They have shorter life-spans, too, because their ability to finish school and seek out other forms of insertion into the job market is compromised on account of poverty, a weak family structure, exposure to the drug trade, and the regions where they live. There are several social difference markers that, taken together, expose a particularly segregated reality: age (young), region (suburban slums), race (Black), and sex (masculine).

There is no shortage of stories from mothers of young Black men who admit to praying every time their sons leave the house, for fear that they might not return alive. Others even pay for a funeral plan, seeking to get a headstart out of the fear of being unable to pay for the burial of the young male members of their nuclear family. Sadly, the statistics justify their fears. According to a report by IPEA, although the period between 1993 and 2007 witnessed an overall increase in life expectancy across the country, White Brazilians continued to live much longer than their Black counterparts. In 2007, despite a general increase in the life expectancy of Brazilians, the Black population remained two percentage points below the average.

In the decade between 2006 and 2016, Brazil witnessed growth of 23.3 percent in the number of deaths among young people. Murder and violent death account for 49.1 percent of all deaths of young men between fifteen and nineteen years of age, and 46 percent of those between twenty and twenty-four years of age. In order to understand the magnitude of these figures, one need only compare it with the percentage of deaths among the generation of Brazilians between forty-five and forty-nine years of age, for whom the toll shrinks to 5.5 percent. In short, the numbers express considerable inequality when it comes to the observance of an individual's rights, and a high level of violence with a very clear target: young men who live in slums on the urban outskirts across the country.

According to the 2017 Index of Youth Vulnerability to Violence (IVJ), the numbers "are evidence of a brutal inequality that affects Black men and women until their dying breath." Inequality is expressed throughout the lifetime of these individuals via various socioeconomic indicators, a brutal combination of social vulnerability and racism that follows them their entire lives. As we can see, inequalities take root within markers such as gender and race, and the intersection between them is still more perverse.

It is important to remember that this treatment of the young Black population is older than it appears. The contexts and motives may differ, but the results, in terms of absolute and proportional number of deaths, are quite familiar. During the period when slavery was still in operation, slaves were, from the age of thirty-five, already designated by their owners as prematurely aged, when indeed they had not perished earlier. The young Black population has historically, therefore, been the most decimated.

Finally, recognizing that lethal violence is heavily directed toward the young Black population—the male population especially, but also the female—and that this fact is related to a series of socioeconomic inequities revolving around race, gender, age, and geographical location, is the first step toward the development of targeted public policies and affirmative action initiatives that can eliminate specific inequities.

The data cited above only go to prove that social exclusion exists in the context of its widespread acceptance, and such exclusion has been shown to be especially pernicious when tolerance for it becomes commonplace. Though a 2018 estimate shows that Black and Brown people account for 55 percent of the population, 130 years after abolition, Brazil still runs a deficit in terms of social inclusion. The long period following emancipation, which in some ways has yet to end, led to the perpetuation of the social exclusion inherited from the slavery era, since there was no investment in the education of recently freed populations or in training such that they might compete on the job market. The result, all these years later, is a country that likes to portray itself as a diverse and culturally inclusive nation—as represented in the country's hodgepodge of rhythms, sports, and culinary dishes—while at the same time it fosters a veiled racism that involves the delegation of the enactment of discrimination to the police.

Thus the country has continued to mix cultural inclusion with social and racial exclusion—a mixture with separation, as in von

Martius's old formula—and to labor under a heavy burden of taboos. The fact of such silencing is borne out in the quantitative data, which offer us a consistent picture concerning the proportion, size, and frequency of violent acts against Black populations. Obviously, however, hard numbers are unable to capture or represent the experience of pain and suffering, or the trauma that lies behind them, and for this reason, taking the year 2018 as an example, I shall pick out a number of cases that, taken together, make even more evident the way in which the fight against racism remains an urgent concern for Brazil's evolution as a republic. They are but a few examples, but they serve to illuminate certain circumstances and repeating patterns.

On March 5, 2018, residents of the area near Acari, in Rio de Janeiro, woke to the sound of gunshots. Arriving at the location where the sound had come from, they found Eduardo Ferreira and Reginaldo Santos with their shirts and shorts torn, lifeless, facedown in the dirt. The police only took the bodies away at seven o'clock that evening, registering the following report: "Black men, strong builds, with broad features and shaved heads." These are summary descriptions that seek to pair stereotype with wrongdoing. The script played out as expected: a subsequent investigation was closed due to insufficient information (and political will).

That same March, on the ninth, a student at the Fundação Getúlio Vargas (FGV) in São Paulo sent an image to his WhatsApp group with the message: "Look at the slave I found in the smoking lounge! Would his owner please come fetch him?" As historian Robert Darnton has shown, the ammunition for jokes like this derives from the displacement of meaning. It is not the thing in itself that provokes laughter, but the inversion of assumptions that remain submerged in the old, persistent theory of "common sense." It is hard to imagine that someone could find such a comment funny. However, from what we can tell, this is no isolated case, but rather part of a pattern. The result? This "funny guy" was suspended, sued by the wronged student, and was punished and forced to pay a fine three years later, in March 2021.

In the city of Belém, during the same month as the incident at FGV, a girl chose as the theme for her fifteenth birthday party a "nostalgic" return to the imperial era. She went all out, dressing as a planter's wife and hiring out Black men and women to dress as domestic slaves. Images of the party went viral, and the resulting furor led the birthday girl's mother to try to justify her daughter's actions. To cite this example is not a matter of assigning blame, but rather of showing the chasm, the social gap, that exists in Brazil. Failing to understand the violent nature of this scene is synonymous with failing to feel another's pain and the weight of discrimination inscribed in such purportedly naive acts.

Racial intolerance is, then, one of the main factors in explaining social inequality in Brazil, aside from being the motive for considerable violence. A democratic society cannot exist where racism thrives. Two more cases may be cited, both in the city of Rio de Janeiro, also during 2018. One of them is enshrouded in anonymity, in the common grave that holds numerous dead individuals who will remain unknown if we fail to give them the burial they deserve. The other turned Brazil upside down.

On the night of March 12, Matheus Melo Castro, twenty-three years of age, was killed after leaving the evangelical church Missão da Fé, located in the Manguinhos favela. Matheus, who was an assistant to the pastor, climbed onto a motorbike that he had paid for with the salary he earned as a garbage collector, and around ten in the evening was met by a Polícia Militar patrol. The military policemen shot him twice, once in the left arm and another time in the chest, but the police did not run to his aid. People living nearby took him in a wheelbarrow to an Urgent Care Post, where he received treatment, but too late. Matheus was a member of the local religious community and had a steady job, but even so he was unable to escape the statistics that reveal the "epidemic" of deaths of young Black men across the country, which remains unseen behind the perverse veil of social and racial invisibility.

Marielle Franco, the first city councilwoman in Rio de Janeiro to be elected via the Party of Socialism and Liberty (PSOL),[1] with the fifth-highest vote count ever, grew up in the favela community of Maré, the largest complex of favelas in the state of Rio de Janeiro. A Black, lesbian single mother and human rights defender in a neglected city, a critic of police actions in underprivileged communities, Franco was executed, two days after the shooting of Matheus, with four shots to the right side of her head. With her was Anderson Pedro Gomes, the driver of the vehicle in which she was traveling, who also died. By this time, Marielle no longer lived in Maré, but she returned there frequently and identified as a child of the favela, challenging value judgments and stereotypes concerning their populations. On the anniversary of the founding of Rio de Janeiro, she posted a photo from a patio in Maré, with the following message: "Congratulations to my beloved city, which sadly has been so mistreated historically, including in recent years. And which, the more she's neglected, the more hostile she grows to women and the Black population."

A sharp wit, Marielle often said that she had turned everything we thought we knew about statistics on its head when she took what little a public education could offer and earned university admission. She took advantage of every opening she found, finished her degree, defended her master's at an elite university, and set out to make a political career, which she did with the determination of those who have never received anything for free, much less on a silver platter. None of this, however, kept her from being killed, or the crime from remaining unsolved to this day: while identities of two suspects in the shooting of Marielle may be known— quite possibly guns-for-hire, both active members of the Polícia Militar, one since retired and collecting a pension, the other dismissed for taking on illegal security "side jobs"—Brazilians still know nothing of who ordered the crime. Police even found 117 M-16 rifles at the residence of a friend of one of the accused in the middle-class Rio neighborhood of Méier: further evidence that having firearms in the home does not lead to peace.

This time, however, the execution was not "swept under the rug." The assassination of Marielle Franco was quickly classified as a "political crime," and news of the incident soon exploded in the hands of the Federal Police. The impact around the country was enormous, and the repercussion global, allowing the activist to escape the obscurity that so often falls over the cases of people who share her skin color, gender, and social background but never attain her political visibility. She became a symbol of minorities' struggle for a more inclusive and civic-minded Brazil. Her motto, "See you in the struggle," became a political rallying cry, as Brazil and the rest of the planet witnessed all sorts of protests on the anniversary of her death.

The slow pace at which the investigation has evolved is related, as far as we can tell, to the proliferation of militias in Rio de Janeiro, a phenomenon of increasing proportions from the early 2000s onward. Brazilian militias, in contrast to historical developments in other countries such as Colombia, are not the result of a civil war. They originated as self-defense organs inside favela communities in response to organized crime's control of the favelas. They soon evolved, however, into criminal paramilitary groups that, claiming to combat crime and drug trafficking, engaged in various kinds of illegal activities while maintaining close ties to the police. Their members tend to be police, vigilantes, prison guards, firemen, and active or reserve military officials who live in the community concerned. These groups' strategies include manipulating residents' fears and local threats to safety, which they manage to do, for example, by extorting money from residents in exchange for protection. But the apparatus is still more complex. Militias are not regional commands alone; they operate with the backing of politicians and community leaders. According to the Violence Research Group at the State University of Rio de Janeiro, at the end of 2009, these groups dominated 41.5 percent of the 1,006 favelas in Rio. The remaining portion were controlled directly by drug cartels (55.9 percent) and "Police Pacification Units." Militias, however, provide the best example of the widespread violence across the country, affecting areas where the law either does not reach or abdicates its duties.

The truth is that there are many Marielles, and the problem—
the intersection of race, gender, and violence—affects all Brazilians
in one way or another and continues to demand an answer. Paradoxically, given her personal success, Marielle Franco is an example
of how social markers such as race (Black), sexual orientation (lesbian), and region (favela "communities" throughout the country)
can lead to the construction of negative stereotypes by those sectors of society that might feel threatened by her prominence. It is
surely no coincidence that, the day before her assassination, outraged at the death of Matheus Melo Castro, the councilwoman had
posted a message on social media: "How many more must die?"

It falls to Brazilian civil society to keep the question from going
unanswered, and to break the authoritarian cycle brought on by
violence by refusing to allow the alarming number of murders (including those of Marielle and Anderson Pedro Gomes) to vanish
into the common grave of oblivion. Marielle Franco represented
the possibility of a more just, inclusive, democratic, and diverse
country, a more tolerant country. Paradoxically, she was killed by
the same violence she so vehemently condemned. For this very
reason, upon her death, a sense of hope for Brazil was buried along
with her. At the same time, however, Marielle lives on in Brazilians' memory: a potent and charismatic harbinger of a new kind
of country.

Violence and Gender Inequality

As is well known, the structural and institutionalized racism across
the country does not merely affect the Black male population;
women, and Black women in particular, have been the favorite
targets of sexual violence in Brazil, which takes on proportions not
unlike those of the violence against men described above.

Sex and gender were previously understood to be synonymous.
For some time now, however, we have understood these as fundamentally distinct concepts; this distinction, in fact, has the power
to impact the lives of many Brazilians. The concept of "sex" is

regularly used to define innate characteristics, according to the perspective of biology: feminine and masculine. "Gender," on the other hand, concerns the roles and social constructions that men and women choose to perform during their lives. In summary, sex is a more firmly fixed category, the visible result of anatomical differences, while gender is a "translation" of sex—it is a socially constructed distinction that surpasses biological features operating according to a network of binary categories.

The category "gender" has been much revised of late. According to Judith Butler, gender is not a social or cultural attribute, but a category created through a series of normative performances that are reinforced by a culture based on heterosexuality. This is why "gender identities" are conceived and operate pragmatically in reality, being associated with various social experiences. Thus, instead of retracing the traditional divisions between men and women, the feminine and the masculine, we begin to build societies that are more plural because they are formed by various familial configurations and the very instability of gender possibilities.

Nonetheless, heteronormative behaviors that seek to extend the concept of sex to other facets of society—such as work, leisure, and power—produce gender imbalances in various forms. Violence is one way in which these asymmetries are expressed. Indeed, there is no shortage of forms of violence that lurk behind the assumptions involved, which ultimately seek to uphold lopsided and noninclusive gender relations.

Nothing works better than statistics to provide us with evidence that gender inequality exists in our society, as widespread as it is routine. Women account for 89 percent of the victims of sexual violence in Brazil. Between 2001 and 2011, fifty thousand women were murdered, according to the Institute of Applied Economic Research. Even so, the term "femicide" was only formally adopted as of March 2015 in recognition of the existence of premeditated lethal crimes committed specifically against women.

Statute 13104 of Brazil's federal legal code classifies the murder of women (where their condition as women is key) as a hate crime and does not allow a reduction in sentence for those convicted. A law alone cannot bring such a frequent phenomenon under control, however. Several studies confirm the shameful prevalence of violence against women; a high proportion of these crimes occur in the household and involve the complicity of family members.

The number of cases of femicide—murder on account of one's gender—is alarming: according to data from Relógios da Violência, a public awareness initiative of the Insituto Maria da Penha,[2] every 7.2 seconds a woman is victim of physical violence. The 2015 *Violence Map* calls attention to the fact that in 2013 alone, thirteen women were victims of femicide every day, and nearly 30 percent of these murders were committed by a partner, ex-husband, or former partner. This number represents an increase of 21 percent in relation to the preceding decade, a sign that, contrary to expectations, the problem has only grown worse.

Despite changes to federal law, the reality has changed little, not so differently from the treatment of offenders. Many are classified as "antisocial individuals" or considered "unfit to stand trial"— qualifying them for special treatment. Meanwhile, the habit of violence against women, far from being abnormal, is common in societies that refuse to confront predominant paternalist, chauvinist, and heteronormative values that have remained unchallenged throughout history. The normalization of aggressive, chauvinistic male behavior can be seen in a recent survey, in which 30 percent of Brazilian men surveyed expressed the belief that a woman who wears revealing clothing is responsible for harassment or is asking to be the victim of violence: an age-old excuse, and one that blames the victim.

The situation looks even more critical if we separate out these high rates of femicide by race. According to data from the *2015 Violence Map*, there was a 54 percent increase in the murder of Black women between 2003 and 2013, while murders of White women registered a drop of 9.8 percent; while according to the 2017 Youth Violence Vulnerability Index, Black women between fifteen and twenty-nine years of age in Brazil are 2.19 times more likely to be murdered than their White counterparts.

There are also important regional differences. Leading the list of states with the highest femicide rates nationwide is Rio Grande do Norte, where young Black women die 8.11 times more frequently than young White women, followed by Amazonas state, where the relative risk is 6.97 times greater. In third place is Paraíba, where young Black women are 5.65 times more likely to be killed. Fourth is the Federal District, where the relative risk is 4.72 times greater.

There are other risks to being a woman in Brazil, as well. Every day, five women do not survive childbirth and four women die from complications related to abortions. Each decade, Brazil's public health system spends R$486 million (US$85.7 million) on patients admitted for these complications, with 75 percent of cases involving voluntary abortions. (Abortion is illegal in Brazil, with few exceptions.)

These alarming numbers reinforce the idea that the only way to confront gender violence is through sound public policies that focus on contributing factors, such as work, family, health, income, racial equity, and opportunity. Educating the public on these issues is also an important step, to the extent that it can help to reduce misogynistic behaviors—expressions of hate, disdain, or prejudice against women, independently of age, race, or place.

Misogyny takes many forms, from social exclusion to gender violence. It can be found in equal doses in the old patriarchal moorings of Brazilian society, which, even today, bring with them the guarantee of male privilege, the normalization of violence against women, and continued efforts toward their sexual objectification. These are the deep roots of Brazil's authoritarianism, which has always carried with it a shameful relationship to gender questions. Women were supposed act as "princesses," obeying and submitting to their husbands, while men are the eternal "princes," conscious of their dominance and authority (and, yet again, any resemblance to current times is no mere coincidence).

In general, the better women manage to establish their independence and autonomy, the stronger reactions from men and displays of misogyny have grown. Meanwhile, men's dominance over the public sphere is indisputable. A good reference point is the scarcity of women in political life. After the 2018 elections, only fifty-five of Brazil's 513 federal deputies were women: a mere 10.7 percent. In a study of 138 countries, Brazil occupied 115th position in terms of women's political representation. Saudi Arabia, which only passed a law against domestic violence in 2013, ranked higher than Brazil on this list, as did Iraq and Afghanistan.

Practice in the political world corresponds to what we see in everyday reality: it is the product of an attitude, deep-seated and enduring, that seeks to render insignificant, if not altogether void, the presence of women in the country's principal institutions; and when this no longer applies, the resulting sense of lost privilege can give way to violence, not only physical, but also symbolic and moral.

Since the end of the 1970s, women have definitively broken free from the social position that had been predetermined for them in Brazil—that of passivity or victimhood—and, organizing into movements, have begun to demand equal rights and opportunities in work and leisure, within the home and beyond it. In the twenty-first century, Black feminism too has taken hold, calling greater attention to the particularities of the situation affecting these women, including issues related to racism in Brazil. As the politician, academic, anthropologist and Black feminist Lélia Gonzalez (1953–94) asserted, "Aside from everything else, here's the deal: I'm Black and I'm a woman. This doesn't mean I'm your brown sugar, some cleaning woman you can order about, or your sweet old mammy. Write that down, that's my message to Black women in Brazil."

Rape Culture, or When the Prince Doesn't Marry the Princess

In what is considered the first official example of writing to come out of Brazil—a letter that Pero Vaz de Caminha addressed to the king of Portugal between April 28 and May 1 of the year 1500—the scrivener on Pedro Álvares Cabral's vessel asserts that everyone in that land walked about "naked, without the least covering for their private parts." It was the Indigenous peoples' beauty and lack of clothing, especially in the case of native women, that quickly attracted the attentions of the first colonizers.

One of the first known engravings in the Americas, dating to around 1580, also sought to imagine this "friendly" encounter between the Old and New worlds (fig. 8). In the image, the European is depicted as a white man in possession of a range of objects symbolic of civilization: the astrolabe, the caravel, the standard, shoes, and abundant clothing. America, on the other hand, is embodied as a woman, practically nude and lying in a hammock, characterizing the New World as languid and indolent, merely awaiting the arrival of the Old. The associations with backwardness are equally overt: the lack of vestments covering America's body, bare feet, exotic animals gathered around, and, especially, the scenes of cannibalism in the background. But there is another significant detail: America is extending one of her arms toward the Conquistador, as though desiring to be "invaded" and inviting the European to do so. In *Imperial Leather*, anthropologist Anne McClintock makes the provocative assertion that this illustration represents the first great symbolic rape in the history of the Americas. The nudity of the "girl" and her "surrender" would serve as justification for the violent colonization that was about to begin and that would change forever the face of the continent.

This is not the place to construct a simple timeline, a single linear history of cause and immediate effect based on a single point of view: that of the European colonizer. It would be better to reflect on accounts that trickled out, that were not incorporated into Brazil's official memory, or, put another way, have not been considered, but that have given rise to "rape culture" in Brazil.

Culture operates as second nature; it brands us like a tattoo. Its participation in our daily lives is so "natural" that we forget that it is the result of many political, social, and human constructs. The term "rape culture" was used for the first time in the 1970s by activists of so-called second-wave feminism. The intent was to issue a warning about the prevalence of this kind of violence and to show

FIGURE 8. Theodoor Galle, *Allegory of America*, Netherlandish, c. 1600, engraving (plate 1 of 19 from *New Inventions of Modern Times* [*Nova Reperta*]), 27 × 20 cm, after a drawing by Jan van der Straet (Stradamus), c. 1580. New York, The Metropolitan Museum of Art.

that it was a hate crime for which society ought to have zero tolerance.

We have yet, however, to identify the foundations of the normalization of rape in Brazil. The beginning of this story is tied to the colonial project, whose efficacy was predicated on the widespread use of compulsory slave labor: Indigenous or African. As a result, as we have seen throughout this book, power was concentrated in the hands of a few, and inequality—racial, ethnic, regional, and also gender- and sex-based—became an essential characteristic. In the first place, colonization was almost entirely implemented by men. The European men who arrived were either single or had embarked without their families, with the aim of taming this immense "land of the future" full of mystery and peril. Secondly, the male slave population was always greater than the female population—to the tune of 70 percent to 30 percent—occasioning an unmistakable gender imbalance.

Such disproportion would redound in increasingly violent consequences in the colonial setting, in which positions of authority led to the normalization of differentiation and internal hierarchies. The enslaved could be bought, sold, auctioned, bartered, mistreated. The female body, for its part, relatively scarce in Afro-Atlantic societies, was soon incorporated into this internal logic of the "traffic in souls." Regarded as fonts of wealth, Indigenous and Black women—put to use in the fields, in the plantation house, in the cities, and in the mines—also served their masters as instruments of pleasure and sexual gratification. The system's sweeping violence found a particular locus in the sexuality exercised by slave-owners in the master's quarters.

The environment of fear, the reality of sexual assault and rape, would not remain confined, however, to the slavery era; they remained common to the present day. According to data from IPEA, 88 percent of the victims of sexual assault are women, 70 percent are children or adolescents, 46 percent lack a primary school education, and 51 percent are people of color. Moreover, 24 percent of registered crimes list fathers or stepfathers as the perpetrators, 32 percent of cases involve a friend or acquaintance of the victim, and many of these acts are committed by two or more people: 10.5 percent where victims are children, 16.2 percent where they are adolescents, and 15.4 percent in the case of adults. This violence also tends to follow a schedule: rapes are more commonly committed on Mondays, cases of child abuse between noon and midnight, and those involving adults between six in the afternoon and six the next morning.

The *2018 Atlas of Violence* presents similar numbers. It tells us that 68 percent of cases of sexual violence registered in the public health system involve the rape of minors, nearly a third of the perpetrators of crimes against children (up to age thirteen) are friends or acquaintances, and another 30 percent are close family members such as fathers, mothers, stepfathers, and brothers. Studies show that in 54.9 percent of reported cases in which the perpetrator is known to the victim, the rapes have been occurring for some time, with 78.5 percent of them occurring in the victim's own home.

It is true that this is not an exclusively Brazilian problem. But in this matter, Brazil trails other countries throughout the Americas, such as Costa Rica, Peru, Jamaica, and the United States. Each of these countries, however, has its own history, and Brazil's is characterized by an alarming rate of crimes to this day, when a lack of confidence in the police, a fear of reprisals, and scant protection for citizens prevail. The immediate consequence of the fragility of Brazil's institutions is that only 35 percent of victims file a complaint to the relevant authorities, thus tethering the country to a scandalous number of unreported crimes.

Even so, according to the 2015 *Annual Report on Public Security in Brazil*, an average of one rape was reported every eleven minutes. According to data from the Ministry of Health, every four minutes a woman seeks medical attention at a public health facility as a result of sexual violence. Estimates vary, but in general it is thought that the figures cover only 10 percent of the total crimes. Following this line of thinking, if we add up such data to make a projection, we arrive at the astounding rate of nearly half a million rapes each year across the country.

In 2016, the Ministry of Health saw an average of ten group rape reports daily in the public health system, and it should furthermore be taken into account that 30 percent of municipalities do not report any data of this kind to the government. In the same survey it was also pointed out that in the city of São Paulo, a rape occurs in a public space every eleven hours. In the state of Rio de Janeiro, there is a case of rape in school every five days, and 62 percent of the victims are under twelve years of age. In the São Paulo metro, according to the *Estado de S. Paulo* newspaper, in 2016 alone there were four cases of sexual assault reported per week. In 2015, the Women's Support Hotline received calls from

749,024 individuals, or one every forty-two seconds. Since 2005, there have been nearly five million calls.

The past has bequeathed the country a heavy burden that has no relation to mere circumstance. So ubiquitous is rape culture today—involving not only criminal acts themselves but also denial and silence, individual and collective, in the face of the crime—that it might even appear insurmountable. It is not, however; and it's necessary to transpose hard figures to understand how each example conceals its own tragedies, traumas, and resentments. The lives of these victims is and will continue to be marked by shame and, many times, by the guilt brought on by keeping the secret that the rape was committed by people who were close to them in some way, such as friends, relatives, politicians, religious leaders, celebrities, colleagues, acquaintances, neighbors, and "everyday" citizens, often shielded by widespread social acceptance. The result of such indifference and omission is not only the perpetuation of rape culture, but a growing "culture of fear": 65 percent of the total population and 85 percent of women residing in major urban centers report being afraid of leaving the house and potentially suffering a sexual assault.

It is easy to condemn a patriarchal society and a history of slavery. It is harder to face these as persistent problems in both rural settings and our modernized cities. In this story, the princess and prince *do not* live happily ever after.

Femicide

Femicide can be defined as "the killing of a woman for the simple reason that she is a woman." The motives are generally tied to feelings of hate, contempt, or a sense of loss of control. These are ultimately intimate emotional motives, but they have common roots in patriarchal, authoritarian, sexist societies characterized by the assignation of discriminatory roles to women. Such motives also reflect the perversity of the historically unequal power dynamics between women and men.

In colonial times, Brazilian society displayed a demonstrable inequality between sexes. As we have seen, not only did male colonizers arrive in greater numbers, but a majority of the enslaved were also men. Such disproportion produced a society given to violent forms of sexual relations, shaped by a rigorous and discriminatory division between men and women. White women were to remain serving their husbands at the "hearth and home," quickly bearing children and aging more quickly still. As for Black women, the prejudice found in a popular expression of the day weighed over them: "White women are for marrying, Black women for working, and mulattas for fornicating." Another proverb delineated the social spaces accorded women while at the same time reinforcing a gender hierarchy that was widely in effect: "Black women at the stove, mulattas between the sheets, and White women at the altar."

Beyond the stereotypes and prejudiced views distilled in them, these would-be proverbs also indirectly foment violent practices against women, a matter of routine in a society where power is concentrated among men. The notion of the absolute power that a landowner amassed on his rural properties extended to other territories, such as control over women, be they his wife, girlfriend, or partner, or enslaved or emancipated women. If the era in general was notable for its permissiveness, in the sense that all sorts of conduct were accepted, for the rural Brazilian landowner such permissiveness was greater still, as he was invested with several powers: economic, political, social, and sexual.

This patriarchal model was sustained until recently, perpetuating throughout the country a common understanding of power and efforts to maintain a strict system of subordination when it came to gender roles. Every society designates different places for women and men. In Brazil, the advent of the language of civil rights in the 1970s led to women's advancement to new positions and posts, and to their active struggle against what were tangible patterns of gender imbalance.

The problem persists, however, when these social places are given differing weight and importance. In the case of the Brazilian social experience, men's roles have been overvalued to the detriment of women, which produces relations characterized by violence. Further, many men began to feel threatened or even insecure in the face of the growing autonomy and independence of their wives, girlfriends, partners, and female acquaintances and colleagues, whose major objective was no longer to shine in the reclusive domestic sphere. The relationship is proportional: the more women reach higher positions at work and outside the home, the greater the volume of femicides. In this way, gender violence represents not only a relationship of domination and male power but an effort to impose submissiveness upon women. It reveals how the distinct roles imposed on feminine and masculine spaces, and the way these were solidified throughout Brazilian history, reinforced by patriarchy, resulted in the establishment of frequently violent models of relations between the sexes.

This attempt to control women, not only in private but in public, led to the internalization of certain roles across the society, via widely shared mores and distinct educational models for men and women. Codes of conduct and order were created and instilled, traditional norms that implied the continuation of "rituals of surrender" but also "chasteness," a daily life confined to the home and a devotion to motherhood, as though this alone were a woman's purpose. As these customs became increasingly entrenched, openings to establish more equitable relations and gender interdependence became increasingly rare. Besides this, the legitimization of these social patterns led the paterfamilias of the past and present day to also feel justified in his use of force, doled out in the silence of his own home and in the deafening silence of social acceptance.

It took many years for the country to become fully aware of the magnitude of this violence. The implementation of the Maria da Penha Law in 2006 was one of the first measures taken to recognize and criminalize domestic and family violence. The law also instituted, for the first time, mechanisms to prevent, punish, and eradicate this type of abuse, "independently of class, race, ethnicity, sexual orientation, income, culture, education, age, or religion." Its objective is to assure the "right to life, safety, health, sustenance, education, culture, shelter, justice, sport, leisure, work, citizenship, freedom, dignity, respect, and family and community life."

However, the implementation of this law hardly means the job is done, since the country still lacks preventive measures against these crimes, such as initiatives to educate the public and a comprehensive support network for victims. If, on the one hand, femicide has been classified as a hate crime by the Brazilian penal code since 2015, on the other, the new law, though important, is incapable of putting an end to such offenses, widespread as they are. There is still a high rate of under-reporting by abused women but also by family members or friends of victims, while at the same time many perpetrators are shielded, and justice delayed.

The number of femicides remains high in Brazil—4.8 for every hundred thousand women, according to data relating to 2013 but published in 2015, and still a shameful rate of 4.3 per hundred thousand in 2017. The former figure placed the country fifth in world rankings, while according to information from the World Health Organization broken down by ethnicity, the number of Black women murdered from 2003 to 2013 grew by 54 percent, from 1,864 cases to 2,875. During the same period, the annual number of homicides involving White women fell by 9.8 percent, from 1,747 in 2003 to 1,576 in 2013. The latest WHO report recorded 4,473 murders in the first degree in 2017, 946 of them femicides. This figure represents an increase of 6. 5 percent relative to 2016, when there were 4,201 homicides reported (812 of which were femicides).

Such figures reveal that a woman is killed every two hours in Brazil. Though the country has made advances in terms of public policies to limit femicide, it remains a long way from having adopted a full-on strategy to combat this type of crime.

Misogynistic declarations are a daily reality and have encroached on the political sphere, still dominated by men and by women who do not see in feminist movements, whatever shape they take and no matter the groups they represent, a just cause and campaign for rights.

Etymologically, the word "misogyny" comes from Greek, *misogynía*, a combination of *mîsos*—hate—and *gyné*—woman. This aversion to the female sex, which frequently assumes morbid and pathological proportions, is directly tied to the violence committed against women for so long. Misogyny is, accordingly, the principal cause of a considerable portion of crimes committed against women in Brazil, which have taken a variety of forms— from physical, emotional, and psychological attacks to mutilations, sexual abuse, torture, and harassment—but are often shielded by a veil of tacit complicity.

Only a concerted effort by civil society can bring an end to this cycle that we have inherited from the colonial period but honed in modern times. Increased education, the establishment of networks of support and protection for victims, an improvement in the conduct of the authorities involved in the investigation and prosecution of such crimes, health policy focused on supporting victims, and public awareness campaigns are some of solutions recommended by specialists. It is meanwhile important to recognize that feminist social movements have already succeeded in shaking Brazilian society on several fronts.

Despite gains, recent authoritarian governments have flourished in Brazil thanks to nostalgia for "the good old days," a time of "traditional family values," but in essence they merely announce a newfangled dystopia: one that divides by hate rather uniting by goodwill. This is not, however, a battle to be waged only by women. If Brazilians do not join together to take on misogyny and femicide, the latter will continue to occur as "chronicles of various tragedies foretold"—tragedies that could, through collective action, be avoided.

LGBTQ Individuals: A Favorite
Target of Authoritarian Politicians

In 2015 alone, 318 gay people were killed in Brazil, according to the NGO Grupo Gay da Bahia, which maps homicides committed against the gay population; among the victims, 52 percent were gay men, 37 percent cross-dressers, 16 percent lesbian, and 10 percent bisexual. This is just one more aspect of the violence plaguing the nation.

Crimes against lesbian, gay, bisexual, transgender, and queer (LGBTQ) people are common across the country, characterized as it is by the disgust for these groups, despite significant advances in recent years when it comes to their inclusion in the broader public agenda, the creation of mechanisms to combat hate crimes, and public policies and programs to combat discrimination.

Brazil, however, presents a paradox when it comes to thinking about these issues. Year after year, the city of São Paulo hosts the largest pride parade in the world; yet 445 LGBTQ people were killed in the country in 2017. As the anthropologist Renan Quinalha has shown, while Brazilians like to present themselves as open to a range and variety of sexualities, preferences, and identities, they nevertheless stand by as crimes against those who do not fit a heteronormative model remain widespread. Likewise, at the same time as Brazil was marking the fortieth anniversary of its LGBTQ movement—making it one of the oldest, and perhaps most daring, having formed under the dictatorship—the country witnessed the election of government leaders who have no qualms about mixing politics and issues of moral or sexual conduct.

If we wish to find evidence of the existence and continuation of such paradoxes, we need look no further than the escalation in physical violence suffered by these populations. In 2017, the Grupo Gay da Bahia reported that a LGBTQ person is killed in Brazil every nineteen hours. According to a study by the NGO Transgender Europe, there were 486 murders of cross-dressers and transgender individuals in Brazil between January 2008 and

April 2013; this is four times the number in Mexico, the country with the second-highest number of registered crimes of this kind.

Organizations such as the International Lesbian, Gay, Bisexual, Trans and Intersex Association–Latin America and the Caribbean (ILGA–LAC), as well as international organizations tied to the United Nations and the Inter-American Commission on Human Rights, have regularly warned of the violence against LGBTQ individuals committed by those outside the law, by state authorities, by individuals, or by social groups that profess beliefs antithetical to the sexual and gender diversity guaranteed by the Brazilian constitution.

Another way of measuring prejudice and institutionalized exclusion is by the lack of a targeted public policy to address this form of crime. Not publicizing and not measuring are forms of ignorance or disdain. There is little in the way of public data, and few trustworthy sources, whether at the state or national level, on homophobic violence. We have only certain mapping tools developed by nongovernmental organizations working in this area, which themselves rely on news articles for their data.

This alone is an important indicator of the silence around crimes committed against these groups. They seem to represent a threat to other segments of Brazilian society that still take pride in the expression of a chauvinism that defines their social relationships, attributing their positions to religions that promote patriarchal tradition and a narrow definition of the family as (the correct) standards for one's behavior and social interactions. The scale of under-reporting of these incidents, then, comes as no surprise. It demonstrates that many victims prefer silence to exposure and humiliating treatment at the hands of authorities.

While there is no easy explanation for a certain widespread scorn for gay, lesbian, bisexual, and transgender people across certain sectors of Brazilian society, it is more difficult still to pin down the motives that lead someone to kill, rape, or torture these individuals, all the more because, for the most part, both media reports and governmental authorities ultimately consider sexual orientation and gender identity of the victim as incidental rather than decisive factors in explaining the commission of a crime. Still, if we take into account the number and frequency of incidents recorded by the press and NGOs alone, we already have sufficient evidence to confirm the existence of a violent practice in Brazil that we might define as "gender-based hate crime." Whatever the name, these are crimes narrowly focused against the LGBTQ population.

As long as victims of this type of aggression cannot count on effective ways to report such crimes, or the guarantee their identities will be protected, the current state of affairs is likely to remain unchanged and even deteriorate, especially at a moment when political polarization, which also tends to encroach on Brazilians' daily life, has taken the form of a sort of sexual and normative hysteria—a moral battle.

The number of deaths of transgender women and cross-dressers due to gender violence is so high that some defend the adoption of a special term when attempting to explain the frequency of these murders: "transfemicide." This reflects the fact that, in the overwhelming majority of cases, there are no legal procedures to investigate such crimes, families do not claim the bodies, and news programs opt to use victims' legal names, disregarding their gender identity even at the hour of their death.

Though consensual relations between individuals of the same sex are not criminalized in Brazil, and despite the constitution's guarantees of gender equality and protective measures for women, legislation touching on the transgender population is only now beginning its journey to law. It is urgent to recognize the existence of an considerable gap between social practices and changes to the culture, which, though significant, have yet to result in legislation that provides specific protections for these populations.

In sharp contrast to this neglect, a variety of civil society organizations and international organs have focused attention on the growing cruelty affecting Brazil's LGBTQ community. Cases range from verbal attacks to violence on the streets, involving acts such as impalement, genital mutilation, torture, stoning, knifings, or attacks employing blunt objects. According to the 2013 Report on Homophobic Violence in Brazil, in 2012 authorities recorded 3,084 complaints regarding 9,982 violations directed at the LGBTQ population. (A single complaint can be used to register multiple transgressions.) Between January 2013 and March 31, 2014, the Inter-American Commission on Human Rights tracked a wave of violence affecting the lesbian, gay, bisexual, transgender, and inter-sex (LGBTI) community across the Americas and counted at least 594 assassinations of LGBT people, or crimes perceived to be such, as well as another 176 serious but not lethal attacks. Of these attacks, fifty-five were, or were thought to be, directed at lesbian women. In a statement to the press, the Commission staked out the following position: "The common denominator of these violent acts is the perception of the perpetrator that the victim has transgressed accept-able gender norms (in function of their gender identity/presentation or sexual orientation)." Again, and this time across the continent, the report is incomplete, since "a majority of OAS member states do not collect data about violence against the LGBT community." In these cases, and in light of significant under-reporting, the solu-tion was, once more, to refer to complementary sources, such as news reports, reports from civil society organizations, and other forms of monitoring.

The Commission further called attention to the high degree of cruelty in such crimes and in cases of police abuse, including tor-ture and inhumane and degrading treatment, as well as verbal and physical attacks. Diving deeper into the data, the same report in-dicates that the targets of the vast majority of murders were gay men and transgender women, or those perceived to be so. The report also highlights the serious lack of reporting, in all cases, as well as many examples of abuse at the hands of sexual partners. Of the 594 murders throughout the continent, Brazil accounted for 336, according to the report. One possible conclusion is that in Brazil people may have been enabled to easily report such crimes but nevertheless lack effective protection.

Further data produced by Brazilian organizations reveal the same paradox: the staggering levels of violence defy formal national protection policies. According to the Brazilian Lesbian League, it is estimated that nearly 6 percent of rape victims who called the federal government's Disque 100 (Dial 100) hotline during the year 2012 were lesbian; between 2012 and 2014, this proportion rose to 9 percent. Within these statistics, there is a considerable percentage of complaints involving "corrective rape," in which the theory that female homosexuality derives from "poor example" and can be "fixed" through violent, nonconsensual sexual relations with "real men" is offered as justification. Additionally, though there are demands for the explicit recognition of homosexuality in the Maria da Penha Statute, this law is little used to safeguard the rights of lesbian, bisexual, and transgender women. Data from the Women's Help Hotline "Call 180" show that in 2013, for example, among all answered calls, less than 1 percent involved same-sex relationships.

It seems clear, then, that violence against LGBTQ people is the result of a complex web of practices and beliefs, of a still-prevalent sexism in Brazilian society, of a dearth of related educational policies, and of the lack of pertinent legislation. There are local-level initiatives on the part of some states, but responsibility belongs squarely to the federal legislative branch—the National Congress.

The São Paulo state government, for example, enacted Statute No. 10948/01, which punishes any citizens—including public servants, regular citizens, or members of the military—and any organization or public or private entity based in the state with warnings, fines, and suspension or even cancellation of their business license should they be caught harassing LGBTQ people. In addition, State Decree No. 55588/10 provides transgender people and cross-dressers with the option of using their name of preference in dealings with the state's public organs. As a result, public servants are required to address these individuals by this preferred name, facing disciplinary action in the event that they fail to do so.

On August 31, 2001, the National Council to Combat Discrimination and Promote the Rights of Lesbian, Gay, Bisexual, Transgender People (CNCD/LGBT) was established, via executive
order 2216-37, as one of the agencies tied to the Presidential
Secretariat for Human Rights (SDH/PR). On December 9, 2010,
the federal government conferred new powers and a new structure
on the CNCD/LGBT via Federal Decree 7388, since policies pertaining to the promotion of racial equality and the Indigenous
population were being implemented by other organs. To attend to
the longstanding demands of the Brazilian LGBTQ community,
and with the aim of strengthening public policies directed toward
this population, the CNCD/LGBT adopted as its mission the
formulation and proposal of national policies focused on combating discrimination and on the advancement and defense of
LGBTQ rights.

Meanwhile, however, as I write, political projects impacting the
LGBTQ community have been changed for the worse, as policies
promoting the rights of the LGBTQ population are rescinded by
the National Council to End Discrimination, which included the
National Directorate for the Rights of Lesbian, Gay, Bisexual,
Transvestite, and Transsexual Persons. In other words, while during Michel Temer's time in the presidency the CNCD/LGBT
remained part of the fundamental structure of the Ministry of
Human Rights, the new government elected in 2018 made clear on
multiple occasions its opposition to the inclusion of such issues in
schools, in government policy, and in society itself. Rather, it has
sought to undermine courses, programs, professors, and books
dedicated to these subjects, whose merit they besmirch with use
of the patently denigratory expression "gender ideology."

The prevailing sentiment seems to be an enormous disdain for
the struggles and demands of LGBTQ people, who at present have
no designated institutional representation in the federal government. In this sense, it is rather revealing that the current Executive
Order 870 fails to make explicit that this population is included in
human rights directives and policies, as they were before. In fact,

the executive order stipulates that the protection of LGBTQ rights falls to National Secretariat for Global Protection of the Ministry for Women, the Family, and Human Rights, representing a clear loss in status within the federal framework for the protection of human rights.

Lesbian, gay, bisexual, transgender, and intersex people may be part of the "ethnic and social minorities" represented by the Ministry for Women, the Family, and Human Rights. Still, the executive order governing the remit of this ministry created by the new government makes no clear reference to this group. On the contrary, the Ministry's basic structure is composed of a number of secretariats and councils (the National Secretariat on Policy for Women; the National Secretariat on the Family; the National Secretariat for the Rights of Children and Adolescents; the National Youth Secretariat; the National Secretariat for Global Protection; the National Secretariat for Racial Equity Policy; the National Secretariat for the Rights of People with Disabilities; the National Secretariat for the Advancement and Defense of the Rights of the Elderly; the National Council for Racial Equity; the National Council on Human Rights; the National Council to End Discrimination; the National Council on the Rights of Children and Adolescents; the National Council on the Rights of People with Disabilities; The National Council on the Rights of the Elderly; the National Committee to Prevent and Eradicate Torture; the National Organization for the Prevention and Eradication of Torture; the National Council on Traditional Communities and Peoples; the National Council for Indigenous Policy; the National Council on Women's Rights; and the National Youth Council)—all this without any indication as to the institutional home for the development and implementation of policy for the LGBTQ population.

Education, protection, inclusion, and autonomy are the only measures that can guarantee that these sectors of the population (and new political players) are no longer the target of attacks and instead become full citizens whose rights are guaranteed. While everyone suffers under the current national politics of negligence, most affected are those who, in addition to identifying as LGBTQ, are vulnerable due to other factors, such as poverty, racial background, lack of access to education, or special needs.

In the context of a growing number of notably conservative political practices, in which fallacies and false political demands multiply, such as the so-called gay kit (which never existed), it is these social minorities who are most at risk, since they are defined as people who inhabit a space beyond the norms and standards of the "traditional family," the source of much mythologizing in recent years. Combating discourses that transform gender realities into mere "ideology" (with the understanding of this as a false truth) and demanding that rights previously conquered are protected and maintained is a collective responsibility, even more so at moments when a normative and moralistic standard has rendered violent behavior and actions against LGBTQ groups invisible and routine, constituting moreover attacks against democracy and the right to difference. It can be agreed, therefore, that this is an issue that not only concerns LGBTQ people but is a priority for all Brazilians who share a commitment to inclusive, republican values and to human rights more generally.

History shows that the more authoritarian a political regime is, the greater is the tendency to intensify attempts at exercising control over sexualities, bodies, and diversity itself. The problem of violence and appeals for safety were, as we have previously discussed, the most prominent themes in the 2018 election, and invariably featured in the stump speeches of those candidates who emerged as winners. Nonetheless, selective ideas about who deserves justice, and public silence at the criminalization of certain identities, provide a sampling of the way violence and the fight against it in Brazil break down not only by color, age, and social class, but also by sex and gender.

8

Intolerance

ANYONE WHO HAS TRAVELED outside Brazil and identified themselves as Brazilian, or who has spoken with foreigners traveling to the country, has certainly encountered a series of cheery descriptions of this tropical land. The idea is that this is a nation averse to conflict, peaceful by nature, democratic in terms of the coexistence of genders, races, and ethnicities—in sum, a sort of "paradise of tolerance" in the face of an unforgiving world.

Alas, these generalizations are no match for a rural land battle, a police baton in the cities, an argument between politicians, an armed assault, a traffic argument, a survey by ethnicity that reveals the structural inequality that persists there.

Brazil is also, as we have seen, a country with a violent past, whose watchword was never the "inclusion" of different peoples, but above all their "submission," even at the price of the erasure of a great many cultures. Treaties, constitutions, and other documents from the sixteenth and seventeenth centuries reveal the harshness of colonial coexistence and the way in which this socialization impacted the country: on the one hand, an attempt at annihilation, on the other its justification as a necessary dominance.

Luís Vaz de Camões (1524–79/80) was the author of what is now considered the greatest Portuguese epic: *Os Lusíadas* (The Lusiads), a work he likely concluded in 1556 but which was published for the first time in 1572. In this saga of the then-powerful Portuguese Empire, which finds itself "forced" to wage war against its declared enemies, all of its conquests, from the Crusades against the "Moors," to control over North Africa, and even colonial movements of discovery, are justified. In the third strophe of Canto I, Camões describes the maritime epic in terms of a sort of national virtue: "Cease all that antique Muse hath sung, for now a better Brav'ry rears its bolder brow" (in the translation by Richard Burton, of *Thousand Nights and a Night* fame). This is how the violent practices of Lusitanian colonizers were explained and "exalted," from the standpoint of a moral notion of "mission," in the original sense of the term: "sent to perform a service or carry on an activity on another's behalf." This would be the "true mission" that would fall to the Portuguese, and the most important, despite the consequences it produced.

Jesuit Antônio Vieira (1608–97), meanwhile, who arrived in Brazil in 1616 and in 1623 joined the Society of Jesus, dedicated his life to the task of catechizing the pagans of this new land: a Portuguese America. At a difficult moment for the Church in Europe, expanding the Christian faith among the Indigenous peoples of the New World, and thus revitalizing Catholicism, was one aim of this religious man, who maintained direct relations with native populations. In fact, Father Vieira soon became an opponent of the exploitation and enslavement of Indigenous peoples and eventually came to further doubt the work of European colonizers. In his 1657 "Sermon of the Holy Spirit," rather than laud the success of colonization, the Jesuit did the opposite: he recognized the arduous and difficult task of bringing the "true faith" to these disparate "Brazils."

There is an especially meaningful passage in which the religious man describes at length the dissimilarities between marble statues and myrtle-tree sculptures, using these to establish parallels with the shock of the encounter between two starkly different cultures living in close proximity: that of the colonizers and that of the Indigenous. The sermon begins with a differentiation between New Christians and Old Christians. Next, it explores another pair of differences: between the lasting faith of the Europeans and the malleability of the native peoples of Brazil. To evangelize the pagans in Europe was an arduous, painful, and costly task; still, the result was lasting, hard and rigid as white marble. Catechizing the "Brazils," meanwhile, was an entirely different matter. It resembled taming the myrtle, a tree amenable to pruning, immediately taking on the desired shape, but which at the first sign of neglect returned to its original form.

This was, and still is, a powerful image for thinking about and characterizing Indigenous peoples, who at first appeared easy to catechize but soon returned to their "primitive state." The Tumpinambá certainly resisted, in their way, the education offered by the Jesuits and efforts to recruit them for the work that the *caraíbas*—or Europeans—imposed upon them, putting a personal stamp on their new faith, "translating" into their own terms the teachings they received. As anthropologist Eduardo Viveiros de Castro has shown us, the lack of commitment on the part of the Indigenous "forced" religious officials to engage in constant re-evangelization. Nonetheless, in the words of Castro, "inconstancy is a constant in the savage equation."

The difference between a marble statue and a myrtle-tree sculpture is, in fact, a powerful metaphor for colonization. On one side is the supposed superiority of the European, represented by marble, understood to be a prized, expensive, and everlasting material; on the other is the refusal to submit of the native peoples, who, although posing no opposition to conversion, adapted the religion as best they could, without consent to the annulment of their own knowledge. In this case, "adapting" is synonymous with reacting and rebelling, or not blindly consuming another's faith—an indication that there was nothing peaceful about the contact between Europeans and the "pagans."

The two classic works of the colonial age just cited help us to reflect on a pattern of behavior that still rears its head, in distinct and renewed forms, in our current age. Whatever its precise form, the denial of violence against and intolerance for the Other—those who are different—relies upon a "varnish," used to justify, even laud, domination, while simultaneously whitewashing and minimizing it. Perhaps for this reason, there were for a remarkably long time those who claimed slavery as practiced in Brazil was "better," when in reality it is not possible to describe such a system in positive terms, as "more benevolent"; the racism practiced there as "less perverse," even in the face of data that reveal the opposite to be true; gender coexistence as "idyllic," despite ongoing violence; the relationship with Indigenous peoples as "friendly," despite history's clear indications otherwise; and even Brazil's military dictatorship as "mild."

Meanwhile, this denial of friction is a telltale symptom. It involves an attempt to describe the country in terms of its unresolved conflicts, yet stripping them of, or attenuating, their violent baggage. A good example can be found in the common expression "the Indigenous problem." According to Anthony Seeger and Eduardo Viveiros de Castro, such an expression is, at a minimum, "deceptive: it could suggest that the Indians 'create' a problem for the society at large, when in fact it's just the opposite. The 'problem,' in reality, is the country."

Negative framing is a form of intolerance, since it does not so much as allow criticism and friction to register: after all, it seems, there is no problem, there is no confrontation. This way of silencing unresolved conflicts and contradictions has been inscribed upon a society that prefers to render the ostensive invisible. In *Raízes do Brasil*, Sérgio Buarque de Holanda spoke of "cordiality," and "affability, hospitality, generosity, virtues touted by foreigners who visit our country," amounting to a "definitive trait of our national character." The historian goes onto explain that it would however be a mistake to imagine such virtues as a matter merely of civility in the sense of "good manners". Rather, they were the expression of "an exceptionally rich and boundless emotional depth," the result of a "vibrant and fecund ancestral influence of patterns of human coexistence informed by patriarchal rural society." It is a civility, he continues, that involves an element of coercion, a form of courtesy that is a far cry from politeness. For

Buarque de Holanda, appearances can be deceptive, amounting to "a guise that allows each individual to keep his or her sensibility and emotions intact."

There is no room, then, for praise of this "cordiality," given that it circumvents hierarchies only to quietly reinforce them. Brazilian society, having long tolerated slavery and the accumulation of large swaths of rural land, has preserved, even in modern times, a sort of national ritual opposition to social, gender, religious, or racial distinctions, while in actual daily practice reinforcing separation.

If this historical burden cannot entirely explain the present, it helps to shed light on Brazil's current predicament, wherein the same logic reigns, though now duly inverted. In place of a "ritual of tolerance," we now practice the opposite: confrontation and open expression of a polarization that, as we have seen throughout this book, has always been present, if muted, throughout the country's history. Perhaps for this reason, today many Brazilians do not bother to maintain their pacific reputation; they prefer to parade their intolerance.

In this, in fact, Brazilians have added their voices to a broader chorus. Many authoritarian movements emerging at present rely on the creation of mythologies of the State sustained by the logic of polarization: "us" and "them," or, more precisely, "them versus us" or "us versus them." Such stances exacerbate dualities and reinforce the standardization of random differences, forging new realities. "Them" is assumed to include the lazy, the corrupt, thieves, ideologues, the unscrupulous, and parasites; while a great "us" is activated on an oppositional basis, embracing everything to be found at the opposite pole. The unspoken rule is that as soon as a "them" is identified, a reassuring—because righteous, just, and exemplary—"us" soon follows.

This belief in binaries potentially divides the world to the tune of refrains that can only work by continuous exploitation of equally binary narratives: the honest versus the corrupt, good versus evil, the family versus individual degenerates, those who identify with a religion versus agnostics and others lacking faith, the new versus the old. These polarities generate a logic of love and hate that contaminates not only the understanding and appraisal of public institutions but also everyday personal relations.

Binary logic produces, furthermore, a belligerent sense of opposition that leads to distrust of everything that is not a part of one particular moral community: the press, intellectuals, the university, science, nongovernmental organizations, minorities, and the recently enfranchised. In their place, the down-to-earth common man reigns supreme: he who barbecues on weekends, attends church on Sundays, is on first-name terms with his barber, is close to his family, which resembles rather a united faction—who leads a daily life like that of those who voted for him. "He's our kind of people," in the words of a common refrain from the 2018 presidential campaign.

The use of social rather than traditional media aggravates the partitioning of communication. In the online free-for-all, there is no time for checking facts, documents, and sources, or for intellectual discussion, or calm consideration rather than decisions made in the heat of the moment. On the contrary, communication takes on the form of propaganda, which tends to exacerbate polarization even further. The success of such propaganda increases in tandem with the use of recognizable watchwords conveying fear, hate, safety; or the more it pushes conspiracy theories that generate such sentiments.

For this reason, to gain visibility in these digital spheres, it is enough to promote plausible political narratives, bureaucratic dystopias; they need only employ a simplified language, as succinct as it is direct. It is also advisable to choose a good enemy, one against which a group can direct all its anger and antagonism, attacking this Other's position to legitimize its own. A common feature of such narratives is a clear break with objective reality: it is better to create one's own, as long as it maintains the us-versus-them division and an emotional connection to fallacious convictions.

These are "rhetorics of divisiveness," in the words of psychoanalyst and academic Christian Ingo Lenz Dunker, which have the tendency to transform political adversaries into enemies to be neutralized or, if possible, eliminated altogether. Any hyperbole and all manner of theories are fair means in service of this goal. That "them" includes not just the corrupt, but also murderers, those lacking moral scruples, opens the way for all sorts of allegations and fabrications, as long as they help to stir the pot of these "war narratives."

While the use of the internet is somewhat novel and was massively important to the 2018 elections, there is nothing original about a strategy of confrontation, and it certainly is not some invention unique to Brazilian nationalism. This strategy is part and parcel of authoritarian discourses, which make use of theories whose origins need not be verified, as the philosopher Hannah Arendt explains in *Essays in Understanding*, a collection written between 1930 and 1954:

> For such a fabrication of a lying reality no one was prepared. The essential characteristic of fascist propaganda was never its lies, for this is something more or less common to propaganda everywhere and of every time. . . . The essential thing was that they exploited the age-old Occidental prejudice which confuses reality with truth, and made that "true" which until then could only be stated as a lie.

This sort of political platform, which aims for division at the expense of consensus and which exploits prejudice rather than confronting it, ultimately amplifies and exacerbates intolerance, which can be characterized as an inability, or a lack of the will, to recognize and respect differences in opinion, religious beliefs, values, and sexual preference. Politically, intolerance appears as a simple refusal to accept different points of view, or an attempt to erase them altogether. Not infrequently, such behavior relies on prejudice and widespread stereotypes for support. Racisms, sexisms, misogyny, anti-Semitism, homophobia, religious or political opportunism, and antipathy toward foreigners are well-known forms of social intolerance.

At the very moment when we thought that democracy had established itself as the best political system and a fundamental value—since its aim is the protection of freedom, equality, and the state of law, even if subject to constant shortcomings—we have been witnessing the growth of intolerance throughout the world, and notably in Brazil. And intolerance, of whatever kind—racial, religious, social, gender-based—is a violation of Article 7 of the Universal Declaration of Human Rights, which states, "All are equal before the law and are entitled without any discrimination to equal protection of the law. All are entitled to equal protection against any discrimination in violation of this Declaration and against any incitement to such discrimination." It also violates Article V of Brazil's 1988 constitution, which guarantees that "all are equal before the law, without any distinction, guaranteeing all Brazilians and foreigners living in Brazil the inviolable right to life, liberty, equality, safety, and property."

If we can assert that intolerance is not a sentiment or an existential position that develops overnight, and, as we have tried to show, that it has roots in the distant, the less distant, and the more recent Brazilian past—despite the habitual national denial of conflict—it is also imperative to recognize that Brazilians have now stopped concealing such sentiments, making public declarations of them with increasing frequency. This, perhaps, is the real news: what was once recondite and furtive has become the occasion for pride and self-satisfaction.

It should be noted first of all that this change in behavior tends to accelerate and become more visible at moments of open political polarization. Second, despite the continued formal functioning of Brazilian institutions, the country still lacks a truly democratic political culture that might channel this type of tension and transform it into public policy. Finally, the prolonged economic crisis Brazil is experiencing, of which the first warning signs were in 2013, and which took hold in 2014 as a full recession, a decrease in income levels, and an increase in unemployment, underlined the potential for a politics that had been little exploited up until that point: a politics of aversion. Repudiation of the corruption so commonly featured on news programs, repudiation of the lack of safety in the streets, repudiation of the growth of organized crime, repudiation of a chaotic government overtaken by private interests, repudiation of favor-trading politicians, repudiation of intellectuals and the press, repudiation of the newly enfranchised: a repudiation of everything, in the end, that fails to describe or represent "us."

Aversion is not in itself necessarily a bad sentiment: it would be a good thing, after all, if Brazilians were to develop an aversion to racism, femicide, gender crimes, or the military dictatorship, which erased the rights of all Brazilians. The crux of the problem will remain, however, if dissatisfaction only engenders greater dissatisfaction, channeled against a supposed "common enemy"—by necessity an "Other" much different from "us."

This is in fact reflected in the shape that public protests took as they swept the country in 2013. Few people noticed at the time, but already there were two opposing sides on the avenues that never came together. Prior to 2013 the street was the domain of movements of the left; suddenly, however, the spectrum of protest was simultaneously broadened and reduced: it expanded in the sense that it now included new demands, but it was constricted insofar as the public arena became clearly divided, such that the two opposing groups would never share the same space.

Democracy, ever since the Greeks, has been conceived of as a work in progress, requiring constant reworking and development. The existence of a healthy representative democracy for thirty consecutive years has not vaccinated Brazilian society against the division between, on the one hand, a more progressive society that respects human rights, and on the other, one that has grown weary of living with an economic recession while its members watch case after case on TV of corruption at the heart of the government, weary of seeing crime increase in both scale and frequency in sprawling urban slums and public safety deteriorating. This weariness in turn gave way to resentment and the direct display of conservative values—the values of those who truly want to "conserve" things, undoing what had appeared to be a shared utopia in terms of understanding, preserving, and expanding civil rights. They also attacked the political world and the homogeneity of Brazil's politicians—in general middle-class, heteronormative, older men.

A new dystopia having taken shape in the world, it made its way to Brazil, manifesting itself via a growing conviction that those who had held power until then lacked "social credibility" or had lost it on account of their inaction. In other words, with the manufacturing of this sort of general lack of faith comes the impression that everything that existed up until that point had no meaning, was lacking, and that it was therefore necessary to demand that which had been "taken" or "stolen" from Brazilian citizens. And so the figure of the "debt collector" (as in the 1979 Rubem Fonseca novel) gained traction: he who has few responsibilities yet demands his rights. The protests that swept the streets in 2013 had many facets and involved many groups and grievances from across Brazilian society. Difference is not a problem (on the contrary, it is part of the game), but intolerance is. What is certain is that ever since the impeachment of President Dilma Rousseff in 2016, the lid was lifted from a cauldron of resentments, which boiled over into a politics of deliberate hate and polarization.

Ever since then, a movement that previously had lived in secrecy has surfaced and begun to spew intransigence, having no qualms about declaring its lack of respect for differences in beliefs, sexual preference, and political opinions. The other side also grew increasingly inflexible, the left revealing its own degree of intolerance and adopting an increasingly polarizing discourse. If there was a time when we believed in the idea, discussed above, that Brazilians were a peaceful and tolerant people, few today would indulge in such bravado. Reports abound of increased violence against the LGBTQ community, of hostile reactions to the inclusion of those with disabilities in society, of xenophobic protests against immigrants and foreigners, of cases of bullying in schools and offices motivated by racial, gender, or even political differences, and we have seen too a multiplication of crimes against sacred candomblé sites.

According to a January 13, 2019 article in the *Folha de S. Paulo*, intolerance-related crimes reached a peak during the 2018 elections. During the campaign months—August, September, and October—there were sixteen cases per day: more than triple the 4.7 daily cases reported to police during the first semester of the year. The numbers peaked in October, during the first and second rounds of the election, with 568 police reports, an average of just over eighteen cases per day. Total crimes reported during the month represent 67 percent of all reports during the first six months of that year, and more than triple those registered in October 2017. Incidents of religious intolerance grew by 171 percent in relation to the total number of incidents during the preceding three-month period, homophobic incidents by 75 percent, and intolerance against immigrants and foreigners by 83 percent. Police reports related to color and racial prejudice grew by 15 percent.

Data from Disque 100—the federal government's crime hotline—show that the religions suffering the highest number of attacks were those of African origin, which were targeted in nearly 35 percent of the cases during the first semester of 2018. Harassment, attacks on *terreiros*, or religious sites, and the destruction of votive offerings are an unfortunate part of the history of candomblé in Brazil. While the religion was officially recognized during the Vargas era, it has suffered an intensification of attacks in the current political climate.

The escalation of violence also reveals the growth of intolerance. The Presidential Secretariat for Human Rights has shown that every three days a complaint of religious intolerance is registered. A report by the Grupo Gay da Bahia informs us that in 2017 the country registered a murder victim every nineteen hours. The number of cases of individuals obliged to conceal Pride badges on account of increasing attacks—from insults to physical aggression—has also risen. Foreigners visiting from Latin

America, Haiti, or Africa have also felt the bitter effects of Brazil-ians' new belligerence: in the year 2015 alone, there was a 63 percent increase in cases related to xenophobia, though only 1 percent came before a court.

Intolerance has similarly spread across social media. According to the Brazilian Internet Steering Committee, between August and October 2018, one in every three minors with access to the internet knew of someone who had experienced discrimination. Those sur-veyed reported cases of prejudice due to color or race (24 percent), appearance (16 percent), and homosexuality (13 percent). Another poll conducted around the same time, over the same period, by SaferNet, the NGO that defends human rights across Brazilian cyberspace, reveals that thirty-nine thousand pages with racist content and incitements to violence were reported for human rights violations.

The data confirm that people who until recently had felt inhib-ited in some way from demonstrating their intolerance now feel at ease, even encouraged to do so. Such a pendulum swing remains difficult to explain, however. When did Brazilians abandon their image of cordiality to devolve into the very picture of intransi-gence and aversion to difference? There is no clear answer, not least because, as we have seen, the original attitude was always a political and cultural performance rather than a faithful portrait of a society free of friction and unresolved conflict.

One crucial element can help us understand the growth of in-tolerance across the country: the deficit in quality basic education. Statistics from the Brazilian Public Safety Forum and from Data-folha polling agency for 2018 indicate that Brazilian society, on a scale of zero to ten, is currently at 8.1 in its tendency to endorse highly authoritarian positions. According to the Forum's chief ex-ecutive Renato Sérgio de Lima, the country is home to a majority that advocates violence as a form of governance and, paradoxically, judges it to be the best way to "create a peaceful society, in a sort of moral and political vendetta." The same study indicates meanwhile that the less schooling an individual has completed, the more likely he or she is to place faith in authoritarian solutions that leave little room for dialogue. After all, it is at school that students learn to coexist despite their differences and respect those who do not share the same family experiences and forms of socialization.

The response to the political, economic, social, and cultural crisis in which the country finds itself—and the effective combating of authoritarian social models, as well those of the political nature—will only come from a more inclusive and egalitarian national political vision. Only investment in solid, ample, and equitable educational provision can topple the cynicism that has taken hold of Brazilian society and move it toward the admirable utopia of one that is better informed, better educated, more critical, and capable of dialogue.

Intolerance makes fragile the rule of law, which demands respect for different ideas, experiences, practices, preferences, and customs. Democracies work better, write Steven Levitsky and Daniel Ziblatt, and survive much longer when constitutions are reinforced by unwritten democratic norms. Authoritarianism, for its part, represents the antithesis of democracy. Inspired by the 1988 Constitution and thirty years of democratic rule, Brazil has consolidated its three branches of government, made its institutions more robust, and fostered social acceptance of diversity. Still, there are signs that its institutions and even its constitution are not working as they should, and any democratic process, after all, by its very nature, is incomplete, inconclusive, and requires constant vigilance.

In the absence of better alternatives, learning from our differences continues to be a golden rule of citizenship and is part of the strengthening of Brazilian society's democratic foundations. To buy into polarization, incentivizing intolerance in the form of hate speech and reinforcement of social binaries, meanwhile, is to act against the common good, and work to sow division that will diminish the country, not make it greater.

When the End Is
Also a Beginning

THE GHOSTS OF OUR PRESENT

Brazil has a mighty past ahead of it.

—MILLÔR FERNANDES

Every history is a history of regret.

—CARLOS DRUMMOND DE ANDRADE

HISTORY TENDS to be defined as a discipline with a great capacity for "remembering." Few remember, however, how much it is capable of forgetting. There are also those who characterize history as the science of change across time. Almost no one, meanwhile, points to its potential to genuinely reiterate and repeat. Nor can Brazilian history escape the fundamental ambiguities that, at the same time as it is formed of a chain of events that build upon one another and conjure substantial changes, it is also replete with selective memories and lacunas, emphases and erasures, reliable accounts and glaring omissions, and that while in the course of the march of time cumulative changes stand out, underscored by isolated facts and events—changes in regime; coups; economic, social, and cultural transformations—it is not difficult to note the existence of structural problems and contradictions that remain basically unchanged, and so shamefully repeat themselves: the concentration of wealth and inequality, structural racism, domestic violence, and patrimonialism.

"The past never was, the past lives on," affirmed then-federal deputy Gilberto Freyre on the floor of Brazil's 1946 Constitutional Convention, in this case paying nostalgic homage to the days of yesteryear. It is this very past that now and then returns to cast its shadow, however: not as a virtue, but rather as a wandering ghost unsure of its destination. Brazil's slaveholding past, the specter of colonialism, the structures of bossism and patriarchy, of unabated corruption, of racial discrimination, gender-, sex-, and religious-based intolerance—all of these elements together tend to reappear, more alive than ever, expressed in the authoritarian governments that now and then appear on the Brazilian political scene.

Since the youthful beginnings of the Brazilian republic, although there have been many moments of greater political "normality," there have been not a few occasions when democratic rule went unrealized, and the government operated as if in a state of exception. So it was during the military republic of Deodoro da Fonseca (1889–91) and Floriano Peixoto (1891–94), both of whom governed for a portion of their terms via martial law. So it was in the 1920s, too, when martial law weighed over nearly the entire presidency of Artur Bernardes, and again under the Estado Novo dictatorship, which lasted from 1937 to 1945, when power was centralized in the hands of Getúlio Vargas and a new constitution imposed. Finally, we cannot forget the 1964 civil-military coup that deposed a legitimately elected government and installed a dictatorship that, with the promulgation of Institution Act No. 5 in 1968, suspended freedom of expression and other rights of Brazilian citizens. Perhaps now Brazil is undergoing yet another chapter in this, its history of authoritarianism, with a convincing conservative and reactionary swing delivered via the ballot box during the 2018 presidential poll.

Every government seeks to frame history in its favor, and it is no accident that governments with authoritarian tendencies tend to *create their own* histories—returning to the past in search of a mythic and ennobling narrative, with little concern for facts and figures—as a way to increase their own standing. In so doing, they recast the nation's past as a golden age (which it certainly was not), or other such "before times" (in the wonderful expression of French writer Frédéric Mistral): a paradise ruled according to patriarchal values, perpetuated across large swaths of land via extended and adopted family living nearby. These "before times" are easily transformed on the political plane into a notional era of paternalistic ties based on a closed and strictly hierarchical social group—a tender "family lexicon" that presents the leader as a father figure, tied to his brothers, children, and friends, in a community of self-styled crusaders. In summary, this type of historical narrative represents the projection of a certain civilization, a certain order, a specific social harmony with the power to guarantee the continuation of a world that never in fact existed.

This is the portrait of a past made legend. These are no more than dreams that appear as one more variation of an act of remembrance without any commitment to the present. So selective is the memory of the time invoked that it no longer belongs to history proper, but merely amounts to a certain way of remembering that history. It is an exalted, glorious history of what never was, which evokes a memory beyond time, or creates a time beyond reproach; but it should be remembered that every political moment forges its own historical reading, and that while the resulting narratives make use of many memories, they also contain several omissions, lacunae, selections, and the insertion of certain political beliefs in the place of others. The era evoked is more properly the "era of memory"—a time of unshakeable conviction where can be found a certain idealized past of lost plenitude. For this reason, the shamelessly glorifying reading of this "before time" abolishes all contradictions, any sort of violence or suffering, and so becomes myth: myth as both an interpretive framework and a form of mobilization.

202 THE GHOSTS OF OUR PRESENT

It is also an exercise in narrative and political imagination with remarkable application today, since it is founded on a nostalgia for "the good old times" and projects onto the present an image of ruins. Far from being a paradigm employed only by anachronistic regimes, this model has been ammunition for a series of authoritarian political policies that have been gaining steam across various regions of the planet. What they have in common is a base of religious, cultural, and ethnic ultranationalism, and the characteristic of delegating power and political representation to their supreme leader, soon mythicized: he who speaks for and in the place of everyone.

Memory is both a cultural product and a practice that inscribes itself on the body and is passed on as "tradition." For this reason, it is not present only in literary or historical texts. It takes form in ritual performances, which construct social memories of great power. The use of national symbols such as clothing, for example, a custom that became a reference point among Brazilian conservatives, is conducted via a memory whose drama plays out on the body.

Wherever one looks—in Recep Tayyip Erdoğan's Turkey, in Jarosław Kaczyński's Poland, in Viktor Orbán's Hungary, in Donald Trump's United States, with Matteo Salvini in Italy, Rodrigo Duterte in the Philippines, Benjamin Netanyahu in Israel, and Nicolás Maduro in Venezuela—it has become increasingly easy to find governments that, without any direct coordination, dialogue through their analogous political models: a sort of authoritarian populism, which has been testing the institutional resilience of democratic institutions in their respective countries.

These new governments have, similarly, found recourse in a host of common strategies: the selection of a glorious and mythic past; the fomenting of a grassroots anti-intellectualism and anti-journalism; a return to patriarchal society by exalting the concepts of hierarchy and order; the use of state police, or, if necessary, militias to control not only criminals but also the politically disaffected; a veritable sexual hysteria that blames women, gays,

THE GHOSTS OF OUR PRESENT 203

cross-dressers, and other minorities for the moral degeneration of their nations; an appeal to victimization (theirs and that of their allies), urging the people to rise up against bogeymen of the past; the incentive to polarization that divides the population between "them" and "us," establishing this "us" as doers and "them" as usurpers; the extensive use of political propaganda that reveals a disdain for facts, preferring instead to invent their own; the normalization of certain native communities and the concomitant aversion to immigrants, who are quickly transformed into "foreigners"; and the manipulation of the State, its institutions and laws, with an eye to perpetuating control of the machine and guaranteeing a nostalgic return to the values of land, family, and tradition, as though these represented pure, unchanging, and necessarily virtuous sentiments.

This was the glue that held together the fascist and Nazi governments of the 1930s and 40s, which invented a mythical past to justify their present actions, and it has served as a paradigm for a series of contemporary political leaders, for whom we still lack a precise name or terminology. Some analysts have suggested the term "dictocracies," to explain the rise of governments who wield a perverse combination of democratic rule and populist authoritarian practices. Nor is it inappropriate for them to have been referred to as the "new populists." What is involved is the following of legal norms up to a certain point, at which they are shaken loose via justifications that skirt the law.

For political scientist Juan Linz, young democracies do not resemble those in which the constitution and institutions function routinely; they instead teeter between dictatorship and democracy. This type of argument derives from the conviction that democracy does not depend on electoral majorities alone, nor is it limited to winning an election within the democratic order. It is also based on rules that would inhibit the creation of political, economic, and social hegemonies and the urge of a government to attack various social causes and newly enfranchised groups. In other words, democracy implies more than mere majorities at the ballot box. It is necessary to guarantee and reinforce institutionalization, so that successive reelection, the perpetuation of single parties in government, or the election of populist leaders results in more than a game to gain and maintain power and leads instead to the establishment of a true and robust democracy. Democracy is not a game that ends in ties. Its efficacy is dependent upon a continual process of critical reassessment and revision of precepts according to the demands of a continually evolving situation.

The emergency brought on by this wave of conservative governments that have inundated contemporary politics is not limited to a return to the past, nor the mere reincarnation of fascisms and populisms left behind in the first half of the twentieth century. It is inarguably a phenomenon that is as modern as it is complex. The populists of today take advantage of new forms of virtual communication by alleging that they need no intermediaries in their communication with the people; they have no scruples in manipulating and exploiting fake news as though they spoke of indisputable truths; they buy into the image of themselves as straight shooters and reformers, and attempt to blot out their own misdeeds; they accuse everyone else of corruption, despite their own entanglements; they anoint themselves as the "new" regardless of how many years they have made their living in politics; they abuse moralistic messages and use religion, family, and nation as a crutch. In the opinion of political philosopher Ruy Fausto, we find ourselves before a "new regression" that ensures oppression and exploitation, marking the return to models it once appeared we had overcome.

While these new statesmen choose a past "to call their own," then, and wield history as a tool to raise their own standing, perhaps it falls to political analysts, journalists, and social historians— and not to regimes, which, after all, are fleeting—to take on a more critical role and commitment to documenting history. In *The Age of Extremes*, Eric Hobsbawm defined historians as "professional remembrancers of what their fellow-citizens wish to forget." Peter Burke, meanwhile, calls our attention to a more humorous but no less apt characterization: "There used to be an official called the 'Remembrancer.' The title was actually a euphemism for debt collector. The official's job was to remind people of what they would have liked to forget."

If the purpose of history is thus "to leave a reminder" of that which we often make an effort to forget, in Brazil's case it is certainly worthwhile to leave a good "reminder" about the past of a country whose social structures and legacies little resemble a rich tropical Arcadia. As we have seen, many factors combined to bequeath to its inhabitants a present with fragile institutions. This fragility helped to foment corrupt practices that became ingrained in the heart of the system, mixing public and private interests with state business: wrongdoing is no longer merely a frequent phenomenon, but integral to the image of politicians and the political system. At the same time, a yawning and persistent wealth gap led to inequities in access to land, education, shelter, health, transport, and civil rights. Finally, it cannot be forgotten that at various moments in Brazil's history, authoritarian intervention has been justified in the name of national security. The problem is that at such moments, when political tempers are running high, the rights of Brazilians tend to be vilified alongside democratic rule itself.

We cannot deny that today Brazil is quite clearly a less unequal country than it was:[1] poverty has been reduced, education and health are better than they were in the past. Access to material goods has also grown, as a result of public policies over the last thirty years increasingly concerned with a more equitable redistribution of income. Notwithstanding this, however, the country's social indicators remain alarming. Though GDP is the ninth largest in the world, 40 percent of its Black population under fourteen still lives in poverty. Brazil tolerates the most violent police force in the world—its police forces arrest, kill, and die more than any others—and has the third largest prison population on the planet. Death certificates tend to have a certain color, too, as 70 percent of violent deaths, whether at the hands of police or of drug-traffickers, involve Black youth. The incidence of femicide, rape, murder, and assault against the LGBTQ community is still extremely high and is reflected in the low levels of representation of women and transgender individuals in the National Congress. Similar conditions apply to the Indigenous population, which still is kept invisible both socially and in terms of political representation, and today has its right to the land repeatedly contested.

Despite an increase in access to childhood education and the fact that 90 percent of children up to the age of three now attend some form of preschool, only 30 percent of these have access to daycare facilities. Nearly 55 percent of students still have serious trouble reading at the end of their third year of middle-school education, while the best private schools prepare the children of the elite for admission to the best—in this case, public—universities. Unemployment rose 12 percent in January 2019, to affect directly 12.7 million Brazilians. The cultural industries remain sidelined and are no longer deemed worthy of representation by a dedicated ministry. Such characteristic features of the society, persisting through five hundred years of Brazilian history, tend to become exaggerated during recessions, notably when there is a lack of political will to tackle them, and no shortage of playing to the crowd.

Yet, if the crisis that began in 2013 continues to torment Brazilians day in and day out, it also contains a seed of hope. Indeed the word "crisis," of Greek origin, carries the meaning of "decisive point," in the sense of approaching, but with a chance of stepping back from, the abyss—though of course not every crisis is provoked by recession, injustice, and unemployment. As Alexis de Tocqueville (1805–59) explained in his classic text *Democracy in America*, followed many years later by Barrington Moore Jr. (1913–2015) in *Injustice: The Social Bases of Obedience and Revolt*, social insurrections often take place soon after periods of improvement in social conditions, when there is an effort to solidify and extend hard-won rights. History has shown us that no one renounces rights and, at such moments, the newest beneficiaries tend to demand that theirs be respected.

The Brazilian experience is not untypical: people flooded the streets of the country's major cities in 2013 to demand more rights in terms of health, education, shelter, and transportation, all prescribed in the constitution. They also criticized politicians, parties, and institutions. Not even football, revered nationally notwithstanding the exorbitant salaries of some players, survived unscathed. I consider it no coincidence that during this same period, the country witnessed the beginning of a process of intensive social radicalization, in which Brazilians demonstrated growing disregard for and dwindling commitment to institutions, parties, politics, and politicians. On both the right and left, demands boiled over into resentment. Cynicism and a social vacuum, in turn, only provided more fertile ground for the ascent of self-declared outsiders, authoritarian politicians, opportunists, and populists who claim to be above the fray, despite very much playing and feeding off the same political game as everyone else. Since they cannot produce broad consensus across civil society, they bet instead, following the lessons of other emerging governments, on conflict and division.

Certainly, the 2013 protests and the political crisis that deepened with the impeachment of President Dilma Rousseff, as well as the Mensalão and Car Wash scandals, negatively impacted the image of politics across the board and were responsible for the general atmosphere of distrust. In countries with authoritarian traditions, however, crises are capable of reviving and renewing longstanding historical precedents, involving a disregard for the law and a distrust of institutions, and which point to dogmatic solutions masquerading as forms of "national salvation." At such moments, constitutions suffer, as does their capacity to serve in the coordination of conflicts and to balance the influence of political actors. Constitutions are more than collections of rules; they work, in the words of law professor Oscar Vilhena Vieira, as "mechanisms that aspire to promote democracy, regulate the exercise of power, and establish parameters of justice that ought to govern the relationship between people and between citizens the

State." They also have the capacity, as long as they are resilient, to moderate internal conflicts in a democratic manner.

Every constitution, like democracy itself, is imperfect, unfinished, and capable of being improved in its own way. The Brazilian model is extensive, and represents the result of a constitutional assembly that began on February 1, 1987 and remained in session until October 5, 1988, with the mission not only of bringing an end to the dictatorship but of providing a solid foundation for a reestablishment of democracy. Its mission was twofold: to create institutions robust enough to withstand political crises, and to establish guarantees for the recognition and exercise of the rights and liberties of Brazilians. Baptized "the People's Constitution," it is detailed and ambitious, seeking to take into account the many faces of this immense country.

Much like Brazil itself, the 1988 Constitution has its faults. It left the agrarian structure untouched, gave the armed forces control over matters of their own interest, and kept the illiterate ineligible for office—though it did approve their right to vote. It also preserved centralization under the executive, producing a sprawling state that, years later, opened the door to "supremocracy," to use a term coined by Oscar Vilhena Vieira. One result is that, notwithstanding an exhaustive and programmatic constitution, recent years have seen a concentration of powers in the judicial sphere, upsetting the balance that ought to reign among the three branches of government. If the judiciary cannot be accused of "usurpation of power," since it has not made a break with its constitutionally prescribed role, the broadening of the authority of tribunals when compared to those of presidential administrations and the National Congress has nevertheless had the immediate consequence that magistrates sometimes overstep their bounds or abuse their power, despite technically observing judicial norms. It has also led judges to transform themselves into national heroes in the war on corruption, but also to use their power for personal advantage or to satisfy certain political bents.

Nevertheless, and in spite of these "buts," the 1988 Constitution remains the best examplar of a Brazil that made a solid democratic commitment at various levels of social relations, as well as establishing sophisticated policies for the defense of human rights. It is attentive to political minorities, advanced in terms of environmental issues, and committed to the legal means and instruments of direct public participation. The body of law created at the time was a reaction, as we have seen, to the military dictatorship, which for twenty-one years had kept Brazilians from the full exercise of democracy and citizenship, and it signaled the birth of a different kind of country, open to new social actors and agents, who also participated in its construction.

Among other things, the constitution stipulated equality between men and women; an end to torture; the right of reply and indemnification for material or moral damages, or damage to one's image; and intellectual, artistic, scientific, and media freedom. It made racism a crime subject neither to bail for the offender nor a statute of limitations; determined the inviolable right to privacy and reputation; outlawed the violation of private communications; permitted access to government information and the creation of associations, and asserted the right to property; put an end to political, artistic, and ideological censorship; and established freedom of conscience, thought, religion, and political and intellectual belief.

Freedom, that most difficult of conditions to attain and maintain, in this country that long lived with slavery, thus takes the form of its constitution, a sort of safe-conduct to citizenship. Article V was absolutely necessary in the face of residual fears of the return of authoritarian regimes; and it remains crucial in the current moment.

Ever since the approval of the People's Constitution, the country has staked its future on a process that has been characterized by important victories: an impressive increase in the catalog of rights and an enduring commitment to transforming society, based on the social inclusion of millions of Brazilians who came to benefit from a new level of income and consumption. The complexity and breadth of the 1988 Constitution do not represent an impediment to reforms and adaptations; in fact, since its ratification, the number of amendments has reached one hundred. In a constitutional democracy, moreover, conflict and difference are part of the democratic process, as are forms of redress. Perhaps this is why Brazil has experienced, in the years since 1988, such a consistent and lasting period of public freedoms and solid democratic institutions.

Much has been accomplished, and, as we have seen in this brief book, much remains to be done. Nowhere is there a model or system impervious to the work of time. For this reason, a democracy functions more effectively, and survives longer, when its constitution is reinforced by shared democratic norms, both written and unwritten. Citizens will also be better equipped for active participation if we reinforce the foundations for a quality public education that is inclusive and attentive to the country's social diversities, and responsive to its most vulnerable populations, such as the Indigenous, the dispossessed, and people with disabilities. In a better-educated country, citizens will show a greater commitment to the republican spirit, in the sense of not obstructing the transit and demarcation between public and private spaces.

Only by doing this can an atmosphere of tolerance be created: when representatives of different parties are understood as legitimate rivals and thus reinforce the republican pact to which they ought to aspire. Polarization, as we have sought to explain, has the power to kill democracy, generate a rhetoric of division, and lead to the election of demagogues who do not represent the desire for justice, safety, ethics, and equality, which, I would posit, belong to all Brazilians.

The way out of the crisis that the country has experienced since 2013 can only be in the form of an ample and democratic constitutional pact, involving multiple sectors of society, via—in a country as accustomed as Brazil is to injustice—a progressive implementation of rights and of the strengthening of institutions. Constitutions act as mechanisms that seek to regulate the exercise of power, establishing parameters of justice that govern the relationships among people and between citizens and the State, and whose ultimate aim is the improvement and fortification of democracy—which is inherently imperfect. As I complete the writing of this book-length essay, the democratic rule of law has not been breached, formally at least, given that elections were contested at the ballot box and Brazil's institutions continue their routine work. However, democracy is not confined to the act of electing officials; it survives by feeding from the environment that helps to instate it, and this has taken a few hits. Manifestations of a "flirtation" with nostalgia for dictatorship that clings to a mythologized past; the messianic character of certain political representatives; attacks on minority groups, among them the Indigenous, Black men and women, and homosexual, queer, and transgender people; disrespect for forms of religion that depart from the Judeo-Christian tradition; the expansion of powers to keep historical documents classified; limitations placed on teachers alongside allegations of ideological indoctrination; the relaxation of firearm laws; the celebration of the exile of political adversaries: these have only raised fears for those who cherish democratic values and human rights. Fear works, it must be said, as the logical and practical opponent of utopias.

Each time a crisis rears its head, the deficit in Brazil's republican spirit is exposed once more at the roots of the national political community. At such moments, Brazilians feel the acute lack of an ethical agenda capable of transforming their electoral system and partisan behavior; of tackling corruption within and beyond government; of combating the violence that continues to assail their freedom to circulate in the streets. The problem is that, in the midst of these fragilities, the republic itself remains vulnerable. The country is experiencing a period of democratic recession, of social division around matters of personal conduct—fertile ground for opportunistic politicians to manipulate historical wounds with false declarations of nostalgia for an age that can never return, insofar as it ever existed in the first place.

The challenge for Brazilians is immense. Without a solid foundation and a targeted agenda, it will be difficult to address some of these themes. It will be necessary to incentivize civic-minded diversity; to combat inequality and social, cultural, and religious intolerance; to expand projects in the area of education and healthcare; to make firm commitments to the shoring up of institutions; to push back against government conduct that attacks and threatens democracy; and to demand constitutional guarantees.

Changes in the party in power, which makes possible the alternation between governments of the left and right, is healthy, and is part of the democratic regime; nor is this the first time that the country finds itself in a new political phase after the one-time opposition takes power. The greater problem lies in the danger of falling prey to the siren song of authoritarian-style governments, which make appeals based on morality and promise easy fixes. We are in need of fewer charismatic leaders, and of more conscious and active citizens.

The rights we call our own have never been rights freely granted, and these new times require—of all Brazilians—vigilance, civic duty, and a great deal of hope. Brazilian civil society has shown signs that it knows how to organize and fight for these rights. Women are not going to return to the stove, Black men and women who earned university degrees and now find themselves in leadership positions will not retreat from their posts, the LGBTQ population will continue to walk arm-in-arm through the streets, Indigenous peoples will fight and ensure their rights to their lands are recognized, and leaders of Muslim and Afro-Brazilian religious communities will openly worship their gods.

All crises have the potential to cause not only economic deficits but social, political, and cultural deficits as well. But all crises are capable of creating an opening, no matter how small, for hope. As Guimarães Rosa told us in *Grande sertão: veredas*, "The course of life leaves nothing untouched, this is life: it goes hot and cold; it sweeps us up then sets us down; it soothes to later unnerve. It demands only one thing of us: courage."

São Paulo, March 1, 2019

METHODOLOGICAL AFTERWORD

AN ANTHROPOLOGY OF HISTORY
AND OF THE PRESENT

In Praise of Anachronism

Brazilian Authoritarianism was written during the 2018 election and the first six months of Jair Bolsonaro's presidency. It is, for that reason, a book marked by the "temperature" of its immediate context and written in the awareness that writing "a history of the present" is always a test for social scientists, who generally prefer to work with processes that have come to a close and not those still under way. This is the reason, for example, that the book does not address the "denialism" of the Brazilian government in the face of wildfires in the Amazon and in the Pantanal, or its minimization of the number of deaths caused by COVID-19, making light of the deadly disease and the nation's collective grief.

Nor, in contrast to the preface and this afterword added for the present English-language edition of this book, did I include in the body of the original text (or in its translation here) details of the references on which it was based—though I did include a lengthy list of works consulted in a bibliography (see below)—not least because the book was written at the request of a Brazilian publishing house that had asked for a book that could speak to a wider public (favoring a quicker pace and the absence of bibliographical notes), though it was not for this reason less demanding in terms of its data and conclusions.

Certainly, however, the book resulted from a methodological approach strongly inspired by works that occupy the borderland between anthropology and history, between synchronic and diachronic perspectives, between framework and event. The theoretical premises that guide this book are based on two fundamental assumptions. The first is that the history of a country is a story of change—that familiar dance of facts and events—but that it is also essential to be attentive to systems that endure, repeat, or are reinforced over time. The second is the observation that "Brazil has a mighty past ahead of it." In other words, the country has inherited many legacies from "bygone eras" that continue to resonate and have meaning in "the history of now."

In this sense, *Brazilian Authoritarianism* dialogues with and is inspired by what the French critic Georges Didi-Huberman calls "praise of anachronism."[1] We return to the past with contemporary problems and pose questions about our own time. We might say, then, that this book sets up a rhetorical question that can be summarized by the concept of "a present of the past." This is because, in Didi-Huberman's words, it is impossible to anticipate the reconstruction of the "exact past," since "every past . . . should be engaged in an anthropology of time."[2]

According to Didi-Huberman, it is memory, anachronistic in effect as it reconstructs time, that is summoned and interrogated by the historian, and not the past itself. For him, then, anachronism is not some errant variant of time but rather a necessary detour, a methodology of study: there is heuristic promise in it, since in every narrative, in every image, various ages are present. History is thus seen as a reflection of temporally impure, complex, overdetermined social structures featuring polychronic, heterochronic, or anachronistic components.

As Michel-Rolph Trouillot argues, every "presentism" is a form of anachronism, since the past is constantly remade in the present, and in the process of writing history, as a representation of changes occurring over time.[3] In the act of narration, the historian links negotiation and power to our understanding of past events, even the more recent past, creating intelligibility so that the present, too, might be understood. We refer to history, therefore, not as a remittal to a proven or fixed past. As Trouillot explains, "historical authenticity resides not in the fidelity to an alleged past but in an honesty vis-à-vis the present as it re-presents that past."[4]

This is also a perspective inspired by the concept of the "chronotype," formulated by Mikhail Bakhtin, which points to "the fundamental interconnection of temporal relations and space,"[5] and the idea of "position," which concerns the distinct moments and spaces in which the events analyzed take place.

Here, then, I propose a more direct analysis, in terms of the themes of "temporality," "synchronic and diachronic analysis," and "History" (or the lack thereof) itself. To put it another way, the purpose of this afterword is to explore a methodological question essential to this book: that is, the way in which anthropology, as a discipline, conceives of history, and vice versa; or, the way in which some schools of anthropology—and different writers— have dialogued with various histories: a Western history—so to speak (and only in a provisional sense)—based on chronology and documentary proof; a history that is above all a social category (and speaks to the notion of temporality common to all societies); and a reaction to the philosophy of history, which made way for the concept of "historicities." In other words, in the face of ethnographic experience, it becomes impossible to think of history in the singular.

Let us start at the beginning, however. If we engage in the methodological debate outlined above, based on a historical anthropology, or an anthropological history, the first possibility that arises is to contrast two more obvious notions of time and, as we have seen, of history: one as repetition and another as its opposite— "nonrepetition." Just as we know that living things are born, grow, and die (and that these life changes are ineluctable), we can say that certain natural phenomena repeat (the seasons, day becomes night and vice-versa). A parallel can be drawn with the familiar distinction between the peoples supposedly "with" or "without" history: those defined by change ("hot societies" or "peoples with a history") or those characterized by repetition—designated "cold societies" by Claude Lévi-Strauss and "stagnant" by Claude Lefort.[6] But even this debate has long since been abandoned, along with the misunderstanding that surrounded it. Lefort showed how he would seek out not "empirical realities" but rather "models," just as Lévi-Strauss sought to make explicit (at various moments) how such classification served above all to name differences between cultures: "there was no pretense to define real categories but only, via a heuristic, two stages that, to paraphrase Rousseau, 'do not exist, never existed, and never will exist.'"[7]

Meanwhile this dichotomy allows us to contrast fundamental notions such as the universal and the particular. This because history can be understood as a *universal* category, since the common experience of the material passage of time is consensual, but also as *particular* at the level of the events, when occurrences are assigned cultural value. History can also be understood as a *discipline*, a technique, that works with documents and facts related to the past, but also as an *analytical category*—in other words, as a synonym for notions of time or temporality. In this case, and in the terms of the sociologist Émile Durkheim, writing at the end of the nineteenth century, we are engaging with a "basic category of thought": there is no society without it, but each culture experiences it in its own different way.[8]

As we can see, from the outset—to repurpose Lévi-Strauss's famous expression—history appears "good for thinking."[9] Insofar as it studies genealogies, rituals, and symbologies, history also allows us to envision the ways in which humanity is one—universal—but diverse in its many forms.

Now let us move our focus to this book. What is important is not to choose between the many definitions we have discussed above, but rather to rethink how the discipline of anthropology has (or has not) understood or registered history in other societies, as well as in our own: we are talking about many times, various historicities. These include histories that change in response to the rapid pace of events, but also those that repeat, returning to fundamental frameworks and contradictions that remain unresolved.

Thus I resume my central inquiry: What name should be given to the many presents in anthropological production, and how do these influence and determine historiographic experience? There are, in principle, many times: "our own," so to say, a Euro-American time, sequential and cumulative but that, despite arguments to the contrary, does not escape repetition; Nuer time which, as E. E. Evans-Pritchard shows, turns back upon itself;[10] time according to the Mendi, a people living in New Guinea who, as Marshall Sahlins notes, quoting Rena Lederman, "have interacted with foreigners without losing their sense of themselves," bringing everything to converge in their own time;[11] the pendular model found by Edmund Leach among the Kachin, where time is represented discontinuously, a repetition of inversions (day and night, winter and summer, dry and rainy, age and youth);[12] and time according to the Piaroa, as described by Joanna Overing, sometimes linear sometimes not.[13] Such a perspective makes it possible to question the evolutionary notion of cumulative, linked time that never repeats. I am proposing, however, a sort of "anthropology of history" so as to put in check our very formal rejection of anachronism. The aim is also to explain the theoretical perspectives that stitched this book together in an attempt to speak of the present through the past and of a history that looks toward the future yet reflects much of its past.

An Anthropology of History

It can be argued that what might be considered the first school of anthropology—the social evolutionist school—incorporated a historical, diachronic approach into its model. On the way from barbarism to civilization, many distinct and fixed stages were crossed, which also staked out the path that several civilizations later followed—inescapably, it was often asserted—to a single destination: the Western model of civilization and progress. Accordingly, different peoples ought to progress via the same successive, unique, and obligatory stages, and for this very reason, "human culture" always appeared, in the relevant literature, in the singular and cumulative form.[14]

Indeed, the early days of the discipline, at the end of the nineteenth century, coincide with the adoption of this evolutionist model of analysis and the illusion of "primitivism." This anthropology *avant la lettre* was the search for a single history—allusive and external to its object—founded on the idea that certain societies had remained at evolutionary ground zero: that they were living fossils, testament to the past of our own society. The Western model, characterized by a cumulative and technological evolution—this last criterion the exclusive yardstick by which to define the imperative progress—later became the trademark of a humanity defined by its unity, despite its many divisions due to inequality. It was at this time, too, that the members of these "societies without a State" came to be characterized as "primitive and eternal children."[15] After all, as they were frozen in history, there was no reason to ask about their history. As the historian of Brazil's imperial period Francisco Varnhagen explained, "Of such peoples in infancy there is no history: there is only ethnography."[16]

It was perhaps on account of the conjectural model of history that this school defended—and that became a paradigm for the era, with its hypothesis of a fixed and obligatory evolution common to all humanity—that American cultural anthropologists on the one hand and British functionalists on the other have sought to distance themselves so deliberately from history. In their view, evolutionism not only presented historical reconstitutions without any evidence, but was also predicated upon societies where the past would be irrelevant; for this reason, they advocated for recourse instead to the "ethnographic present."

Franz Boas, for example, concluded that, in the face of our disappointment at not knowing how the past unfolded, it would be better to disavow attempts at understanding history.[17] In his view, rather than assume that similar phenomena could be attributed to the same causes, it was necessary to ask for specifics and developments particular to the societies concerned, then to conduct a limited comparative analysis. It was the emphasis upon cultures considered individually that offered a solution, in its opposition to major generalizing models that rendered appeals to history mere speculation, an instrument to unify entirely different human realities.

According to Boas, for all that the evolutionist school had called for the adoption of a "historical model," it was not possible in the study of cultures to arrive at history via ethnography. In the anthropologist's opinion, in the domain of ethnography—which focuses on nonliterate societies—no historical facts appear available.[18] In other words, while history was important, it did not come within reach of the ethnographer.[19] But what history did Boas have in mind, in the end? Would it not be precisely Western history (divided chronologically and supported by written records) and, as a matter of principle, not to be found in the cultures he studied? Boas would never ignore the importance of history; he merely seemed to be resigned to its absence. As he explained, "It would be an error to claim, as some anthropologists do, that for this reason historical study is irrelevant. The two sides of our problem require equal attention, for we desire to know not only the dynamics of existing societies, but also how they came to be what they are."[20]

As Lévi-Strauss jibed, in his text "History and Anthropology," Boas had expressed disappointment at having to renounce his aspiration to understand "not only how things are, but how they have come to be."[21] The question, the French ethnologist teased, was whether a history of the present was possible without recourse to the past—an understanding of the present without retracing its development. It was a matter, then, of introducing a methodological turn: to think of other histories (plural) with concepts of time different from those known and defined by Western historians.

Still more radical was the position of those composing the so-called British functionalist school, who in the face of this challenge appear to have opted to deprive themselves of any diachronic analysis. A. R. Radcliffe-Brown, for example, radicalized the argument by also generalizing it: recourse to history would only bring "subjectivity" to any scientific analysis. To this end, he even established a radical distance between disciplines: "Ethnography differs from history in that the ethnographer derives his knowledge, or some major part of it, from direct observation of or contact with the people about whom he writes, and not, like the historian, from written records."[22] History, meanwhile, was "the study of records and monuments for the purpose of providing knowledge about conditions and events of the past."[23] Taking up the same theme from the standpoint of method alone, Radcliffe-Brown purged history from his analysis and in its place opted for "the ethnographic present":

> The acceptability of a historical explanation depends on the fullness and reliability of the historical record. In the primitive societies that are studied by social anthropology there are no historical records. We have no knowledge of the development of social institutions among the Australian aborigines for example. Anthropologists, thinking of their study as a kind of historical study, fall back on conjecture and imagination."[24]

Once again it was Lévi-Strauss who satirized this type of paradox claiming, in a 1949 article, that "a little history . . . is better than no history at all."[25] Ethnology and ethnography would, then, become models of the present, synchronic models, subject to a significant degree to the absence of written documents, while it would fall to history to limit itself to the past and abandon analysis of the present. But the problem was not exclusively one of methodology, since it implied ignorance of the fact that history also existed in the present tense, or, additionally, that other histories and temporalities were inscribed in ethnography itself and in the immediate context.

E. E. Evans-Pritchard would find another solution in the series of lectures he gave for the BBC in 1950. Calling the debate between anthropology and history a "domestic quarrel," the ethnographer remade the borders at the same time as he diluted them. He reflected that "to know a society's past gives one a deeper understanding of the nature of its social life at the present time; for history is not merely a succession of changes but . . . a growth. The past is contained in the present as the present is in the future."[26] Evans-Pritchard again took up, in this way, the topic of history and introduced a new key point: history dealt with processes of development, and from this perspective no society exists that does not construct its history, even if synchronically. Informed by French historiography, the English anthropologist concluded that "history is not a succession of events, it is the links between them."[27] Or, better yet, it is the ways in which societies produce their own arguments and structures that persist in the extended time of anachronism.

In some sense, this is the methodology followed in Evans-Pritchard's study *The Nuer*, when, still in the 1940s, he confronted the specificity of the category "time" in this North African society. In this work, he seeks to understand how concepts such as time and space are determined by the physical environment but also, and at the same time, according to structural principles. For this reason, the longest times or periods are nearly always structural, while the briefest times are ecological—with interactions between both. Further, while structural time is progressive and cumulative, ecological time appears cyclical and constrained.[28]

Evans-Pritchard's proposal seems to suggest another way to conceive time and, overall, a broader way of conceiving history: not "our history" (or the history of the subject of knowledge), but a history internal to the group—a history constructed according to native categories. Incidentally, in his "Marett Lecture," given in 1950, Evans-Pritchard would return to this theme, arguing that the term "history" contains two meanings. By the first, history came to be a "collective representation of events," and, accordingly, is

not so distant from the notion of myth. It was the second definition that the anthropologist would oppose, however: the idea that
history is a discipline interested only in collecting and interpreting
documents. In light of this, Evans-Pritchard would, without citing
names, return to the question expressed by Franz Boas. After all,
concluding that nineteenth-century studies were less than careful
in their historic reconstructions did not entail history's obligatory
abolition.[29] On the contrary: in a 1961 article appropriately entitled "Anthropology and History," Evans-Pritchard outlines the
impasses resulting from an anthropology that went from being
ahistoric to antihistoric, involving the largely uncritical use of
documentary sources, a lack of effort in reconstructing a past according to records and oral tradition, the accepted thinking that
before European domination native populations were static—
frozen in time—ignorance of the fact that the past is part of the
present, and the certainty that it was possible simply to abolish
social change. In effect, the English anthropologist insisted, "the
process of change could not adequately have been understood
unless placed in the crucible of history. . . . Those who ignore history condemn themselves to not knowing the present."[30] Updat-
ing himself, Evans-Pritchard cites Lévi-Strauss's 1949 essay "Race
and History," and then refers to Louis Dumont to summarize his
point of view: "History is the movement whereby a society reveals
itself for what it is."[31]

In fact, Evans-Pritchard was more worried about some of the
consequences of what he called "the ignorance of history," not
least because, in his opinion, the two disciplines had similar objectives: "to translate ideas into other terms and render them intelli-
gible." He warned, "In recent years there has been a growing interest among anthropologists in the history of the simpler peoples
they have studied, either from the point of view of history as a
record of events which have brought about social changes or from
the point of view of history as a representation of these events."[32]

The question, then, could not be reduced to a quarrel between
disciplines, but involved reflecting on narrative regimes: How to

tell a synchronic history always in anachronistic form? How to replace history in the singular with history in the plural? This problem seemed, however, to be the order of the day—such that, simultaneously, Lévi-Strauss would be writing the first of his texts to be entitled "History and Anthropology." In this essay, which served as the introduction to *Structural Anthropology*—a collection of articles written from 1944 to 1956—the ethnologist rewrote the discipline's own history to include history, or the lack thereof, as one of its axes. It was not Evans-Pritchard with whom the French ethnologist was dialoguing, however, in his well-known and highly criticized 1949 article. In this essay, it is British functionalism—and it is known that Radcliffe-Brown vehemently objected to this common grouping, which he claimed was an invention of Malinowski[33]—that seems to be called into in question: "We might ask," Lévi- Strauss affirmed, "whether, by banning all history on the premise that ethnologists' history is not worthy of consideration, they have not gone to too great extremes."[34]

With this text, the ethnologist initiated an entirely new critique, no longer methodological but epistemological, of social evolutionism and what might be termed the philosophy of history. As Lévi-Strauss would write in *Race and History*, "all human societies have behind them a past of approximately equal length. . . . This ellipsis simply means that their history is and will always be unknown to us, not that they actually have no history. . . . In actual fact, there are no peoples still in their childhood; all are adult, even those who have not kept a diary of their childhood and adolescence."[35]

For Lévi-Strauss, then, peoples without history do not exist; what exists are different ways in which societies *represent themselves* in relation to history: some reserve a special place for history, others deny its importance. We find ourselves faced with different "ways" of conceiving of history and temporality itself: one progressive, which accumulates findings and inventions—and therefore confers a central role to temporality—and another, equally active, but which dissolves in something of a spiral movement.

Meanwhile, even recognizing two models of history, there is not sufficient support for the notion of peoples "without history," and much less for the supposed existence of differences of nature—or essence—between these different societies.

This is also the position of Claude Lefort who, in this context, published the text "The Forms of History." Taking up notions from Lévi-Strauss, Lefort introduced the concept of "historicities." Different cultures would have different "historicities," since one could confirm variations between a history governed by a principle of conservation or repetition and a history—such as ours—that, by definition, opens space for the new; between, that is, a visible history—a reading of change—and an invisible history (which erases all vestiges of itself). For these and other reasons, Lefort would claim that it was incorrect to speak of history in the singular. "There are societies whose form remained indubitably the same for millenia and which, despite the most varied events for which they were the theater . . . are organized according to this refusal of the historic."[36] Lefort defined these societies as "without history" not to conclude that they had not undergone change, but to place in relief their tendency to "neutralize the effects of change." According to this conclusion, "the 'stagnant' societies did not situate themselves beyond the era of historical development, they determined the conditions of their stagnation."[37]

Differently, therefore, from Hegel, for whom history begins with the Western nation-state, Lefort is interested in the duration of societies that refuse history—or at least, this Western model of history. For this reason, ethnology would shed light on the existence of distinct historicities, seeking to access not primitive forms of human evolution but rather comparable elements among ways of becoming: forms of temporality. Lefort closes his essay by showing how we all find ourselves before "a common humanity, caught up in similar questions, though finding different solutions in response."[38]

With these considerations in mind, it is worth returning, yet again, to Lévi-Strauss's "History and Anthropology," with which

Lefort himself maintained a dialogue. Originally published in the *Revue de metaphysique et de morale*, the essay not only signaled the specific nature of the ethnology that Lévi-Strauss sought to practice but also prefaced what he considered the fundamental dilemma of anthropology: "the problem of reconstructing a past whose history we are incapable of grasping confronts ethnology more particularly; the problem of writing the history of a present without a past confronts ethnography."[39] In this article, which, as we have seen, opens the famous collection *Structural Anthropology*, one of Lévi-Strauss's claims was that localized studies would only be justified as a prelude to more general inquiries. The absence of written documents, then, could be overcome to some extent by comparative study.

The essay began, therefore, by declaring a harmonious coexistence between anthropology and history. After all, in the ethnologist's eyes, the similarities between the two disciplines were much more evident than their differences: both study other societies, in general those in which we have not lived—whether in time or space. Further, Lévi-Strauss easily discarded other dichotomies between the disciplines: of time (in the case of history), and of space (in the case of anthropology). According to the French structuralist, "in both cases we are dealing with systems of representations which differ for each member of the group and which, on the whole, differ from the representations of the investigator."[40]

The debate then began to play out in an increasingly narrow direction. The difference between the two disciplines appears not to lie in their object (the Other), still less their objective (the manifold), nor even their methods (more or fewer documents). Meanwhile, a new dichotomy was beginning to appear: "History organizes its data in relation to conscious expressions of social life, while anthropology proceeds by examining its unconscious foundations."[41] According to this perspective, history, as a discipline, would have a relationship to anthropology like that of ethnography to ethnology. The difference, however, was not one of technique. With this distinction, Lévi-Strauss established the foundations of a structural

anthropology and at the same time declared his intellectual project. Seeking his principal foundations in structural linguistics, the
ethnologist not only created a clean slate (in his own way) for
anthropological production but disqualified a certain type of historiography that was being developed at that time, with a new
distinction: anthropology traveled from the particular to the universal and history from the explicit to the implicit.

The essay appeared strategic not in its intent to disqualify historical practice, but rather in its affirmation of the structuralist
model. Forty years later, the French master would again defend his
position: "As a starting point for my article I took the following
extremes into consideration: history as traditionally conceived . . .
on the one hand; and on the other ethnology as we practice it with
the help of structuralist analysis." It was not, he said, that he was
unaware of the works of Lucien Febvre and his followers: "My
article intended to show that a fatal and decrepit opposition ought
to give way to works that ethnologists and historians today can
realize side by side."[42]

Lévi-Strauss would himself attempt to revisit the question in a
new article presented on July 2, 1983, on the occasion of a conference series in honor of Marc Bloch.[43] Though it had the same
title—"History and Anthropology"—there are no explicit references to the previous text and, differently from the first, this essay
begins with (brief) praise for the oeuvre of Bloch. Once again,
Lévi-Strauss examines what he calls "the close relationship between ethnology and history," and draws three new distinctions.
First, history addressed complex societies while anthropology ex-
amined archaic ones. Further, history filtered through the analyses
of the powerful classes in the way anthropology would deal with
the popular universe. And finally—and here we are not properly
speaking of a distinction—"it was thanks to anthropology that historians realized the importance of these obscure manifestations."

The debate then moves to the following issue: "All societies
are historical but only some openly admit it; others prefer to
ignore it."[44] Consequently, societies could be classified not

according to their degree of historicity, but rather according to the way in which they "represent" it: the way in which collective thought opens to history; or in which some societies view it as a threat and seek to undo it, or view it as an instrument to transform the present.

Here there is an important change in the argument: taking time as an analytic category, there is no society that is not historic. Furthermore, to choose structuralism does not mean to refuse history. This was how Lévi-Strauss deployed concepts like that of *house*, which for him contained, at the same time, structure and history, alliance and kinship. Consequently, in analyzing marriage among cousins across societies in different eras and locations, he demonstrates how societies "heat up" or "cool off"—that is, open themselves or close themselves off to history, according to agency, manipulation of the languages of kinship, and the expansion of alliances.

What is important here is that Lévi-Strauss, without abandoning his method, found new points of convergence between the two disciplines. He concluded, "As it is hardly plausible that human societies divide in two neat categories, some corresponding to structure, others to historic events, to doubt that structural analysis applies to some [societies] leads to rejecting it in all cases."[45] There are, in this sense, no essential differences, and, in Lévi-Strauss's own words, "All that the historian or ethnographer can do, and all that we can expect of either of them, is to expand a specific experience to the dimensions of a more general one."[46]

The category of time, then, refers to the very relativity that exists between cultures: there is no society that does not conceive of time; they vary according to the way they represent it. But this is only a first step. In reality, the problem of history, with its various meanings, reveals the way Lévi-Strauss deployed ethnology, with the aim of developing a critique of the universalizing role that history assumed in Western society. If up to this point we have basically worked with two categories—the "history of historians"[47] (or a disciplinary technique), and history as an analytic concept (or as temporality)—it is possible to add the critique that Lévi-Strauss went on to make to the philosophy of history.[48]

And so, in opposing the idea that there was some privileged meaning to be found in history, some defining feature of humanity itself, the ethnologist published a final chapter in *The Savage Mind*, addressed to history as practiced by the philosopher Jean-Paul Sartre. Lévi-Strauss here dialogues with the philosophy of history and, above all, with a certain rationalist reading of history: "a good deal of egocentricity and naivety is necessary to believe that man has taken refuge in a single one of the historical or geographical modes of his existence."[49] The accusation against Sartre, in particular, is that he is isolating our society from others when he seeks to invoke "historical consciousness" as a universal: "The anthropologist respects history, but he does not accord it a special value. . . . Even history which claims to be universal is still only a juxtaposition of a few local histories. . . . History is therefore never history, but history-for."[50] Every history is a selection, and our own Western conception could be reduced to a single code: chronology. To this end, one need only contrast this model to the singularity of the "savage mind": its timeless character, its way of capturing the world in its synchronic and diachronic totality, its way of instilling a circular time.

Lévi-Strauss thus arrived at fundamental conclusions in this debate that distinguished between forms of designating historicity and identified the problems inherent in assuming there to be a single history that would, putatively, be universal. Taking diversity as his starting point, the anthropologist calls attention to the existence of as many histories as there are cultures, religions, and kinship systems. For this reason, the distinction between "cold" and "hot" history is but one way to think of alterity. "It does not postulate, between societies, a difference in nature . . . but refers to the subjective attitudes that societies adopt towards history, to the variable ways in which they conceive it."[51] According to Lévi-Strauss, what changes is rather the ways in which societies represent themselves before history.[52]

More than indict the bad conscience of a philosophy of history, as the last redoubt of Western philosophy, or merely remind us that each society dictates its own passage of time, in this text Lévi-Strauss declares, as Marcio Goldman explains, that

> distinct historicities peculiar to each society or culture constitute the private form through which these societies react to the ineluctable fact that they are either in time or in the process of becoming. In this sense, both "the history of historians" and "the philosophy of history" are constituent parts of our private form of historicity or, at least, of the dominant form in the West for many centuries now.[53]

Anchoring his analyses in concrete societies, Lévi-Strauss shows us, then, how, for structuralism, historical transformations take form through inversions of logic, according to which the elements of our experience of the concrete world are constantly remade, permitting changes in representations.[54] According to his definition, "structural analysis does not reject history. On the contrary, it grants it a pre-eminent place."[55]

The debate would continue and gain new exponents of this structural history, which is not linear but turns back upon itself and its past in the present. Among these, it is worth noting anthropologist Marshall Sahlins, who defined himself as a "historical structuralist," seeking to understand how cultures carry their own readings and historicities. Temporality itself is taken up by Sahlins, in its social capacity, given the impossibility, in his view, of separating synchronic perspectives from diachronic ones. In his *Historical Metaphors and Mythical Realities* (1986) in particular, Sahlins first entered the debate between structure and history. As he wrote, "The great challenge to a historical anthropology is not merely to know how events are ordered by culture, but how, in that process, the culture is reordered. How does the reproduction of a structure become its transformation?"[56] The challenge was therefore to call attention to the way in which any historical rereading is always based on previous structures and questions of the present. "People act upon circumstances according to their own cultural presuppositions, the socially given categories of persons and things."[57]

In *Islands of History*, Sahlins calls this process "the functional re-evaluation of the categories." In other words, "History is culturally ordered, differently so in different societies. . . . The converse is also true: cultural schemes are historically ordered."[58] This problem would lead not so much to the explosion of the concept of history by the anthropological experience of culture, as to its introduction into historical experience, breaking wide open the anthropological concept of culture and including structure—in other words, the organization of the current situation in terms of the past. It is this that Sahlins calls "the structure of the conjuncture":[59] the way in which cultures react to an event (a culturally significant occurrence), bringing the immediate context into dialogue with previously existing cultural and social structures. History is, in this way, constructed as much within a society as between societies, which reestablish past structures in the orchestration of the present. It is also via this perspective that the anthropologist introduces the notion of "cultural dynamic," which proposes that the production of content is related to the present context but is retranslated according to previous models to be found in the past.

Sahlins's work further points to the question of power. In his explanation of the deep roots of certain symbols, rituals, and representations, he demonstrates how anthropological study, in its search for fixed values, neither need nor ought to shut its eyes to history and change. Finally, he reveals the way in which political practice carries, by its very logic, symbolic and ritual dimensions that articulate past and present and thereby exert their power.

Following a parallel line of thought, Clifford Geertz realizes, in *Negara: The Theatre State in Nineteenth-Century Bali*, an excursion that looks from present to past. Reframing the history of Indonesia in terms of the practice of the Negara, the anthropologist not only develops a critique of Western political philosophy, but defines his own concept of history: "The history of a great civilization can be depicted as a series of major events—wars, reigns, and revolutions. . . . Or it can be depicted as a succession not of dates, places, and prominent persons, but of general phases of sociocultural development."[60] The first approach corresponds to the genre of historiography defined as *evenementielle*. The second, meanwhile, understands historical change as a relatively continuous *social and cultural process*.

On the other hand, in the revelation of the symbolic dimensions of state power in Indonesia would reside the possibility of finding alternative ways of thinking about power and the Western version of the state.[61] Analyzing the relevance of state ceremony, performed as grand political theater, Geertz puts into perspective, within the limits of history, our Western concept of power, "heir despite itself to the sixteenth century, [to which] most of modern political theory clings."[62] The ceremony, he explains, is an experience that includes and involves "an extended, socially constructed gloss, a collective representation."[63]

Geertz's analysis in *Negara* represents a way of finding "peripheric" and native forms of speaking of politics and powers and of showing, following this line of inquiry, other historicities, recognized, in this case, by a method as particular as it is contested: "doing history backward."[64] Here I cite Geertz in his 1968 book *Islam Observed*:

> What we want to know is, again, by what mechanisms and from what causes these extraordinary transformations have taken place. And for this we need to train our primary attention neither on indices, stages, traits, nor trends, but on processes, on the way in which things stop being what they are and become instead something else. . . . In a sense, to pose the problem as I have—how our countries got to where they are from where they were—is to do history backward. . . . Life, as Kierkegaard said, is lived forward but understood backward.[65]

In sum, what we are underlining are models that show how processes of the present are determined and recognized via structures of the past. Particularly in Brazil, the object of my research, a series of investigations has reconsidered approaches to this "history of the encounter" and questioned the image of native Brazilians as "passive elements" in their own history. We may recall the anthologies of Manuela Carneira da Cunha, Bruce Albert and Alcida Ramos, Bruna Frenchetto and Michael Heckenberger, and the article by Eduardo Viveiro de Castro and Manuela Carneiro da Cunha whose focus is not only the (Western) history of Brazil's Indigenous, but an Indigenous history on its own terms.[66] There is, as well, an entire series of writings attentive to the political aspects of domination, including the works of John Monteiro, Robin Wright (who analyzed the various forms of conversion among Indigenous peoples), Pedro Puntoni (who showed the role of the Indigenous in the development of colonial northeast Brazil), Cristina Pompa (who addressed, based especially on documents from missionaries, the role of the "Tapuias" of the backlands of the Northeast in the seventeenth century), and Beatriz Perrone-Moisés, in her look at colonial-era legislation."[67]

We might also mention the research of Joanna Overing, which defends, according to Piaroa theories of history, "a (modified) relativist stance, such as that of Vernant who argues that different types of cultural order have their own historical practice."[68] In addition, a history that can more properly be called Indigenous has been gaining strength, one that, rather than considering the entire discourse about non-European peoples useful only for illuminating our "representations of the Other," asks instead how, in the words of Eduard Viveiros de Castro, these "Others represent their Others: Others that are Others because their Others are other than our own (us, for example)."[69] An example can be found in David Kopenawa's *The Falling Sky*, which is at once autobiography, shamanic manifesto, and indictment of the destruction of the forest.[70]

This alternative represents a two-way constructivism, whereby the field of anthropology recognizes that its theories have always expressed a pact, continuously negotiated throughout history, between the worlds of the observed and the observer, and that the best anthropology will always be a "symmetrical anthropology," in the terms of Bruno Latour.[71]

History as Myth of Western Modernity

If anthropology is the discipline of Otherness, or, to use Maurice Merleau-Ponty's definition, a "way of thinking when the object is the Other that demands our own transformation,"[72] this permits us to reflect on the way that history allows us to think and understand not just diversity, but many temporalities, among them anachronism and chronology. Thus it is worth returning one last time to Lévi-Strauss and his theory that, for us, it is history that functions as myth. As he said, "History has replaced mythology and fulfills the same function, that for societies without writing and without archives the aim of mythology is to ensure that as closely as possible—complete closeness is obviously impossible—the future will remain faithful to the present and to the past."[73]

History, then, is our great social narrative, or our political ideology. Lévi-Strauss asserts just this with reference to the role played by the French Revolution, which "can be made clear through a comparison between myth and what appears largely to have replaced it in modern societies, namely, politics."[74] The self-awareness of history is part of societies that internalize history's progression, which would make ours a society "pro-history." In this sense it is possible to turn our gaze upon our own society and understand our forms of narrative.

The German historian Reinhart Koselleck, appealing to different models and schools, accomplished a great feat in attempting to historicize the notion of "history." In so doing, he constructed a kind of archeology of notions of history at different periods in time, and describes each. He points out, for example, that it was Cicero (106–43 BCE) who coined the expression *historia magistra vitae*. This expression would in turn engender other metaphors related to history's various tasks: as the witness of time, the light of truth, life of memory, the herald of antiquity. According to Koselleck, since the time of the Greeks, it has been a *topos* that history is the teacher of life, serving in the role of school. This interpretation would be abandoned in modernity, with its ideas of rupture and change.

It was only in the eighteenth century, Koselleck writes, that the term "history" took on new meaning. Up until that point, in German, the word *Historie* was employed when the subject was *historia magistra vitae*, as in a report, a narrative of events. From the eighteenth century onward, the term *Geschichte* came into use, indicating the event itself, and not its recounting. The use of the term then changed: "History [*Geschichte*] as unique event or as a universal relation of events was clearly not capable of instructing in the same manner as history [*Historie*] in the form of exemplary account."[75]

Koselleck notes that history was soon expected to provide a broader representation: it was responsible for shedding light on the seemingly hidden motives that could explain events—not just describe them chronologically. At this point, history (*Geschichte*) becomes defined not as a single, unified history—universal history—but as the history of the world. It is no longer a particular history or histories offering specific models of conduct, but a universal organizational history.

If *Historie* made use of examples from the past such that time could be reapproached and described countless times, *Geschichte* pivots toward the unknown, to a future that can be staked out. Koselleck thus describes the expression "to make history" as a formulation typical of "modern experience."[76] In his view, it is during the eighteenth century, amid this new, self-referring reformulation of modern universal history or "history itself"—this abstract and singular collective composed of all the many histories of humanity in a shared past, present, and future—and in light of the abdication of extra-historical jurisdictions, such as religion or nature, that history comes to be seen as a separate discipline.

This investment in the differentiation of the future in relation to the past, with the increasing speed and magnitude of changes, the feeling of authenticity as historical expectation for the period to come, and the centrality of *action,* joined with the concept of progression, are key components of modernity. Further, upon acquiring its historic quality, time becomes something more than a frame in which events take place. On the contrary, this process—the creation of a *historical time* as part of "history itself"—is defined by Koselleck as the temporalization of history: "Progress and historical consciousness reciprocally temporalize all histories into the singularity of the world-historical process. Without resort to a Hereafter, world history becomes the tribunal of the world, with [this phrase of] Schiller's . . . being immediately invoked and continually cited as evidence of the change. The consciousness of epochal uniqueness likewise entered the long term as a criterion of the later so-called *Neuzeit* (modernity)."[77] "Making history" or "going down in history" are therefore concepts directly connected to the process of temporalization of history and its hegemonic narrative, above all in Western societies.

Anthropologist Bruno Latour, who has systematically analyzed contemporary Western temporality, claimed that

> the modern passage of time is nothing but a particular form of historicity. . . . Anthropology is here to remind us: the passage of time can be interpreted in several ways—as a cycle or as decadence, as a fall or as instability, as a return or as a continuous presence. . . . [The] moderns indeed sense time as an irreversible arrow. . . . As Nietzsche observed long ago, the moderns suffer from the illness of historicism. They want to keep everything, date everything, because they think they have definitively broken with their past. . . . The past remains, therefore, and even returns."[78]

The premise of *Brazilian Authoritarianism* is precisely this, the idea that a country's present is entirely impregnated by its past. Contemporary practices like corruption, bossisms, racisms, femicide, sexisms, intolerance, patrimonialism, and endemic violence are traits of the here and now, but they echo structures of the past.

It is also no accident that the book begins with a controversy over Brazilian national history: the first call for work issued by the Brazilian Historical and Geographical Institute, in 1846, was entitled, appropriately, "How to Write the History of Brazil," a demonstration that for the recently independent country, it was necessary to train engineers, lawyers, and doctors, but also to produce its own narrative based on events that necessarily lived in the past.

Furthermore, for those who were victorious in Brazil's November 2018 elections, history plays a crucial role. It is evoked as though it were a "restorative nostalgia" that seeks to reconstruct a missing "home" and finds its truth in myths and symbols of a past that never in fact existed.[79]

Hans Castorp, the central character in Thomas Mann's *The Magic Mountain*, was a young man whose history recovered a "story [that] . . . belongs to the long ago" and "is already, so to speak, covered with historical mould, and unquestionably to be presented in the tense best suited to a narrative out of the depth of the past."[80] Covered with "historical mould" are Castorp, his cousin Joachim, Claudia, Dr. Behrens, Settembrini, and Naphta, who reside in the Berghof sanatorium, located in the Swiss village of Davos-Platz. There can be found a laboratory of a diseased Europe, where, united by illness, anxieties, illusions, grief, and utopia intersect. High above the earth's surface, time is subject to new rules and to the monotony of a routine of medical examinations, strolls, meals, schedules, and rest regimens.

Immersed in this full schedule, our Castorp, "by nature . . . passive," finds his stay extended in this place where time takes on a different rhythm and duration. As Thomas Mann explains,

> Since histories must be in the past, then the more past the better, it would seem, for them in their character as histories, and for him, the teller of them, rounding wizard of times gone by. With this story, moreover, it stands as it does to-day with human beings, not least among them writers of tales: it is far older than its years; its age may not be measured by length of

days, nor the weight of time on its head reckoned by the rising or setting of suns. In a word, the degree of its antiquity has no ways to do with the passage of time—in which statement the author intentionally touches upon the strange and questionable double nature of that riddling element.[81]

Mann cements his narrative, therefore, with this history, whose length is not measured in days but by this "riddling element" called time. Riddling and problematic, because this history is not so old: written in the years following the First World War, the book relates events that took place not long before it. Mann insists, however, on showing how time "is a riddling thing, and hard it is to expound its essence."[82] The story soon moves on, and Castorp avers that the seven years he spent on top of the mountain appeared no longer than seven days; or that at times, everything he remembered was the exact opposite of what happened: that he had lived in that place much longer than in reality. As the author noted, "Both were probably true: when he looked back, the time seemed both unnaturally long and unnaturally short, or rather it seemed anything but what it actually was—in saying which we assume that time is a natural phenomenon, and that it is admissible to associate with it the conception of actuality."[83] What eluded Castorp was precisely a palpable sense of time, our Western concept of temporality: the month of October that was about to begin, or even the reality of days on a calendar, which follow a process that appears progressive and conclusive.

In Castorp's eyes, "time passed, it ran on, the time flowed onward and so forth—no one in his senses could consider that a narrative."[84] How much time, in the end, did he spend up there? Mann's book obliges us to remember the way in which—among us, as well—time and history, like the time spent on holiday, which passes quickly but stretches on in our memory, are matters to be negotiated: ambiguous in their understanding, plural in their outcomes, swift to change but reiterative, insistent upon returning.

History, understood in the West as a chronological series, as progressive time, is the central theme of our society, which always behaved as a "pro-history" society. For this reason, it is worth paying attention to the central position history plays in our thought: it is a crucial part of our great social narratives and our form of representation, stitching together events. History has also played a strategic part in the narratives of recent governments rooted in populism, technocratism, and authoritarianism, which seek to justify the present via a certain past that has been mythified, sugar-coated—and never took place.

This is a book about history and power, about narratives of the present that mirror and return to the past. It also shows the way in which the production of historical narratives involves uneven levels of participation among competing groups and individuals, who have different levels of access to the means of this form of production. As Trouillot showed, in the case of Haiti's history, "the ultimate mark of power may be its invisibility; the ultimate challenge, the exposition of its roots."[85]

Brazilian Authoritarianism is similarly a work directed toward "anachronistic space," in Anne McClintock's splendid phrase. McClintock establishes a distinction between panoptical time and anachronistic space: with the first, a universal narrative of history is told from an invisible geographical point; in other words, it can be told from anywhere, as long as that place be located in Europe or the West. Anachronistic space functions within panoptical time and is what establishes which societies are considered modern and which remained in archaic time, or, in other words, did not evolve. It is also within the narrative of anachronistic space that the construction of unstable sexualities takes place. It is in this historic time that languor—a characteristic that society has determined to be feminine—comes to be linked to Black and Indigenous populations and acquires negative connotations, such as being a sign of impotent masculinity, in comparison to the White man whose noble and hegemonic masculinity spurs him to constantly set his sights upon and make his path toward new horizons.

This is also the underlying model of the Bolsonaro aesthetic, which has increasingly asserted itself over these last three years of a government that has sought to create criteria of normalization based on heteronormativity, Christian religious traditions, critiques of feminism, rejection of Black and Indigenous movements, and discrediting of science, of the academy, of journalism, and of democratic institutions. But the current president is merely a symptom of an authoritarian Brazil whose history of the present sheds light on structures of the past.

It was Thomas Mann who showed, atop his Magic Mountain, the way in which history "is far older than its years." It is fundamental above all to governments that prefer to invent their own narrative of the past and thus justify their actions in the present. Here, my intention has been precisely the contrary: to locate in this past and its vestiges structures that, in their obstinacy, insist on leaving their mark on the present.

APPENDIX

GLOSSARY OF BRAZILIAN POLITICAL PARTIES

THE BRAZILIAN political system might bewilder readers in the US or UK upon first glance. Rather than a pair, or handful, of electorally viable political parties, Brazil has no fewer than thirty-three. This has a considerable impact upon the ability of the executive to govern, and most administrations rely on broad coalitions of ideologically disparate political parties to advance their priorities. As is shown in this book, this is often also a driver of political corruption. The list below is limited to those parties that are referenced in the book.

Avante. The name translates as "Forward" or "Onward." This small centrist to center-left party was founded in 1989 after splitting from the Brazilian Labor Party.

Brazilian Democratic Movement (MDB; formerly PMDB): Movimento Democrático Brasileiro. Growing out of the only legal opposition party during the dictatorship that ruled the country from 1964 to 1985, the MDB is centrist to center-right party. In a political system that necessitates alliances to allow presidents to govern, the MDB has been a kingmaker for much of the last thirty years, forming alliances first with Fernando Henrique Cardoso's PSDB from 1994 to 2002, and then with the Workers' Party from 2002 to 2016, when party leader and then-vice president Michel Temer conspired with opposition politicians to remove Dilma Rousseff from office.

Brazilian Social Democracy Party (PSDB): Partido da Social-Democracia Brasileira. The party of former president Fernando Henrique Cardoso, the PSDB was founded in the aftermath of the military dictatorship that came to an end in 1985. Originally a center to center-left party, it has increasingly drifted rightward, especially following the election of the PT's Lula to the presidency in 2002. It is, with the PT and the MDB, one of the three major Brazilian political parties. It is currently a liberal, center-right party.

Brazilian Socialist Party (PSB): Partido Socialista Brasileiro. Its name notwithstanding, the PSB is now a centrist party.

Brazilian Labor Party (PTB): Partido Trabalhista Brasileiro. A progressive party, founded in 1981. Abolished during the dictatorship that ruled from 1964 to 1985, the party in its previous, original formation was that of president-cum-dictator Getúlio Vargas, who was responsible for instituting labor laws that largely persist to this day. In the 2018 elections, Ciro Gomes—a former member of prior PT governments—ran for the presidency, but did not make it through to the runoff.

Christian Labor Party (PTC): Partido Trabalhista Cristão. A right-wing party founded in 1985, the PTC was originally founded as the Youth Party, changing its name in 1989 to the National Reconstruction Party and electing Fernando Collor to the presidency that year in the first direct elections since the end of a twenty-year dictatorship in 1985. Since Collor's 1992 impeachment on corruption charges, the party has failed to elect federal representatives, even after changing to its current name in 2000.

Communist Party of Brazil (PCdoB): Partido Comunista do Brasil. A progressive political party founded in 1958 and officially recognized in 1988, following the military dictatorship. It officially identifies as a Marxist-Leninist party.

Democratic Social Party (PDS): Partido Democrático Social. A conservative party established in 1979 as a continuation of ARENA, the official party of the dictatorship that ruled Brazil from 1964 to 1985. In 1993, the party ceased to exist when it merged with the Christian Democratic Party to form the now-defunct Reform Progressive Party.

Democrats (DEM): Democratas. A right-wing party that can be traced back to the National Renewal Alliance (ARENA), the official party during the dictatorship that lasted from 1964 to 1985.

Free Fatherland Party (PPL): Partido Pátria Livre. A center-left party with strong nationalist tendencies founded in 2009 and dissolved in 2019

Patriots (PATRI): Patriots. A right-wing party founded in 2012 with hardline views on national defense, as well as on issues of violence and crime, and opposed to the landless and Indigenous rights movements.

Pode. A center-right party that has since changed its name to Podemos (We Can), inspired by a Barack Obama campaign slogan.

Progressive Republican Party (PRP): Partido Republicano Progressista. A center-right party founded in 1991. The party merged with PATRI in 2018.

Progressive Party (PP): Partido Progressista. A right-wing party.

Republican Party for Social Progress (PROS): Partido Republican da Ordem Social. A centrist party founded in 2010 that has supported Workers' Party (PT) presidential runs.

Republicans (PRB): Republicanos. A conservative party with ties to the Universal Church.

Social Christian Party (PSC): Partido Social Cristão. A conservative party founded in 1985.

Social Democratic Party (PSD): Partido Social Democrático. A center-right party founded in 2011 by then São Paulo mayor Gilberto Kassab. On both the national and regional levels, however, the party has aligned with the Workers' Party.

Social Liberal Party (PSL): Partido Social Liberal. A far-right party founded in 1994. Until Jair Bolsonaro joined the party in 2018, it had little success in getting its candidates elected. Bolsonaro split from the party early in his presidency and has, as of April 2021, remained party-less.

Socialism and Liberty Party (PSOL): Partido Socialismo e Liberdade. A democratic socialist party founded by former members of the PT in 2004.

Workers' Party (PT): Partido dos Trabalhadores. A traditionally left-leaning party founded in 1980 that, during the governments of Luiz Inácio Lula da Silva (2003–10) and Dilma Rousseff (2010–16), often governed from the center-left. In the Bolsonaro era, the party is once again left-leaning.

ACKNOWLEDGMENTS

THE AUTHOR would like to thank Érico Melo, Luiz Schwarcz, Otávio Marques da Costa, and also André Botelho, Heloisa Starling, Lucila Lombardi, and Márcia Copola, who manned all positions: defense, offense, strikers, and coaches.

NOTES

Preface: When Fears Become Reality

1. The National Truth Commission was created in accordance with a law passed on November 18, 2011. Officially formed on May 16, 2012, the commission's objective was to investigate the crimes committed by the military dictatorship that ruled Brazil from 1964 to 1985. Importantly, it did not have the authority to prosecute these political crimes committed during the dictatorship, on account of a 1979 amnesty law that pardoned all such crimes. The commission's final report was delivered on December 10, 2014: Human Rights Day. The document constituted official recognition that crimes against humanity such as illegal and arbitrary imprisonment, torture, sexual assault, and executions, among other forms of aggression, were the result of official state policy.

2. Philippe Ariès, *The Hour of Our Death*, trans. Helen Weaver. New York: Knopf, 1981.

3. Walter Benjamin, "Experience and Poverty." In *The Storyteller Essays*, trans. Tess Lewis, ed. Samuel Titan. New York: NYRB, 2019.

4. Ariès, *Hour of Our Death*, p. 559.

5. Interview with George Yancy, *Truthout*, April 30, 2020, available at https://truthout.org/articles/judith-butler-mourning-is-a-political-act-amid-the-pandemic-and-its-disparities/?utm_campaign.

6. José Murilo de Carvalho, *O pecado original da República: Debates, personagens e eventos para compreender o Brasil*, ed. Ana Cecília Impellizieri Martins and Luciano Figueiredo. Rio de Janeiro: Bazar do Tempo, 2016.

Introduction: History Provides No Vaccines

1. In 1808, the Portuguese royal family arrived in Brazil, fleeing Napoleonic troops who would occupy Lisbon soon after their departure. The royals remained in Brazil until 1821, and in 1815, they elevated Brazil to new status as a United Kingdom, entirely changing the standing of the now former colony. This episode is central to understanding the process that would lead to Brazil's hardly revolutionary declaration of independence in 1822.

Chapter 1: Slavery and Racism

2. With the Lei Áurea (Golden law), Brazil became the last country in the Americas to abolish slavery. The law was also an attempt to guarantee that Princess Isabel, the daughter of Dom Pedro II, might take the reins of government of a Third Empire. It was hoped that the popularity of the act might guarantee the continuation of imperial government in Brazil. The plan did not work out, and the monarchy fell in November 1889, a month and a half after slavery came to an end in Brazil.

3. The first federal university in Brazil was founded in 1920: the University of Rio de Janeiro. Following this, twenty federal universities had been established by 1963, ten of them during the administration of Juscelino Kubitschek, eight in 1960, and two in early 1961. These universities were founded on the principle, which persists to this day, of a free, quality public education. It is also important to note that there are in addition forty public state universities in Brazil—fourteen spread across eight states in the Northeast, nine in the Southeast, and an additional nine in the South. These, too, are tuition-fee free and notable for their distinguished faculty and student bodies. Such is the case of the University of São Paulo (USP), for example, which enjoys an international reputation for excellence.

4. In June 2013, Brazil was overwhelmed by a series of popular, nonpartisan protests. It all began in response to an increase in bus fares in São Paulo. Soon, however, other issues entered the picture. Brazilians protested against corruption, in favor of quality public education, for improvements in public transportation, against public expenditure on the World Cup (which Brazil hosted in 2014), and in favor of the public health system. The movement registered a direct hit against then-president Dilma Rousseff, of the Workers' Party, who sought—unsuccessfully—to open a dialogue with the groups involved. The demands were very progressive, but the criticisms made by protestors against the political system were used and abused by street protestors in 2016 who sought, and succeeded in, the deposition of Rousseff.

Chapter 2: Bossism

1. "New Christian" was a designation used by the Portuguese Empire to identify those of Jewish and Muslim descent who were forcefully converted to Christianity by royal decree in 1497.

2. The imperial period in Brazil was divided into two reigns, with an intervening nine-year regency. The Empire was first led by Dom Pedro I, who had led Brazil to political independence in 1822; he would remain in power until 1831, when he left the country on account of various popular protests against him, and to see to the kingdom of Portugal. The second reign began in July 1840 and only came to an end in November 1889 when Dom Pedro II was deposed. Pedro II, in contrast to his father,

was a popular and enduring leader. His error was to delay too long in abolishing slavery, which cost him his reign.

3. The Vale do Paraíba is a region near Rio de Janeiro, then capital of Brazil, which was flooded by coffee planters from the middle of the eighteenth century. Wealthy landowners with vast cohorts of slaves changed the local landscape. A sort of tropical aristocracy also took root, implemented by the monarch Dom Pedro II, who named viscounts, barons, and marquises, thus exercising control over this landowning aristocracy, his right-hand men during the Empire. This aristocracy adopted the fashions and behavior of Paris society, in a veritable performance of power that sought to establish slavery and social hierarchy as natural phenomena.

4. The National Guard was a military force created in 1831, during the Regency period—which corresponds to a gap between Dom Pedro I's departure in 1831 and Dom Pedro II's rise to power in 1840—and demobilized in 1922. It also gained importance during the Paraguay War (1864–71) when the country was compelled to raise an army as a national institution.

Chapter 3: Patrimonialism

1. The Brazilian Empire begins with the political independence of Brazil, in September 1822, when Dom Pedro I assumed political leadership of the country, imposed the first constitution in 1823, and inaugurated a period characterized by many social and political conflicts. Pedro I renounced his title in 1831, as a result of political pressures in Brazil, but also in Portugal, where he was embroiled in a dispute over the succession.

Chapter 4: Corruption

1. Pero Vaz de Caminha (1450–1500), often called simply Caminha, was a Portuguese nobleman who became known as the scrivener on the ship of Pedro Álvares Cabral (1467–1520), and who wrote the letter to King Manuel I informing him of the "discovery" of the New World.

2. The Paraguayan War resulted from an alliance between Brazil, Uruguay, and Argentina against Paraguay. Despite the victory of the so-called Triple Alliance, Brazil suffered tremendous losses in both human and financial terms.

3. The Targeted Plan (*Plano de Metas*) was an economic development plan conceived by President Juscelino Kubitschek, aimed at moving Brazil ahead "fifty years in five."

4. The *caras pintadas* came onto the streets with their faces painted the colors of the national flag: yellow and green.

5. In March 2021, Brazil's supreme court issued a ruling on former president Lula's convictions with regard to Operation Car Wash that suggests a favorable legal

outlook for the former president. His defense, however, faces an uphill task on several dozen fronts when it comes to ensuring the former president remains out of prison and eligible to enter the 2022 presidential contest. On March 8, 2021, supreme court justice Edson Fachin transferred the four Operation Car Wash proceedings involving Lula to federal courts in Brasília, quashing existing convictions for corruption and money laundering related to two real estate properties in São Paulo state. The following day, the court annulled all investigations and proceedings against the former president, ruling that the presiding judge in those cases, Sérgio Moro, had been partial in his rulings. The former judge, who served as minister of justice in Jair Bolsonaro's administration from January 2019 to April 2020, is now flirting with a presidential run in 2022. In his decision, Fachin wrote that "in this particular case, we must recognize with urgent intellectual honesty that this decision may invalidate all rulings made by the former magistrate [Moro]," establishing that Operation Car Wash was guilty of political persecution in its singling out of the former president. Fachin also criticized the "spectacle" created around Lula's arrest, ordered by the judge in March 2016; Moro's leaking of conversations among Lula's defense team; the leaking of a conversation between Lula and former president Dilma Rousseff regarding Lula's nomination as her chief of staff (an action with grave consequences for the eventual impeachment of Rousseff); and the unsealing of testimony from Lula's former minister Antonio Palocci during the 2018 presidential campaign. In a statement, Lula's defense claimed he had been "the target of numerous illegalities committed by Moro." At time of writing this note for the English-language edition of this book, Operation Car Wash has been practically dismantled and its methods criticized as partial and illegal.

Chapter 5: Social Inequality

1. The Additional Act of 1834 (Ato Adicional de 1834) is the popular name given to Statute No. 16, which came into effect on October 12, 1834 and revised the constitution in effect up to that point. It was passed three years after the abdication of Emperor Dom Pedro I, at a moment when the country was divided on account of nativist movements that had gained a hold in various provinces. Aside from creating the Sole Regency, maintaining Senate terms for life, and establishing a "Neutral District" separate from the province of Rio de Janeiro, this Act dissolved the Council of the Imperial State of Brazil and created provincial legislative assemblies, which conferred greater autonomy upon the provinces in a clear move toward political decentralization.

2. SENAI—Serviço nacional de aprendizagem industrial (National industrial training service)—and SENAC—Serviço nacional de aprendizagem comercial (National commercial training service)—are institutions focused on apprenticeship and social advancement. They are part of the so-called S-System and offer both technical training and regular courses. SENAI is a technical school aimed at training students for industrial lines of work; SENAC is a professional school that offers technical and

liberal studies courses in several areas, but with the ultimate aim of meeting the needs of business..

Chapter 6: Violence

1. José de Ancheita was born on March 19, 1534, in Tenerife, in the Canary Islands. He joined the Society of Jesus in 1551, and two years later was sent to Brazil as part of the retinue of Duarte da Costa—the second governor-general of Portugal's American colony. His great mission was to "convert the pagans," bringing the "true faith" to Brazil's Indigenous. On January 25, 1554, he founded, with Pedro Manoel da Nóbrega, a Jesuit school in Piratininga, where a village soon grew. He was sent to São Vicente to learn the Tupi language so as to convert local populations to Catholicism. During his time in Brazil, he lived in what are now the states of São Paulo, Rio de Janeiro, and Espírito Santo. In 1595, he wrote *Grammatical Art of the Most Common Language on the Brazilian Coast*, the first Tupi-Guarani grammar. He also wrote poetry, letters, and legal texts. He died on June 9, 1597, in Espírito Santo.

Chapter 7: Race and Gender

1. The Party of Socialism and Liberty (PSOL) was founded in June 2004, obtaining its definitive recognition by the Electoral Court in September 2015. It is a left-leaning party that defends democratic socialism.

2. Maria da Penha Maia Fernandes (born in Fortaleza, Ceará in 1945) was a pharmacy worker trapped in an abusive relationship with her partner, who tried to kill her twice in 1983. After the first attempt, she was left paraplegic. Her partner was eventually convicted for his crime. In addition to being a victim of the sort of domestic violence affecting many Brazilian women, today she is a leader in the fight for women's rights. On August 7, 2006, a statute was signed into law that carries her name: the Lei Maria da Penha. It is an important weapon in combating violence against women. She now also leads an NGO—the Instituto Maria da Penha—committed to this struggle.

When the End Is Also a Beginning: The Ghosts of Our Present

1. Since this book was first written, the situation has worsened due to the COVID-19 pandemic, which exacerbated inequality.

Methodological Afterword

1. Georges Didi-Huberman, *The Surviving Image: Phantoms of Time and Time of Phantoms; Aby Warburg's History of Art*, trans. Harvey Mendelsohn. University Park, PA: Penn State University Press, 2016.

2. Georges Didi-Huberman, *Devant le temps*. Paris: Les Éditions de Minuit, 2000, p. 36.

3. Michel-Rolph Trouillot, *Silencing the Past: Power and the Production of History*. Boston: Beacon Press, 1995.

4. Ibid., p. 148.

5. Mikhail Bakhtin,, *Questões de literaturae estética: A teoria do romance*. São Paulo: Editora Unesp, 1998, p. 211.

6. Claude Lévi-Strauss, *Totemism*, trans. Rodney Needham. New York: Beacon Press, 1971; Claude Lefort, *Les formes de l'histoire: Essais d'anthropologie politique*. Paris: Gallimard, 1978.

7. Claude Lévi-Strauss, "Histoire et Ethnologie." *Annales ESC* 38, no. 6, pp. 1217–31: 1219.

8. See Émile Durkheim, "Individual Representations and Collective Representations" [1898]. In Émile Durkheim, *Sociology and Philosophy*, trans. D. F. Pocock. New York: Free Press, 1974, pp. 1–34. For a good analysis of this concept, see Heloisa Pontes, "Durkheim: Uma análise dos fundamentos simbólicos da vida social e dos fundamentos sociais do simbolismo." *Cadernos de Campos (São Paulo 1991)* 3, no. 3, 1993, pp. 89–102.

9. Claude Lévi-Strauss, *The Savage Mind*, trans. (for) George Weidenfeld & Nicolson Ltd, Chicago: University of Chicago Press, 1966.

10. E. E. Evans-Pritchard, *The Nuer: A Description of the Modes of Livelihood and Political Institutions of a Nilotic People*. Oxford: Oxford University Press, 1969.

11. Marshall Sahlins, "O 'pessimismo sentimental' e a experiência etnográfica: Por que a cultura não é um 'objeto' em extinção," part 1, trans. Déborah Danowski and Eduardo Viveiros de Castro. *Mana* 3, no. 1, April 1997, https://doi.org/10.1590/S0104 -93131997000100002; Rena Lederman, *What Gifts Engender: Social Relations and Politics in Mendi, Highland Papua New Guinea*. Cambridge: Cambridge University Press, 1986, p. 9.

12. E. R. Leach, "Two Essays concerning the Symbolic Representation of Time." In E. R. Leach, *Rethinking Anthropology*. New York: Humanities Press, 1971 (repr.), pp. 124–36.

13. Joanna Overing, "Myth as History: A Problem of Time, Reality, and Other Matters," pp. 2–3. PDF available at https://www.academia.edu/10411486/Myth_as _History_A_Problem_of_Reality_and_Other_Matters.

14. In the decade between 1861 and 1871, a number of works appeared that are today considered the field's first classics: Maine's *Ancient Law* (1861), Bachofen's *Das Mutterrecht* (1861), Fustel de Coulanges's *La cité antique* (1864), McLennan's *Primitive Marriage* (1865), Tylor's *Researches into the Early History of Mankind* (1865), Morgan's *The Systems of Consanguinity* (1871), and others.

15. Manuela Carneiro Cunha, "Introdução a uma história indígena." In *História dos índios no Brasil*, ed. Manuela Carneiro da Cunha. São Paulo: Companhia das Letras, 1992, pp. 9–24: 11.

16. Francisco Adolfo de Varnhagen,. *História geral do Brasil*. São Paulo, Melhoramentos, 1978 [1854], p. 30.

17. "[A]ll the history of primitive people that any ethnologist has ever developed is reconstruction and cannot be anything else." Franz Boas, "History and Science in Anthropology: A Reply." *American Anthropologist*, 38, no. 1, 1936, pp. 137–41: 140.

18. Franz Boas, "The Methods of Ethnology." *American Anthropologist*, 22, no. 4, 1920, pp. 311–21.

19. Franz Boas, "The Aims of Anthropological Research" [1932]. In Franz Boas, *Race, Language and Culture*. New York: The Free Press, 1966 (repr.), pp. 243–59.

20. Ibid., p. 255.

21. Claude Lévi-Strauss, "Introduction: History and Anthropology" [1949]. In Claude Lévi-Strauss, *Structural Anthropology*, trans. Claire Jacobson and Brooke Grundfest Schoepf (revised edn). New York: Basic Books, 1974, pp. 1–17: 8.

22. A. R. Radcliffe-Brown, *Structure and Function in Primitive Society: Essays and Addresses*. New York: Free Press, 1965, p. 2.

23. Ibid., p. 3.

24. Ibid.

25. Lévi-Strauss, "Introduction: History and Anthropology," p. 12.

26. E. E. Evans-Pritchard, "Anthropology and History." In *Essays in Social Anthropology*, London, Faber and Faber, pp. 46–65: 48.

27. Ibid.

28. Evans-Pritchard *The Nuer*.

29. Evans-Pritchard, "Anthropology and History," p. 21.

30. Ibid., p. 56.

31. Ibid., p. 65; Louis Dumont, "For a Sociology of India." *Contributions to Indian Sociology* 1, 1957, pp. 7–22: 21.

32. Evans-Pritchard, "Anthropology and History," p. 65; Dumont, "For a Sociology," p. 63.

33. On this, see Radcliffe-Brown, *Structure and Function*, p. 279.

34. Lévi-Strauss, "Introduction: History and Anthropology," p. 11.

35. Claude Lévi-Strauss, *Race and History*. Paris: UNESCO, 1952, p. 23.

36. Claude Lefort, *As formas da história*, trans. Rubens Enderle, Nélio Schneider, and Luciano Martorano. São Paulo: Brasiliense, 1979, p. 17.

37. Ibid. pp.17–18.

38. Ibid., p. 18.

39. Lévi-Strauss, "Introduction: History and Anthropology," p. 3.

40. Ibid., p. 16.

41. Ibid., p. 18.

42. Claude Lévi-Strauss and Didier Eribon, *De perto e de longe*. Rio de Janeiro: Nova Fronteira, 1990, p. 157.

43. This essay was published in 1983, in the journal *Annales*.

44. Lévi-Strauss, "Histoire et Ethnologie," p. 1218.

45. Ibid., p. 1229.

46. Lévi-Strauss "Introduction: History and Anthropology," p. 17.

47. Marcio Goldman, "Lévi-Strauss e os sentidos da história." *Revista de Antropologia* 42, nos 1–2, 1998; Idem, "Lévi-Strauss e os sentidos da história." In Marcio Goldman, *Alguma antropologia*. Rio de Janeiro: Relume Dumará, 1999, pp. 55–64.

48. Lévi-Strauss would return to this theme in other works, such as "History and Anthropology" (1949), *Race and History* (1952), *The First Class* (1960), the first two chapters of *The Savage Mind* (1962), the second "History and Anthropology" (1983), "A Different View" (published in the journal *L'Homme* in 1983), *The Story of Lynx* (1991), and "Voltas ao pasado" (1998 interview for the journal *Mana*).

49. Claude Lévi-Strauss, "History and Dialectic." In Lévi-Strauss, *Savage Mind*, pp. 245–70.

50. Ibid. This provocation recalls the positions of Paul Veyne: "The nationalist hailing of the past is not a universal fact, there are other possible alcohols. . . . Let us not make history a phenomenology of the mind, let us not take accidental sequences for the displaying of an essence." Paul Veyne, *Writing History: Essay on Epistemology*, trans. Mina Moore-Rinvolucri. Middletown, CT: Wesleyan University Press, 1984.

51. Claude Lévi-Strauss, "Lévi-Strauss nos 90 voltas ao passado," *Mana* 4, no. 2, 1998, pp. 107–17: 108

52. Ibid., p. 109.

53. Goldman, *Alguma antropologia*, p. 232

54. The reach of this type of proposal becomes clear from the 1960s onward, with the publication of the first volume of an analysis of the mythology of the American continent: *As Mitológicas*. In this work, the idea of transformation appears at the beginning of the first volume, as a central part of the analysis that follows: "We configure the group of transformations of each sequence, whether within the myth itself, or elucidating the relations of isomorphism between sequences taken from various myths originating in a single population." Claude Lévi-Strauss, *Mitológas 1: O cru e o cozido*. São Paulo: Cosac Naify, 2004, pp. 20–21.

55. Claude Lévi-Strauss, "A harmonia das esferas." In *Mitológas 2: Do mel às cinzas*. São Paulo: Cosac Naify, 2005, pp. 397–448: 401–8.

56. Marshall Sahlins, *Historical Metaphors and Mythical Realities: Structure in the Early History of the Sandwich Islands Kingdom (Canada, Origins and Options)*. Ann Arbor: University of Michigan Press, 1981, p. 8.

57. Ibid., p. 72.

58. Marshall Sahlins, *Islands of History*. Chicago: University of Chicago Press, 1987, p. xvii.

59. Ibid.

60. Clifford Geertz, *Negara: The Theatre State in Nineteenth-Century Bali*. Princeton, NJ: Princeton University Press, 1981, p. 5.

61. Geertz, *Negara*.

62. Ibid., p. 134.

63. Ibid., p. 135.

64. See Clifford Geertz, *Islam Observed: Religious Development in Morocco and Indonesia*. Chicago: University of Chicago Press, 1971.

65. Ibid., pp. 59–60.

66. Carneiro da Cunha, Manuela (ed.), *História dos índios no Brasil*. São Paulo: Companhia das Letras, 1992; Manuela Carneiro da Cunha, and Eduardo Viveiro de Castro, "Vingança e temporalidade: Os Tupinambás." *Anuário Antropológico 85*, 1986, pp. 57–78; Bruce Albert and Alcida Ramos, *Pacificando o branco: Cosmologias do contato no Norte Amazônico*. São Paulo: Editora Unesp, 2002; Bruna Franchetto and Michael Heckenberger (eds), *Os povos do Alto Xingu: História e cultura*. Rio de Janeiro: Editora da UFRJ, 2001.

67. John Monteiro, "Tupis, Tapuias e historiadores: Estudos de história indígena e do indigenismo." Dissertation (Tese de livre docência), University of Campinas, 2001; Robin Wright (ed.), *Transformando os deuses: Os múltiplos sentidos da conversão entre os índios do Brasil*. Campinas: Unicamp, 1999; Pedro Puntoni, *A guerra dos bárbaros: Povos indígenas e colonização do sertão; Nordeste do Brasil, 1650–1720*. São Paulo: Hucitec/Edusp; Beatriz Perrone-Moysés, "Índios livres e índios escravos: Os princípios da legislação indigenista do período colonial (séculos XVI a XVIII)." In Carneiro da Cunha (ed.), *História dos índios*, pp. 115–32.

68. Overing, "Myth as History," p. 3. I would like to clarify that I do not accept Overing's criticisms of Lévi-Strauss alleging that he classifies the peoples of the Amazon as "lacking history."

69. Eduardo Viveiros de Castro, "Etnologia brasileira." In *O que ler na ciência social brasileira (1970–1995)*, ed. Sergio Miceli, vol. 1: *Antropologia*. São Paulo: Editora Sumaré, 1999, pp. 109–223: 155

70. David Kopenawa and Bruce Albert, *A queda do céu: Palavras de um xamã Yanomami*. São Paulo: Companhia das Letras, 2019

71. Viveiros de Castro, "Etnologia brasileira," p. 156; Bruno Latour and Catherine Porter, *We Have Never Been Modern*. Cambridge, MA: Harvard University Press, 1993.

72. Maurice Merleau-Ponty, "De Mauss a Claude Lévi-Strauss" [1960]. In Maurice Merleau-Ponty, *Textos escolhidos*, trans. Marilena de Souza Chauí (Os pensadores). São Paulo: Abril Cultural, 1984, pp. 193–206: 199–200.

73. Claude Lévi-Strauss, *Myth and Meaning: Five Talks for Radio*, Toronto: University of Toronto Press, 1978, p. 43.

74. Claude Lévi-Strauss, "The Structural Study of Myth." *Journal of American Folklore* 68, no. 270, 1955, pp. 428–44: 430.

75. Reinhart Koselleck, *Futures Past: On the Semantics of Historical Time*, trans. Keith Tribe (Studies in Contemporary German Social Thought.). New York: Columbia University Press, 2004, p. 28.

76. Ibid., p. 200.

77. Ibid., p. 254.

78. Latour and Porter, *We Have Never*, pp. 68–69.

79. Svetlana Boym, *The Future of Nostalgia*. New York: Basic Books, 2002, Parts 1 and 3.

80. Thomas Mann, *The Magic Mountain*, trans. H. T. Lowe-Porter. New York: Penguin, 1976, Foreword.

81. Ibid.

82. Ibid., p. 141.

83. Ibid., p. 219.

84. Ibid., p. 541.

85. Trouillot, *Silencing the Past*, p. xix.

BIBLIOGRAPHY

Abranches, Sérgio. *Presidencialismo de coalizão: Raízes e evolução do modelo político brasileiro* [Coalitional presidentialism: Roots and evolution of the Brazilian political model]. Companhia das Letras, 2018.

———. "Polarização radicalizada e ruptura eleitoral" [Radical polarization and democratic rupture]. In *Democracia em risco?*, pp.11–34.

Adorno, Sergio. "Violência e crime: Sob o domínio do medo na sociedade brasileira" [Violence and crime: The dominance of fear in Brazilian society]. In Botelho and Schwarcz (eds), *Agenda brasileira*, pp. 554–65.

Agranonik, Marilyn. "Desigualdades no acesso à saúde" [Inequality in access to healthcare]. *Carta de Conjuntura FEE*, August 2016, http://carta.fee.tche.br /article/desigualdades-no-acesso-a-saude/.

Alencar, José de. *Iracema*. Penguin/Companhia das Letras, 2016.

Alencastro, Luiz Felipe de. "L'Empire du Brésil" [The Brazilian empire]. In *Le Concept d'empire* [The concept of empire], ed. Maurice Duverver. PUF, 1980, pp. 301–10.

———. "Le Commerce des vivants: Traités d'esclaves et 'pax lusitana' dans l'Atlantique sud" [Trading in the living: Slave treaties and "pax lusitana" in the southern Atlantic]. PhD dissertation, Université de Paris X, 1986.

———. "As populações africanas no Brasil" [African populations in Brazil]. Text drafted for the related chapter of the "Plano nacional de cultura" [National culture plan] presented to the National Congress by the Brazilian Ministry of Culture December 15, 2006; available at https://www.yumpu.com/pt/document /read/12637740/as-populacoes-africanas-no-brasilpdf-casa-das-africas.

Almeida, Ronaldo de. "Deus acima de todos" [God first of all]. In *Democracia em risco?*, pp. 35–51.

Almeida, Silvio. *O que é racismo estrutural?* [What is institutional racism?]. Letramento, 2018.

Alonso, Angela. "Protestos em São Paulo de Dilma a Temer" [Protests in São Paulo from Dilma (Rousseff) to (Michel) Temer]. In *República e democracia: Impasses no Brasil contemporâneo* [Republic and democracy: The impasses of contemporary

Brazil], ed. André Botelho and Heloisa Murgel Starling. Editora UFMG, 2017, pp. 413–24.

———. "A comunidade moral bolsonarista" [The Bolsonarist moral community]. In *Democracia em risco?*, pp. 52–70.

Anderson, Benedict. *Comunidades imaginadas: Reflexões sobre a origem e a difusão do nacionalismo* [original title: *Imagined Communities: Reflections on the Origin and Spread of Nationalism*, Verso, 1983], trans. Denise Bottman. Companhia das Letras, 2008.

Andrade, Carlos Drummond de. *Contos plausíveis* [Plausible tales]. Companhia das Letras, 2012.

Antonil, André João and Andrée Mansuy Diniz Silva. *Cultura e opulência do Brasil por suas drogas e minas* [Brazilian culture and opulence via the spice and mining trades]. EDUSP, 2007.

Aranha, Maria Lucia de Arruda. *História da educação* [A history of education]. Moderna, 1989.

Arendt, Hannah. "Verdade e política" [original title: "Truth and Politics"]. In Hannah Arendt, *Entre o passado e o futuro* [original title: *Between Past and Future*, Viking Press, 1961)], trans. Mauro W. Barbosa. Perspectiva, 1979, pp. 282–325.

———. "The Seeds of a Fascist International." In Hannah Arendt, *Essays in Understanding, 1930–1954*, ed. Jerome Kohn. Harcourt, Brace & Co., 1994, pp. 140–50.

———. *Origens do totalitarismo* [original title: *The Origins of Totalitarianism* (Harcourt, Brace & Co., 1951)], trans. Roberto Raposo. Companhia das Letras, 2002.

Ariza, Marília. "Mães infames, rebentos venturosos: Mulheres e crianças, trabalho e emancipação em São Paulo (século XIX)" [Notorious mothers, intrepid offsring: Women and children, work and emancipation in São Paulo (nineteenth century)]. PhD dissertation, Universidade de São Paulo, 2018.

Arruda, Natália Martins et al. "Desigualdade no acesso à saúde entre as áreas urbanas e rurais do Brasil: Uma de composição de fatores entre 1988 e 2008" [Inequality in healthcare access between urban and rural Brazil: A disaggregation of factors from 1998 to 2008]. *Cadernos de Saúde Pública* 34, no. 6 (2018), available at https://www.scielo.br/j/csp/a/zMLkvhHQzMQQHjqFt3D534x/?format =pdf&lang=pt.

Arruti, José Maurício. *Mocambo: Antropologia e história no processo de formação quilombola* [Mocambo: Anthropology and history in the formation of the runaway slave community]. EDUSC, 2006.

Avritzer, Leonardo (ed.). *Corrupção: Ensaios e críticas* [Corruption: Essays and analyses]. Editora UFMG, 2008.

Bacha, Edmar L. and Roberto M. Unger. *Participação, salário e voto: Um projeto de democracia para o Brasil* [Participation, wages, and the vote: A democratic vision for Brazil]. Paz e Terra, 1978.

Barman, Roderick. *Citizen Emperor: Pedro II and the Making of Brazil, 1825–1891.* Stanford University Press, 1999.

Barreto, Lima. *Aventuras do dr. Bogóloff: Episódios da vida de um pseudo-revolucionário russo* [The adventures of Dr. Bogoloff: Episodes in the life of a Russian pseudo-revolutionary]. A. Reis & Cia., 1912.

———. *Diário íntimo* [Private notebook]. Brasiliense, 1956.

Borges, Vavy Pacheco. *O que é história* [What history is]. Brasiliense, 1987.

Botelho, André. *Aprendizado do Brasil: A nação em busca dos seus portadores sociais* [A Brazilian apprenticeship: A nation in search of its social bearers]. Editora da Unicamp, 2002.

———. "Público e privado no pensamento social brasileiro" [The public and the private in Brazilian social thought]. In Botelho and Schwarcz (eds), *Agenda brasileira*, pp. 418–29.

———. "Patrimonialismo brasileiro: Entre o Estado e a sociedade" [Brazilian patri-monialism within the State and society]. In *Dicionário da República* [Dictionary of the Republic], ed. Lilia Moritz Schwarcz and Heloísa Starling. Companhia das Letras, 2019.

——— and Lilia Moritz Schwarcz (eds). *Agenda brasileira: Temas de uma sociedade em mundança* [An agenda for Brazil: Themes of a changing society]. Companhia das Letras, 2011.

Burke, Peter. *Variedades de história cultural* [original title: *Varieties of Cultural History*, Cornell University Press, 1997)], trans. Alda Porto. Civilização Brasileira, 2006.

———. *Testemunha ocular: O uso de imagens como evidência histórica* [original title: *Eyewitnessing: The Uses of Images as Historical Evidence*, Cornell University Press, 2001)], trans. Vera Maria Xavier dos Santos. Editora Unesp, 2017.

Butler, Judith. *Problemas de gênero: Feminismo e subversão da identidade* [original title: *Gender Trouble: Feminism and the Subversion of Identity*, Routledge, 1990)], trans. Renato Aguiar. Civilização Brasileira, 2003.

Cândido, Antônio. "A literatura durante o Império" [Literature during the Empire]. In *História geral da civilização brasileira* [A general history of Brazilian civiliza-tion], ed. Sérgio Buarque de Holanda. Difel, 1967, pp. 343–55.

———. "Dialética da malandragem" [Dialectic of malandroism]. In Antônio Cân-dido, *O discurso e a cidade* [Discourse and the city]. Livraria Duas Cidades, 2004, pp. 17–46.

Carneiro da Cunha, Manuela. "Política indigenista no século xix" [Indigenous policy in the nineteenth century]. In *História dos índios no Brasil* [A history of the Indi-ans in Brazil], ed. Manuela Carneiro da Cunha. Companhia das Letras, 1992, pp. 133–54.

———. "Índios como tema do pensamento social no Brasil" [The Indian in Brazilian social thought]. In Botelho and Schwarcz (eds), *Agenda brasileira*, pp. 278–91.

Carone, Edgard. *O Estado Novo* [The New State]. Bertrand Brasil, 1988.

Carvalho, José Murilo de. *A construção da ordem: A elite política imperial* [The construction of order: The imperial political elite]. Campus, 1980.

————. *A construção da ordem A elite política imperial: Teatro de sombras* [The construction of order: The imperial political elite: shadow puppets]. Editora Relume-Dumará, 1996.

————. *A formação das almas: O imaginário da República no Brasil* [published in English as *The Formation of Souls: Imagery of the Republic in Brazil*, trans. Clifford E. Landers, University of Notre Dame Press, 2012]. Companhia das Letras, 1996.

————. *Cidadania no Brasil: O longo caminho* [Citizenship in Brazil: The long road]. Civilização Brasileira, 2001.

————. *D. Pedro II: Ser ou não ser* [Dom Pedro II: To be or not to be]. Companhia das Letras, 2007.

————. "Mandonismo, coronelismo, clientelismo, República" [Bossism, coronelism, clientelism, republic]. In Botelho and Schwarcz (eds), *Agenda brasileira*, pp. 334–43.

————. *O pecado original da República: Debates, personagens e eventos para compreender o Brasil* [The Republic's original sin: Key debates, figures, and events for understanding Brazil]. Bazar do Tempo, 2017.

Cavalcanti, Nireu Oliveira. *Rio de Janeiro: Centro histórico, 1808–1998: Marcos da colônia* [Rio de Janeiro: The historic center, 1808–1998: Colonial-era landmarks]. Dresdner Bank Brasil, 1998.

Chacon, Vamireh. *História dos partidos brasileiros* [A history of Brazilian political parties]. Editora UnB, 1981.

Correa, Mariza. "Gênero, ou a pulseira de Joaquim Nabuco" [Gender, or Joaquim Nabuco's bracelet]. In Botelho and Schwarcz (eds), *Agenda brasileira*, pp. 224–33.

Cortesão, Jaime. *História da expansão portuguesa* [A history of Portuguese expansion]. Bertrand, 1993.

Costa e Silva, Alberto da. *A Manilha e o Libambo: A África e a escravidão de 1500 a 1700* [Manillas and shackles: Africa and slavery from 1500 to 1700]. Nova Fronteira and Fundação Biblioteca Nacional, 2002.

————. *Um rio chamado Atlântico: A África no Brasil e o Brasil na África* [A river called the Atlantic: Africa in Brazil and Brazil in Africa]. Nova Fronteira, 2006.

Daibert, Bárbara Simões and Robert Daibert Jr. "Extra! Roubaram as joias da imperatriz!" [Extra, extra! The empress's jewels have been stolen!]. *Revista de História da Biblioteca Nacional* no. 21 (June 2007), pp. 68–71.

Damatta, Roberto. *Carnavais, malandros e heróis: Para uma sociologia do dilema brasileiro* [Carnivals, malandros, and heroes: Toward a sociology of the Brazilian dilemma]. Rocco, 1998.

Darnton, Robert. *O grande massacre de gatos, e outros episódios da história cultural francesa* [original title: *The Great Cat Massacre, and Other Episodes in French Cultural History*, Basic Books, 1984)], trans. Sonia Coutinho. Paz e Terra, 1997.

Debert, Guita Grin and Tatiana Santos Perrone. "Questões de poder e as expectativas das vítimas: Dilemas da judicialização da violência de gênero" [Issues of power and victim expectations: The dilemma of judicializing gender violence]. *Revista brasileira de ciências criminais* 150 (2018), pp. 423–47.

Democracia em risco?: 22 ensaios sobre o Brasil hoje [Democracy at risk?: 22 essays on today's Brazil]. Companhia das Letras, 2019

Dolhnikoff, Miriam. *O pacto imperial: Origens do federalismo no Brasil do século XIX* [The imperial pact: The origins of federalism in nineteenth-century Brazil]. Globo, 2005.

Domingues, Petrônio. "Democracia e autoritarismo: Entre o racismo e o antirracismo [Democracy and authoritarianism: Between racism and antiracism]". In *Democracia em risco?*, pp. 98–115.

Drosdoff, Daniel. *Linha dura no Brasil: O governo Médici (1969–1974)* [The hard line in Brazil: The Médici government (1969–1974)]. Global, 1986.

Dunker, Christian Ingo Lenz. "Psicologia das massas digitais e análise do sujeito democrático" [Psychology fo the digital asses and analysis of the democratic subject]. In *Democracia em risco?*, pp. 116–35.

Faoro, Raymundo. "A aventura liberal numa ordem patrimonialista" [The liberal adventure within the patrimonialist order]. *Revista USP* no. 17 (1993), pp. 14–29.

———. *Os donos do poder: Formação do patronato político brasileiro* [Power brokers: The formation of Brazilian political patronage]. Biblioteca Azul, 2012.

Farage, Nadia. *As muralhas dos sertões: Os povos indígenas no rio Branco e a colonização* [The front lines of the frontier: Indigenous peoples in Rio Branco and colonization]. Paz e Terra, 1991.

Fausto, Boris. "A queda do foguete" [The rocket falls back to earth]. In *Democracia em risco?*, pp. 136–46.

Fausto, Carlos. *Os índios antes do Brasil* [The Indians before Brazil]. Zahar, 2012.

Fausto, Ruy. "Depois do temporal [After the Storm]". In *Democracia em risco?*, pp. 147–63.

Fausto, Sergio. "A que ponto chegamos: Da Constituição de 1988 à eleição de Jair Bolsonaro" [How we got here: From the 1988 Constitution to the election of Jair Bolsonaro]. *piauí* 149 (February 2019), pp 22–28.

Fernandes, Florestan. *A integração do Negro na sociedade de classes* [The integration of Black people in society's classes]. 2 vols, EDUSP, 1965.

———. *A revolução burguesa no Brasil: Ensaio de interpretação sociológica* [The bourgeois revolution in Brazil: Attempt at a sociological interpretation]. Zahar, 1975.

Ferraro, Alceu Ravanello and Daniel Kreidlow. "Analfabetismo no Brasil: Configuração e gênese das desigualdades regionais" [Illiteracy in Brazil: The shape and origins of regional inequalities]. *Educação e Realidade* 29, no. 2 (2004), pp. 179–200.

Ferreira, Jorge. *João Goulart: Uma biografia* [João Goulart: A biography]. Civilização Brasileira, 2011.

Ferreira, Naura and Márcia Aguiar. *Gestão da educação: Impasses, perspectivas e compromissos* [Education policy in action: Dilemmas, perspectives, and compromises]. Cortez, 2000.

Fico, Carlos. *Além do golpe: Versões e controvérsias sobre 1964 e a ditadura militar* [Beyond the coup: Tales and controversies surrounding 1964 and the military dictatorship]. Record, 2004.

Franco, Maria Sylvia de Carvalho. *Homens livres na ordem escravocrata* [Free men in the slaveholding order]. Editora Unesp, 1997.

Freire, Américo and Celso Castro. "As bases republicanas dos Estados Unidos do Brasil" [Republican foundations of the United States of Brazil]. In *A República no Brasil* [Republican government in Brazil], ed. Angela de Castro Gomes, Dulce Chaves Pandolfi, and Alberti Verena. Nova Fronteira, 2002, pp. 30–53.

Freyre, Gilberto. *Discursos parlamentares* [Congressional speeches]. Câmara dos Deputados, Centro de Documentação e Informação, 1994.

———. *Casa-grande & senzala* [Big house and slave quarters; published in English as *The Masters and the Slaves: A Study in the Development of Brazilian Civilization*, trans. Samuel Putnam. Knopf, 1946]. Record, 1998 [1933].

Gaspari, Elio. *A ditadura escancarada* [A full-blown dictatorship]. Companhia das Letras, 2002.

Ghiraldelli Jr., Paulo. *História da educação* [A history of education]. Cortez, 2000.

Girardet, Raoul. *Mitos e mitologias políticas* [original title: *Mythes et mythologies politiques*, Éditions du Seuil, 1986], trans. Maria Lúcia Machado. Companhia das Letras, 1998.

Gomes, Ângela de Castro. "A política brasileira em tempos de cólera" [Brazilian politics in times of choler]". In *Democracia em risco?*, pp. 175–94.

——— and Martha Abreu. "A nova 'Velha' República: Um pouco de história e historiografia" [The new "Old" Republic: A bit of history and historiography]. *Tempo* 13, no. 26 (2009), pp. 1–14.

———, Dulce Chaves Pandolfi, and Verena Alberti (eds). *A República no Brasil* [Republican government in Brazil]. Nova Fronteira, 2002.

Gomes, Flávio and Lilia Moritz Schwarcz (eds). *Dicionário da escravidão e liberdade* [Dictionary of slavery and freedom]. Companhia das Letras, 2018.

Green, James N., Ronaldo Trinidade and José Fábio Barbosa da Silva (eds). *Homossexualismo em São Paulo, e outros escritos* [Homosexuality in São Paulo, and other writings], Editora Unesp, 2005.

Guimarães, Antonio Sérgio Alfredo. "A República de 1889: Utopia de branco, medo de preto" [The Republic of 1889: White utopia, Black nightmare]. *Contemporânea: Revista de Sociologia da UFSCar* 1, no. 2 (2011), pp. 17–36.

————. "Desigualdade e diversidade: Os sentidos contrários da ação" [Inequality and diversity: The contradictions of action]. In Botelho and Schwarcz (eds), *Agenda brasileira*, pp. 166–75.

————. "La République de 1889: Utopie de l'homme blanc, peur de l'homme noir. (La liberté est noire, l'égalité, blanche, la fraternité, métisse)" [The Repubic of 1889: White man's utopia, Black man's fear. (Liberty is Black, equality White, fraternity mixed)]. *Brésil (s): Sciences Humaines et Sociales* 1 (2012), pp. 149–68.

Hasenbalg, Carlos and Nelson Valle e Silva. *Origens e destinos: Desigualdades sociais ao longo da vida* [Starting and end Points: Social inequality throughout life]. Topbooks, 2003.

Hobsbawm, Eric. *Era dos extremos: O breve século XX, 1914–1991* [original title: *The Age of Extremes: The Short Twentieth Century, 1914–1991*, Michael Joseph, 1994], trans. Marcos Santarrita. Companhia das Letras, 1995.

Holanda, Sérgio Buarque de. *Raízes do Brasil* [published in English as *Roots of Brazil*, trans. G. Harvey Summ. University of Notre Dame Press, 2012]. Companhia das Letras, 2002 [1936].

————. *Raízes do Brasil: Edição crítica 80 anos* [*Roots of Brazil*: Eightieth anniversary critical edition], ed. Pedro Meira Monteiro and Lilia Moritz Schwarcz. Companhia das Letras, 2016.

Hollanda, Heloisa Buarque de (ed.). *Explosão feminista: Arte, cultura, política e universidade* [Feminist explosion: Art, culture, politics, and the university]. Companhia das Letras, 2018.

Holston, James. *A cidade modernista: Uma crítica de Brasília e sua utopia* [The modernist city: A critique of Brasília and its utopia; original title: *The Modernist City: An Anthropological Critique of Brasilia*, University of Chicago Press, 1989], trans. Marcelo Coelho. Companhia das Letras, 1993.

Humboldt, Alexander von. *Views of Nature, or, Contemplations on the Sublime Phenomena of Creation*, trans. Elise C. Otté and Henry George Bohn. Nabu, 2010 [1850].

Koselleck, Reinhart. *Futuro passado: Contribuição à semântica dos tempos históricos* [original title: *Vergangene Zukunft: Zur Semantik Zeiten*, Suhrkamp, 1979 [1965]; published in English as *Futures Past: On the Semantics of Historical Time*, MIT Press, 1985, trans. Keith Tribe; revised edn Columbia University Press, 2004], trans. Wilma Patrícia Maas and Carlos Almeida Pereira, revised by César Benjamin. Contraponto, 2006.

Leal, Victor Nunes. *Coronelismo, enxada e voto: O município e o regime representativo no Brasil* [Coronelism, the plough, and the ballot box: The city and system of representation in Brazil; published in English as *Coronelismo: The Municipality and Representative Government in Brazil*, Cambridge University Press, 2009]. Companhia das Letras, 2012 [1949].

Lemos, Ronaldo. "Diante da realidade, seis ficções epistemológicas" [Facing reality: Six epistemological fictions]. In *Democracia em risco?*, pp. 195–210.

Leopoldi, Maria Antonieta P. "Crescendo em meio à incerteza: A política econômica do governo jk (1956–60)" [Growth in the face of uncertainty: The economic policy of the Juscelino Kubitschek government, (1956–1960)]. In *O Brasil de JK* [JK's Brazil], ed. Ângela de Castro Gomes. Editora FGV, 2008, pp. 71–99.

Lessa, Renato. *A invenção republicana: Campos Sales, as bases e a decadência da Primeira República brasileira*, [Republican fantasy: Campos Sales, the foundations and fall of the first Brazilian Republic]. Vértice, 1988.

Lévi-Strauss, Claude. *Mito e significado* [original title: *Myth and Meaning*, Routledge, 1978], trans. António Marques Bessa. Edições 70, 1978.

Levitsky, Steven and Daniel Ziblatt. *How Democracies Die*. Crown, 2018.

Lilla, Mark. *O progressista de ontem e o do amanhã: Desafios da democracia liberal no mundo pós-políticas identitárias* [The liberal of yesterday and of tomorrow: Challenges for liberal democracy in a postidentity politics world; original title: *The Once and Future Liberal: After Identity Politics*, Harper, 2017], trans. Berilo Vargas. Companhia das Letras, 2018.

Lima, Oliveira. *D. João VI no Brasil* [Dom João VI in Brazil]. Topbooks, 1996 [1908].

Linz, Juan J. and Alfred Stepan. *The Breakdown of Democratic Regimes: Crisis, Breakdown and Reequilibration*. Johns Hopkins University Press, 1978.

Luna, Francisco Vidal and Herbert S. Klein. *Escravismo no Brasil* [Slavery in Brazil]. Imprensa Oficial, 2010.

Machado, Maria Helena. *O plano e o pânico: Os movimentos sociais na década da abolição* [The plan and the panic: Social movement during the decade of abolition]. EDUSP, 2010.

Maduro Jr., Paulo Rogério. "Taxas de matrícula e gastos em educação no Brasil" (Enrollment fees and educational expenses in Brazil). Master's thesis, Fundação Getulio Vargas, 2007.

Magalhães, Gonçalves de. *A Confederação dos Tamoios* [The Confederation of Tamoios]. Tipografia de Paula Brito, 1856.

Magnoli, Demétrio. "A verdade em fluxo" [Truth in flux]. *Folha de S. Paulo*, January 5, 2019.

Maio, Marcos Chor. "From Bahia to Brazil: The Unesco Race Relations Project." In *Imagining Brazil*, ed. Jessé Souza and Valter Sinda. Lexington Books, 2005, pp. 141–74.

——— and Ricardo Ventura (eds). *Raça, ciência e sociedade* [Race, science, and society]. Editora Fiocruz, 1996.

Malerba, Jurandir. *A corte no exílio: Civilização e poder no Brasil às vésperas da Independência (1808 a 1821)* [Court in exile: Civilization and power in Brazil on the eve of independence (1801–1821)]. Companhia das Letras, 2000.

Marquese, Rafael Bivar. *Feitores do corpo, missionários da mente: Senhores, letrados e o controle dos escravos nas Américas, 1660–1860* [Foremen of the body, missionaries of the mind: Landowners, the literate, and the control of slaves in the Americas, 1660–1860]. Companhia das Letras, 2004.

Martius, Karl von. "Como se deve escrever a história do Brasil" [How to write the history of Brazil]. *Jornal do Instituto Histórico e Geográfico Brasileiro* 6, no. 24 (January 1845), pp. 389–403.

McClintock, Anne. *Couro imperial: Raça, gênero e sexualidade no embate colonial* [original title: *Imperial Leather: Race, Gender and Sexuality in the Colonial Contest*, Routledge, 1995], trans. Plinio Dentzien. Editora da Unicamp, 2010.

Medeiros, Mário. *Pedagogia do desafio* [Challenge pedagogy]. Simpere, 2015.

Mello, Evaldo Cabral. *Rubro veio: O imaginário da restauração pernambucana* [Images of the Pernambuco restoration]. Nova Fronteira, 1986.

Melo, Carlos. "A marcha brasileira para a insensatez" [The Brazilian march toward madness]. In *Democracia em risco?*, pp. 211–29.

Mendes, Conrado Hübner. "A política do pânico e circo" [The politics of "panic et circenses"] In *Democracia em risco?*, pp. 230–46.

Milá, Marc Morgan. "Income Inequality, Growth and Elite Taxation in Brazil: New Evidence Combining Survey and Fiscal Data, 2001–2015". International Policy Centre for Inclusive Growth (IPC-IG), Brasília, 2018, Working Paper available at http://www.ipc-undp.org/pub/eng/WP165_Income_inequality_growth_and _elite_taxation_in_Brasil.pdf.

Miquilin, Isabella de Oliveira Campos et al. "Desigualdades no acesso e uso dos serviços de saúde entre trabalhadores informais e desempregados: Análise da Pnad, 2008, Brasil" [Inequality in access and use of health services among informal workers and the unemployed: An analysis of the 2008 Brazilian National Household Survey]. *Cadernos de Saúde Pública* 29, no. 7 (2018), pp. 1392–1406.

Montaigne, Michel de. *Os ensaios* [original title: *Essais* (1580); (re)published in English as *The Complete Essays*, trans. M. A. Screech, Penguin Classics, 1993], trans. Rosa Freire Aguiar. Penguin/Companhia das Letras, 2010.

Monteiro, John Manuel. *Negros da terra: Índios e bandeirantes nas origens de São Paulo* [Native Blacks: Indians and frontiersmen in the formation of São Paulo]. Companhia das Letras, 1999.

Moore Jr., Barrington. *Injustiça: As bases sociais da obediência e da revolta* [original title: *Injustice: The Social Bases of Obedience and Revolt*, Palgrave Macmillan, 1978], trans. João Roberto Martins Filho. Brasiliense, 1987.

Morel, Marco. *Corrupção mostra a sua cara* [Corruption rears its head]. Casa da Palavra, 2006.

Morrison, Toni. *Amada* [original title: *Beloved*, Knopf, 1987], trans. José Rubens Siqueira. Companhia das Letras, 2007.

Neiva, Pedro and Maurício Izumi. "Perfil profissional e distribuição regional dos senadores brasileiros em dois séculos de história" [Professional profile and regional distribution of Brazilian senators over two centuries]. *Revista Brasileira de Ciências Sociais* 29, no. 84 (2014), pp. 165–88.

Nicolau, Jairo. *Eleições no Brasil: Do Império aos dias atuais* [Elections in Brazil: From the Empire to the present day]. Zahar, 2012.

Nora, Pierre. "Entre memória e história: A problemática dos lugares" [Between memory and history: The problematic of sites; original title: "Entre mémoire et histoire: La problématique des lieux," in Nora (ed.), *Les Lieux de mémoire*, vol. 1: *La République*, pp. xv–xlii], trans. Yara Aun Khoury. *Projeto História*10 (1993), pp. 7–28.

——— (ed.). *Les Lieux de mémoire* [published in English as *The Realms of Memory*, ed. Pierre Nora and Lawrence D. Kritzman, trans. Arthur Goldhammer, 3 vols, Columbia University Press, 1996–98]. 3 vols, Gallimard, 1984–92.

———. *Essais d'ego-histoire* [Ego-history essays]. Gallimard, 1987.

——— and Jacques Le Goff (eds). *Faire de l'Histoire* [Making history]. 3 vols, Gallimard, 1974.

Novais, Fernando A. *Império: A Corte e a Modernidade Nacional* [Empire: The court and national modernity]. 2 vols, Companhia das Letras, 1997–99.

Oliveira, Dalila Andrade. "Educação no Brasil" [Education in Brazil]. In Botelho and Schwarcz (eds), *Agenda brasileira*, pp. 176–87.

Paiva, Vanilda. "Um século de educação republicana" [A century of republican education]. *Pro-Posições* 1, no. 2 (1990), pp. 7–21.

Paula, Liana de. *Punição e cidadania: Adolescentes e liberdade assistida na cidade de São Paulo* [Punishment and citizenship: Adolescents and probation in the city of São Paulo]. Alameda, 2017.

Paula, Sergio Goes de (ed.). *Um monarca da fuzarca: Três versões para um escândalo na corte* [Monarch of pandemonium: Three tales of a court scandal]. Relume-Dumará, 1998.

Piletti, Claudino and Nelson Piletti. *Filosofia e história da educação* [Philosophy and history of education]. Ática, 1987.

Pinto, Célia Regina Jardim. *A banalidade da corrupção: Uma forma de governar o Brasil* [The banality of corruption: A way of governing Brazil]. Editora UFMG, 2011.

Prado júnior, Caio. *Formação do Brasil contemporâneo* [The making of contemporary Brazil]. Companhia das Letras, 2014.

Queiroz, Maria Isaura Pereira de. *O mandonismo local na vida política brasileira, e outros ensaios* [Local bossism in Brazilian political life, and other essays]. Alfa-Ômega, 1976.

Quinalha, Renan. "Desafios para a comunidade e o movimento lgbt no governo Bolsonaro" [Challenges for the LGBT community and movements under the Bolsonaro government]. In *Democracia em risco?*, pp. 256–73.

Ramírez G., María Teresa and Juana Patricia Téllez C. "La educación primaria y secundaria en Colombia en el siglo XX" [Primary and secondary education in Colombia in the twentieth century]. Bogotà: Banco de la República de Colombia, 2006, available at https://ideas.repec.org/p/bdr/borrec/379 .html.

Reginaldo, Lucilene. "Racismo e naturalização das desigualdades: Uma perspectiva histórica" [Racism and naturalization of inequalities: A historical perspective]. *Jornal da Unicamp*, edição web, UNICAMP (Universidade estadal de Campinas), November 21, 2018, https://www.unicamp.br/unicamp/ju/artigos/direitos -humanos/.

Reis, Daniel Aarão. *Ditadura e democracia no Brasil: Do golpe de 1964 à Constituição de 1988* [Dictatorship and democracy in Brazil: From the 1964 coup to the 1988 Constitution]. Zahar, 2014.

———. "As armadilhas da memória e a reconstrução democrática" [The traps of memory and democratic reconstruction]. In *Democracia em risco?*, pp. 274–86.

Reis, João José. *Rebelião escrava no Brasil: A história do Levante dos Malês em 1835* [Slave rebellion in Brazil: The history of the 1835 Malê Revolt]. Companhia das Letras, 2012.

Reis, João José and Flávio dos Santos Gomes. *Liberdade por um fio: História dos quilombos no Brasil* [Freedom by a thread: The history of runaway slave communities in Brazil]. Companhia das Letras, 1996.

Ribeiro, Djamila. *Quem tem medo do feminismo negro?* [Who's afraid of Black feminism?]. Companhia das Letras, 2018.

Ribeiro, Maria Luisa Santos. *História da educação brasileira: A organização escolar* [A history of Brazilian education: The school]. Autores Associados, 1998.

Romeiro, Adriana. *Corrupção e poder no Brasil: Uma história, séculos XVI a XVIII* [Corruption and power in Brazil: A history from the sixteenth to the eighteenth century]. Autêntica, 2017.

Runciman, David. *Como a democracia chega ao fim* [original title: *How Democracy Ends*, Profile Books, 2018], trans. Sergio Flaksman. Todavia, 2018.

Sadek, Maria Tereza Aina. "Justiça e direitos: A construção da igualdade" [Justice and rights: Building equality]. In Botelho and Schwarcz (eds), *Agenda brasileira*, pp. 324–33.

Saggese, Gustavo Santa Roza et al. (eds). *Marcadores sociais da diferença: Gênero, sexualidade, raça e classes em perspectiva antropológica* [Social markers of difference: Gender, sexuality, race, and classes from an anthropological perspective]. Numas, 2018.

Salvador, Frei Vicente do. *História do Brasil* [History of Brazil]. Odebrecht, 2008.

Santos, José Alcides Figueiredo. "Desigualdade racial de saúde e contexto de classe no Brasil" [Racial Health Inequality and Class Context in Brazil]. *Dados: Revista de Ciências Sociais* 54, no. 1 (2011), pp. 5–40.

Schueler, Alessandra F. Martinez de. "Crianças e escolas na passagem do Império para a República" [Children and schools in the transition from Empire to Republic]. *Revista Brasileira de História* 19, no. 37 (1999), pp. 59–84.

Schwarcz, Lilia Moritz. *Retrato em branco e negro: Jornais, escravos e cidadãos em São Paulo no final do século XIX* [Portrait in black and white: Newspapers, slaves, and citizens in São Paulo at the end of the nineteenth century]. Companhia das Letras, 1987.

———. *O espetáculo das raças: Cientistas, instituições e questão racial no Brasil do século XIX* [The spectacle of races: Scientists, institutions, and the race question in nineteenth-century Brazil]. Companhia das Letras, 1993.

———. *As barbas do imperador: D. Pedro II, um monarca nos trópicos* [also published in English, as *The Emperor's Beard: Dom Pedro II and His Tropical Monarchy in Brazil*, trans. John Gledson, Hill and Wang, 2004]. Companhia das Letras, 1998.

———. *Lima Barreto: Triste visionário* [Lima Barreto: Tragic visionary], Companhia das Letras, 2018.

———, Paulo Cesar de Avezedo, and Ângela Marques da Costa. *A longa viagem da biblioteca dos reis: Do terremoto de Lisboa à Independência do Brasil* [The long journey of the kings' library: From the Lisbon earthquake to the independence of Brazil]. Companhia das Letras, 2002.

——— and Heloisa Murgel Starling. *Brasil: Uma biografia* [published in English as *Brazil: A Biography*, Farrar, Straus and Giroux, 2018]. Companhia das Letras, 2015.

——— and Maria Helena P. T. Machado (eds). *Emancipação, inclusão e exclusão: Desafios do passado e do presente* [Emancipation, inclusion, and exclusion: Past and present challenges]. EDUSP, 2018.

Schwartz, Stuart. *Segredos internos: Engenhos e escravos na sociedade colonial, 1550–1835* [Inside secrets: Plantations and slaves in colonial society, 1550–1835]. Companhia das Letras, 1998.

Schwarz, Roberto. *Ao vencedor as batatas: Forma literária e processo social nos inícios do romance brasileiro* [To the winner, the potatoes: Literary form and social process in the early years of the Brazilian novel]. Duas Cidades, 1977.

Seeger, Anthony, Roberto da Matta, and Eduardo B. V. de Castro. "A construção da pessoa nas sociedades indígenas brasileiras" [The construction of the individual in Indigenous Brazilian societies]. *Boletim do Museu Nacional*, Série Antropologia no. 32 (1979), pp. 2–19.

Singer, André and Gustavo Venturi. "Sismografia de um terremoto eleitoral" [Seismograph of an electoral earthquake]. *Democracia em risco?*, pp. 355–71.

Skidmore, Thomas E. *Brasil: De Getúlio a Castello (1930–64)* [Brazil: From Getúlio to Castello, 1930–64; original title: *Politics in Brazil (1930–1964): An Experiment in Democracy*, Oxford University Press, 1967], trans. Berilo Vargas. Companhia das Letras, 2010.

Snyder, Timothy. *The Road to Unfreedom*, Tim Duggan Books, 2018.

Soares, Luiz Eduardo. "Segurança pública: Dimensão essencial do estado democrático de direito" [Public safety: An essential feature of the democratic rule of law]. In Botelho and Schwarcz (eds), *Agenda brasileira*, pp. 492–503.

Solano, Esther. "A bolsonarização do Brasil" [The bolsonaroization of Brazil. In *Democracia em risco?*, pp. 307–21.

Souza, Pedro H. G. Ferreira de. *Uma história de desigualdade: A concentração de renda entre os ricos, 1926–2013* [A history of inequality: Wealth concentration among the rich, 1926–2013]. Hucitec Editora, 2018.

Souza Santos, Andrea Aruska de. *The Politics of Memory: Urban Cultural Heritage in Brazil*. Rowman & Littlefield, 2019.

Stanley, Jason. *How Fascism Works: The Politics of Us and Them*. Random House, 2018.

Starling, Heloisa Murgel. *Ser republicano no Brasil colônia: A história de uma tradição esquecida* [Republican spirit in colonial Brazil: History of a forgotten tradition]. Companhia das Letras, 2018.

———. "O passado que não passou". In *Democracia em risco?*, pp. 337–54.

Telles, Lorena Feres da Silva. "Teresa Benguela e Felipa Crioula estavam grávidas: Maternidade e escravidão no Rio de Janeiro (século XIX)" [Teresa Benguela and Felipa Crioula were pregnant: Motherhood and slavery in nineteenth-century Rio de Janeiro]. PhD dissertation, Universidade de São Paulo, 2019.

Tocqueville, Alexis de. *A democracia na América* [original title: *De la démocratie en Amérique*, 2 vols, Gosselin, 1835–40; first translated into English by Henry Reeve as *Democracy in America* (1835–62), revised by Francis Bowen and further revised and edited by Phillips Bradley, 2 vols, Knopf, 1945], trans. Neil Ribeiro da Silva. Itatiaia, 1962.

Tostes, Vera Lucia Bottrel. *Títulos e brasões: Sinais da nobreza: Titulares brasonados do Império: Rio de Janeiro e São Paulo* [Titles and coats of arms: The symbols of aristocracy. Aristocratic figures of the Empire in Rio de Janeiro and São Paulo]. JC, 1996.

Vainfas, Ronaldo. *Dicionário do Brasil imperial (1822–1889)* [Dictionary of imperial Brazil (1822–1889)]. Objetiva, 2002.

Vasconcellos, Barão Smith de. *Archivo nobiliarchico brasileiro* [Brazilian nobility archive], La Concorde, 1918.

Veyne, Paul. *Como se escreve a história* [original title:*Comment on écrit l'histoire: Essai d'epistemologie*, Éditions du Seuil, 1971; published in English as *Writing History: Essay on Epistemology*, trans. Mina Moore-Rinvolucri, Wesleyan University Press, 1984], in Paul Veyne, *Como se escreve a história e Foucault revoluciona a história*, trans. Alda Baltar and Maria Auxiadora Kneipp, 4th edn. Editora UnB, 1998.

Vieira, Oscar Vilhena. *A batalha dos poderes: Da transição democrática ao mal-estar constitucional* [Battle of powers: From democratic transition to constitutional malaise]. Companhia das Letras, 2018.

Viveiros de Castro, Eduardo. *A inconstância da alma selvagem* [The inconstancy of the savage soul]. Cosac Naify, 2002.

Weber, Max. *Metodologia das ciências sociais* [Methodology of the Social Sciences]. Cortez, 2017.

Wehling, Arno and Maria José C. M. Wehling. *Formação do Brasil colonial* [The making of colonial Brazil]. Nova Fronteira, 2012.

Xavier, Giovana, Juliana Barreto Farias, and Flávio Gomes (eds). *Mulheres negras: No Brasil escravista e do pós-emancipação* [Black women: In Brazil before and after emancipation], Selo Negro, 2012.

INDEX

Page numbers in *italics* refer to figures.

equality (*continued*)
114; Indigenous peoples and, 12, 14,
153, 183; legal, 107; long-term, 26;
protection of, 193; Racial Equality
Statute and, 26; rights and, 24 (*see also*
rights); societal recognition of,
156; Special Secretariat for Racial
Equality Policy (SEPPIR) and,
25–26; tolerance and, 210; universal,
21; Whites and, 19, 29, 174; women
and, 12, 17–18, 113–14, 158, 165, 168,
173–74, 209
Erdoğan, Recep Tayyip, 202
Essays in Understanding (Arendt), 192
Estado de S. Paulo (newspaper), 98, 172
Estado Novo (New State), xix, 122,
126–27, 200
ethical issues, 53–54, 58, 76, 80, 88, 134,
210–11
European Union, 112
Evans-Pritchard, E. E., 217, 221–23
Evolução política do Brasil e outros estudos
(*The political evolution of Brazil and
other studies*) (Júnior), 56
evolutionism, 217–19, 223
execution, 97, 162, 247n1
exports, 31, 57, 68, 80–81

Facebook, xi
Falling Sky, The (Kopenawa), 232
family caucus, 69–71
Faoro, Raymundo, 55, 65–66
Farage, Nádia, 144
Farias, Paulo César, 99
Fausto, Ruy, 204
Fausto, Sergio, 141
favelas, 23, 93, 142, 161–64
favoritism, 43, 87
Federal Council on Education, 127
Federal Police, 101–3, 138, 163
Federal Prosecution Office, 102
femicide, xxi, 157, 166–67, 173, 175–77,
180, 194, 205, 235
femininity, 165, 175, 238

feminism, 25, 168–69, 177, 239
Fernandes, Florestan, 7
Fernandes, Millôr, 199
Fernandes Paranhos Fleury, Sérgio, 97
Ferreira, Eduardo, 160
Ferreira Gomes, José Euclides, 46–47
Ferreira Gomes, Vicente Antenor, 46
Ferreira Gomes, Vicente César, 46
Ferrez, Marc, 38–41, 40
Figueredo Santos, José Alcides, 117–18
Filho, Laurenço, 122
First Republic, 13, 20, 43, 68–69, 89–91,
110, 148
Folha de S. Paulo (newspaper), 46–47,
196
Fonseca, Deodoro da, 200
"Forms of History, The" (Lefort), 224
foundling wheel, 17
France, 14, 81, 113
Franco, Marielle, 161–64
fraud, 42, 67–68, 90–91, 100, 102, 107
freedom of expression, xi, 50, 200
Freedom of Information Act, 136
Free Fatherland Party (PPL), 70, 242
Frenchetto, Bruna, 232
French Revolution, 233
Freyre, Gilberto, 6–7, 200
Functional Illiteracy Indicator (INAF),
130
Fundação Cultural Palmares, 25
Fundação Getúlio Vargas (FGV), 107,
160–61
Fundação João Pinheiro, xx
Fundação Palmares, xii
Fundamental Law of Education,
118–19

G1, 43
Galvão, Ricardo, 12–13
Garrastazu Médici, Emílio, 96, 98
gays, 12, 178–85, 195–96, 202, 206, 212
Gazeta de Noticias (newspaper), 87
Geertz, Clifford, 230–31
Geisel, Ernesto, 92–93

and, 10, 134, 153, 156, 180, 190–95,
198, 203, 210; police and, 186, 196;
prejudice and, 192, 196–97; religious,
187–93, 196, 200, 211–12; repudiation
and, 194; rights and, 193–97; rural
areas and, 186, 189–90; São Paulo
and, 196; sexism and, x, 14, 173,
178–85, 192, 235; slavery and, 187–90;
Universal Declaration of Human
Rights and, 193; Vaz de Camões on,
186–87; Vieira on, 187–88; xenophobia, 195–97
Iracema (Alencar), 146
Iraq, 168
Isabel (princess), 85–86
Isaura de Queiroz, Maria, 49
Islands of History (Sahlins), 230
Israel, 14, 202
Italy, 14, 202

Jamaica, 172
Japan, 116
Jefferson, Roberto, 100
Jesuits, 35, 147, 187–88, 251n1
job market, 2, 115–16, 131, 157, 159
judiciary, 2–3, 105, 208
justice: anthropological view of, 206–7,
210; corruption and, 83, 86–88,
101–2, 105–8, 249n5; criminal courts
and, 23; delayed, 176; distribution
of power and, 50; education and,
26; patrimonialism and, 60, 66;
public silence and, 185; violence and,
143, 150, 153
juvenile offenders, 23

Kachin, 217
Kaczyński, Jarosław, 202
Kaingang, 147–49
Kingdom of Belíndia, 96
Kingdom of Daomé, 62
Kirchner, Cristina, 106
knifings, 181
Kodamaa, Nelma, 103

Kopenawa, David, 232, 255n70
Koselleck, Reinhart, 233–35
Kotscho, Ricardo, 98
Kubitschek, Juscelino, 93, 127, 248n3,
249n3
Kuczynski, Pedro Pablo, 105–6

Labor Court, 69
Labor Minister, 98
Lacerda, Carlos, 92
landowners: agriculture and, 31 (*see also*
agriculture); aristocracy and, 9,
32–33, 35, 55, 249n3; bossism and,
31–36, 41–42, 50; corruption and,
78, 90; masters and, 7, 12, 17–18,
32–41, 171; National Institute for
Land Settlement and Agrarian
Reform (INCRA) and, 45, 134;
patrimonialism and, 55–56, 61–62,
65, 68–69; plantations and, 16, 30–41,
34, 57, 65, 81, 112, 161, 171, 249n3;
power of, x, 9, 31, 34–36, 55–56, 62,
68–69, 90, 112, 174, 249n3; slavery
and, 16 (*see also* slavery); social
inequality and, 112, 119; Vale do
Paraíba and, 35–36, 39, 40, 63, 65,
249n3; violence and, 13, 139, 145,
149, 174
Largo do Machado, 120
latifundia (farm estates), 30, 55
Latin American Faculty of Social
Sciences, 137
Latour, Bruno, 233, 235
Law No. 12711, 26
Law of the Free Womb, 18, 120
lawyers, 59, 64, 236
Leach, Edmund, 217
Lederman, Rena, 217
Lefort, Claude, 216, 224–25
legal issues: arbitrary imprisonment,
247n1; Article 5, 25; corruption, 76,
80–86, 94–110, 249n5; courts and, 2,
26, 54, 57–69, 81–86, 97, 100–108,
119–20, 152, 189, 197, 249n5, 251n1;

Movement for Brazilian Democracy
(MDB), 47, 102, 104, 241
Mozambique, 62
mulattas, 17, 174
Municipal Human Development
Index, xx
murder/homicide: assassinations, 92,
97, 151, 161–64, 181; data on, 22, 135–37,
140–41, 158, 171, 196; exterminations,
145–50; femicide, xxi, 157, 166–67, 173,
175–77, 180, 194, 205, 235; Franco
and, 161–64; gender and, 22, 136,
157–58, 164–67, 173–81, 194, 205, 235;
genocide, xii, 7, 22, 145; increase of,
135, 158; intolerance and, 192, 196;
massacres, xii, 96, 146–47, 149;
racism and, xxi, 22, 166, 176, 205;
Statute 13104 and, 165–66; war
narratives and, 192; of women, 157,
165–67, 173–77, 180, 194, 205, 235; of
youth, 22, 136, 158, 205
Murilo de Carvalho, José, xx, 75
Museu Paulista, 149
Muslims, 212, 231, 248n1
myth: anthropological view of, 201–3,
211, 222, 229; bossism and, 51; common sense theories and, 10–11, 24,
160; cultural constructions of, 8–12,
15, 156–57, 201–3, 211; democracy
and, 7; effects on history of, 8–12,
15, 233–39; Evans-Pritchard on, 222;
four assumptions for, 11; genealogies
and, 32; intolerance and, 190; Levi-
Strauss on, 222, 229; national anthem
and, 9–10; of paradise, 11, 110, 186,
201; patrimonialism and, 54; of
racial democracy, 7, 15, 29, 185, 211;
sexism and, 185; slavery and, 24, 29;
von Martius on, 8, 11, 146; Western
modernity and, 233–39

Namibia, 44
Napoleon, 247n1
National Commerce Confederation,
123–24

National Congress, 72, 182, 206, 208
National Council on Human Rights, 184
National Council on Women's Rights,
184
National Council to Combat Discrim-
ination and Promote the Rights of
Lesbian, Gay, Bisexual, Transgender
People (CNCD/LGBT), 183
National Council to End Discrimination,
183
National Day of Black Consciousness,
26
National Economic Development
Bank, 98
National Educational Policy and
Guidelines Statute, 26
National Educational Policy and
Standards, 127
National Education Plan, 127–30
National Film Agency, xi
National Guard, 42, 66, 249, 249n4
National Household Sample Survey,
xx, 112–13, 116–17, 130
National Indian Foundation
(FUNAI), 150
National Industry Confederation, 107,
123–24
National Information Services, 97
National Information System on
Public Safety, Prison, and Drugs
(SINESP), 140
National Institute for Colonization
and Agrarian Reform, 154
National Institute for Land Settlement
and Agrarian Reform (INCRA), 45,
134
National Institute for Space Research, xii
nationalism, 15, 124, 192, 202, 242, 254n50
National Justice Council, 102
National Secretariat for Global Protec-
tion, 184
National Secretariat on Policy for
Women, 184
National Truth Commission, 247n1
National Youth Council, 184

racism: activists and, 24–25, 27, 29, 151,
163; affirmative action and, xiii, 25,
159; apartheid and, 7, 28; aristocracy
and, 32; colonialism and, 20, 27,
29; commixture and, 6–7, 10, 23;
conservatism and, 25, 28; constitutional issues and, 186; crime and,
24–25, 194, 209; dictatorship and,
24; diversity and, 26–28, 51, 153, 179,
185, 198, 211, 228, 233; education and,
20, 26–28, 157, 159, 171, 176; exclusion
and, 20–24, 27–29, 112, 129, 159, 167,
179; femicide and, 157, 166; Freyre
on, 6–7; imperialism and, 20, 161;
inclusion and, 8, 20, 24, 26–27, 50,
121, 127, 145–46, 150, 156–59, 178,
183–86, 195, 209; income gap and,
xx, 137; intolerance and, 161 (see also
intolerance); legal issues and, 25;
liberalism and, 19; life expectancy
and, 158; Maria da Penha Law and,
175–76; military and, 21, 161; moral
issues and, 19–20, 168, 178, 180, 185;
murder and, 22, 166, 176, 205; myth
of racial democracy and, 7, 15, 29, 185,
211; "new bronze" and, 6; NUMAS
and, 156–57; police and, 23–24, 101,
139, 159–63, 172, 181, 205; poverty
and, xx, 158, 185; prejudice and, 7, 11,
33, 156, 167, 174, 179, 192, 196–97;
prison and, 25, 28, 101, 205; quotas
and, 26; republics and, 20, 24–25,
160; rights and, 20–28, 158, 162, 168,
174, 177–85, 251n2; and "savages," 33,
145–48, 188, 228; scientific models
and, 19; segregation and, 27, 51, 53,
93, 158; slavery and, 16–29, 159–61,
170–74; social Darwinism and,
19; Special Secretariat for Racial
Equality Policy (SEPPIR) and,
25–26; stereotypes and, 32, 41, 162,
164, 169, 192, 238; violence and, xxi,
139, 144, 148, 159–61, 164–68, 176,
211; women and, 12, 25, 41, 113–15,

121, 129, 157–58, 161–68, 174, 176, 212;
and xenophobia, 195–97; youth and,
21–22
Radcliffe-Browne, A. R., 220, 223
Raízes do Brasil (The Roots of Brazil)
(Buarque de Holanda), xix, 34, 54,
189–90
Ramos, Alcida, 232
Ramos, Artur, 7
rape: culture of, 17, 157, 168–73; data
on, 171–72; violence and, 17, 29, 157,
168–73, 179, 182, 205, 247n1
rebellion, 5, 12, 18, 35–38, 62, 118, 144,
148, 188
reform: bossism and, 50; Capanema
Reform, 122; constitutional issues
and, 209; education and, 118–19, 122,
127; fake news and, 204; illiteracy and,
118–19, 122, 130; National Educational
Policy and Standards and, 127;
National Institute for Land Settlement and Agrarian Reform (INCRA)
and, 45, 134; patrimonialism and,
66–67; Saraiva Reform, 67; social
inequality and, 118–19, 122; Statute
for the Reform of Primary and
Secondary Education in the Municipality of the Court and, 119; Vargas
and, 122–26; violence and, 154
Rêgo, Veneziano do, 70
religion: Afro-Brazilian, 212; anthropological view of, 228, 234; Catholicism,
3, 32, 67, 78, 120, 187, 251n1; Christians,
xiii, 32, 70, 187, 191, 211, 239, 248n1;
community of origin and, 155;
intolerance and, 187–93, 196, 200,
211–12; Maria da Penha Law and,
175–76; modernity and, 239; moral
issues and, xiii, 204, 209; Muslims,
212, 231, 248n1; paganism, 187–88,
203, 251n1; political parties and, 70,
242; prayer and, 158; prejudice and,
11; rape culture and, 173; slavery
and, 16, 18; social inequality and,

violence (*continued*)
  voters and, 140–43; Whites and, 139,
    144, 148; women and, xxi, 147, 160–85,
    204–5; youth and, 136, 157–61, 158,
    166–67, 205. *See also* assassinations;
    bullying; execution; femicide;
    genocide; homicide; massacre;
    murder; rape; torture
Violence Research Group, 163
Vital do Rêgo, Veneziano, 72
Viveiros de Castro, Eduardo, 188, 232
von Humboldt, Alexander, 32
von Ihering, Hermann, 149
von Martius, Karl, 4–11, 146, 159–60
voters: bossism and, 42–43; corruption
  and, 90, 94, 104; patrimonialism and,
  66–69, 73; Verification Commission
  and, 68–69; violence and, 140–43;
  yoke-and-oxen vote, 68. *See also*
  elections

Wagner, Richard, xi
Weber, Max, 53–54, 74
Western society: anthropological view
  and, 18–19, 81, 215, 218–19, 224, 227–39;
  Evans-Pritchard on, 217, 221–23;
  Lévi-Strauss on, 219, 224, 227, 229;
  modernity and, 233–39; technology
  and, 218
WhatsApp, 160
Whites: and bossism, 32, 41; and
  equality, 19, 29, 174; Freyre on, 6–7;
  and homicide, 22; and income gap,
  xx, 137; intellectual capacity of, 20;
  life expectancy of, 158; and marriage,
  174; population data on, 21; and
  poverty, xx; and power, 9, 24, 28; and
  racism, 20 (*see also* racism); and
  social class, 27; and social Darwinism,
  19; and social inequality, 113–18, 129;
  and stereotypes, 32, 169, 238; and
  violence, 139, 144, 148, 166–67, 176;
  and women, 41, 113–15, 129, 157, 166–67,
  174, 176. *See also* colonialism; elitism

women: Black, 12, 25, 41, 113–15, 121, 129,
    157–58, 161–68, 174, 176, 212; bossism
    and, 32, 36–37, 41, 44; and crime, 17,
    29, 57, 157, 162–73, 176–82, 205, 209,
    247n1; discrimination against, 12;
    and equality, 12, 17–18, 113–14, 158,
    165, 168, 173–74, 209; historical
    perspective on, 202–3; languor of,
    146, 238; Law of the Free Womb and,
    18, 120; lesbians, 12, 162, 164, 178–85,
    195, 206, 212; Maria da Penha Law
    and, 175–76; and marriage, 32–34,
    64, 227; Ministry for Women, the
    Family, and Human Rights, 184;
    and misogyny, x, 157, 167, 177, 192;
    mulatta, 17, 174; and murder, 157,
    165–67, 173, 175–77, 180, 194, 205,
    235; National Council on Women's
    Rights, 184; National Secretariat
    on Policy for Women, 184; native,
    146–47, 169; and nudity, 169; patriar-
    chal society and, 167, 173–75; political
    representation by, 168, 206; and
    pregnancy, 36; prejudice against, 11,
    167, 174; and race, 12, 25, 41, 113–15,
    121, 129, 157–58, 161–68, 174, 176, 212;
    and rape, 17, 29, 157, 168–73, 179, 182,
    205; and religion, 173, 176, 179; and
    rights, 168, 174, 177, 182, 184, 212,
    251n2; and slavery, 12, 17–18, 25, 29, 36,
    41, 147, 161, 174; and social inequality,
    113–16, 121, 129, 147, 157–58; Statute
    13104 and, 165–66; surrender by, 17,
    147, 169, 175; transgender, 12, 180, 182;
    violence against, xxi, 147, 160–85,
    204–5; White, 41, 113–15, 129, 157,
    166–67, 174, 176. *See also* femicide;
    feminism
Women's Support Hotline, 172–73
Workers' Party (PT), 48, 70–71,
    100–103, 106, 241–43, 248n4
World Health Organization (WHO),
    49, 135, 137, 141, 142, 176
World War I era, xv, 237

World War II era, 7
Wright, Robin, 232

Xavante, 149
xenophobia, 195–97

Yemen, 22
yoke-and-oxen vote, 68
Youssef, Alberto, 103
youth: education and, 131, 133 (*see also* education); Index of Youth Vulnerability to Violence (IVJ) and, 158;

juvenile offenders, 23; murder of, 22, 136, 158, 205; National Youth Council and, 184; National Youth Secretariat and, 184; racism and, 21–22; social inequality and, 119, 126, 131, 133; violence and, 136, 157–61, 167, 205
Youth Party, 242
Youth Violence Vulnerability Index, 166

Zambia, 105
Ziblatt, Daniel, 198

A NOTE ON THE TYPE

This book has been composed in Arno, an Old-style serif typeface in the classic Venetian tradition, designed by Robert Slimbach at Adobe.